Voices from
the Pacific War

VOICES
FROM THE
PACIFIC WAR

◆ ◆ ◆ ◆ ◆

Bluejackets Remember

Bruce M. Petty

Naval Institute Press
Annapolis, Maryland

Naval Institute Press

291 Wood Road

Annapolis, MD 21402

Library of Congress Cataloging-in-Publication Data

Petty, Bruce M., 1945–

    Voices from the Pacific War : Bluejackets remember / Bruce M. Petty.

        p.   cm.

    Includes bibliographical references and index.

    ISBN 1-59114-663-1 (alk. paper)

    1. World War, 1939–1945—Campaigns—Pacific Area. 2. World War, 1939–1945—Naval operations, American. 3. World War, 1939–1945—Personal narratives, American. 4. United States. Navy—Biography. 5. Oral history. I. Title.

    D767.P47 2003

    940.54'26'092273—dc21

                                         2003010784

Printed in the United States of America on acid-free paper ∞

11 10 09 08 07 06 05 04   9 8 7 6 5 4 3 2

First printing

To Dr. Daniele Lonchamp-Petty, wife, mother,
and only breadwinner in the family

CONTENTS

ACKNOWLEDGMENTS

As with my first book, I would like to thank the many hundreds of people who shared their stories with me. I concluded my research with such a wealth of fascinating and interesting interviews that I just could not fit all of them into a single volume. Still, I learned much from each and every person I interviewed. I am especially grateful to those whose stories unfold in the chapters of this book. Their bravery, and that of all their fellow bluejackets, under the most horrific conditions can never be sufficiently honored.

This book never would have been written without the help of my wife, Dr. Daniele Lonchamp-Petty, who as a wife, mother, and sole breadwinner in the family, made it all emotionally and financially possible. Without her I would be just another faceless house dad.

To my dear and faithful friend Dr. Beret E. Strong, my thanks for being there as my unofficial editor, confidante, and confidence builder. She always found time to comment on and edit my scribblings in spite of her own busy schedule as a wife, mother, and documentary filmmaker.

A very special thanks goes to Capt. Tim Wooldridge, USN (Ret.), for reading my original oversized manuscript and pointing me in the right direction. I also want to thank the Naval Institute Press for accepting my manuscript for publication. As a fellow military historian once told me, "Getting published by the Naval Institute Press is like winning an Academy Award," and that is exactly how I feel. Paul Wilderson of the Naval Institute Press deserves special praise for his time, patience, and good advice. Also of the Naval Institute Press, I would like to thank Rebecca Edwards Hinds, Susan Artigiani, Kelly Compo, and Sara Sprinkle. I am sure there are many others at the Naval Institute Press whose names I don't know and whom I never met, who also deserve my thanks. I thank you now.

Lys Ann Shore, who was assigned to copyedit my manuscript also deserves my many thanks for doing such a wonderful job in cleaning up my many typos and catching errors I missed.

I am grateful to Tiny Clarkson, Jim Talbert, and John Cummer of the LCI Association, and their active group of veterans. With their help I was able to obtain some very good oral histories from LCI veterans of the Pacific War.

Although neither one of my books fit his "list," I would like to thank Mark Gatlin of the Smithsonian Institution Press. His interest in my work, and his advice and guidance have been priceless.

For more than twenty-five years John Newbold of Napa Valley, California, in his free time, has interviewed American veterans living at the Veteran's Home in Yountville, California. He started off interviewing Spanish-American War veterans. As they died off, he moved on to World War I veterans, and is now working on the World War II generation. As a one-man operation, he has not had time to transcribe the tomes of oral histories he has collected over the years. They sit, archived at the Veteran's Home, begging for researchers to make use of them. I am grateful that he took time out of his busy schedule to help me.

Dr. Bill Lee from St. Mary's College in Moraga, California, is one of my oldest friends, going back to our university days at the University of California at Santa Barbara. A faux pas in my first book was the failure to mention Bill in the acknowledgments for the long-distance help he provided. I'm a little late, Bill, but thanks.

I am grateful to all the other people who contributed to my efforts to put this book together; I hope I didn't forget anybody this time. The list includes Joseph Abado, Col. Joseph Alexander, USMC (Ret.), Frank Baillie, Dale Barker, Dr. Judy

Bellafaire of Women in the Military Service Association (WIMSA), Elva Belsches, Chris Bommarito, Bill Chapin, Paul Cooper, Elaine and Harry Dallas, Marybeth Lysons Filice, Peter Flahavin of Brisbane, Australia (a Guadalcanal obsessive), Arnel Garcia, Jeffery Gilmartin, John Grause, Brian Grubbs, Tom Hawkins of the UDT-Seals Museum, Mike Lyga, Bill Mozinga, USN (Ret.), Maria Theresita "Thet" Nebre, Joven S. Ramirez Jr., Michael B. Reaso, Henry Sakaida, Ms. Vane Scott, Capt. William Van Dusen, USN (Ret.), Bill Winnekins, and Eugene Zarsuela. I will conclude this list by mentioning Dr. Kathy Broome Williams, a fellow military historian whose Marine Corps father died from wounds received in the last days of fighting on Saipan in July 1944.

On the morning of 7 December 1941 the United States stepped over a line. On one side was a nation of poverty and unemployment, a nation bent on isolating itself from the rest of the world and the world's problems. On the other side was a nation at war and desperate for men and women to work in factories, man ships, and fly airplanes. Suddenly there were a lot of jobs and not enough people. Suddenly America was no longer isolated and uninvolved. The world's problems were, in an instant, America's problems. However, this book starts before that Day of Infamy. It starts with the enlisted men and women of the United States Navy—the bluejackets—who helped in the fight to win the war in the Pacific.

As I discovered from the multitude of oral histories I conducted with men who enlisted before Pearl Harbor, the Great Depression was the main motivating factor in their electing to serve. Poverty made service in the U.S. Navy a desirable option for thousands of young men. For some men it was their only option in a world of limited choices. Many a farm boy ran off to join the navy in order to secure three meals a day, clean sheets to sleep on, and the possibility of learning a trade that would serve him on the outside if and when he chose to leave the military. A chance to see some of the world was another motivating factor. In spite of the horrors some of them experienced during World War

II—some as POWs—a surprisingly large number elected to stay in after the war until they reached retirement age. Many of those who left at the end of World War II were able to make a living in the civilian sector as a result of what they had learned while in the navy. Others took advantage of the G.I. Bill and went to college.

Those who enlisted before Pearl Harbor found themselves in a navy that was underfunded, with few ships and not always enough men to man them at full strength. The number of enlisted men in the navy in the 1920s and 1930s rarely totaled over one hundred thousand at any one time. Some men, I discovered, served their entire navy careers aboard one ship. Their home was not only the navy but also that one ship until they retired or until the ship was decommissioned or sunk in battle.

After Pearl Harbor both men and women joined the navy for a variety of reasons. Some enlisted for the simple reason that they wanted to. As many members of that generation told me, "The Japanese attack on Pearl Harbor made it easy for me to want to enlist." Others joined the navy to avoid the draft. The thought of a bunk on a ship sounded a lot better than the mud floor of a foxhole. That is not to say that the "Greatest Generation" didn't have its draft dodgers and deserters, because it did, but the vast majority of Americans rushed to serve the national effort in whatever way they could. Others had to be prodded along by their local draft board, and as the war progressed, the U.S. Navy, and even the Marine Corps, turned to the draft to fill their growing manpower needs. But regardless of how desirable the navy may have looked to some compared to service in the army or marines, the navy suffered its fair share of casualties, and being on a ship instead of in a foxhole was no guarantee that one would survive the war.

The navy lost more men in the fight for Guadalcanal than did the marines. After suffering multiple torpedo hits from a Japanese submarine, the USS *Juneau* had almost 100 percent casualties, including five brothers from one family. The super-typhoon that struck the fleet near the Philippines in December 1944 resulted in the loss of three destroyers and over eight hundred men, as well as damage and loss of life on other ships. Aircraft carriers, although powerful weapons, were also terribly vulnerable, especially the smaller, thin-skinned escort carriers. When these vessels were hit, the casualties were often high. And in the last major battle of World War II, Okinawa, the navy suffered over ten thousand casualties, mostly from Japanese air attacks, involving thousands of kamikazes. It was a bloody war for the navy, and the last year of the war was the bloodiest of all.

By war's end, over sixteen million Americans had served in the U.S. military, including my mother, father, and most of my uncles. Close to three million Americans served in the Pacific, and a good many of them served in the navy, though how many served in the navy during any given year has been difficult to determine.

Until the loss of the five Sullivan brothers when the USS *Juneau* was sunk in the Solomon Islands in 1942, brothers, including my father and one of his brothers, were allowed to serve together if they so desired. There were even father-and-son enlistments once the United States had entered the war and there was an increasing demand for men. The father was usually referred to as "Pop" by the rest of the crew.

Also, as a response to the call to arms and the need for more and more men to serve, a growing number of underage individuals enlisted in all branches of the military. The youngest known to have served in the U.S. Navy was Calvin Graham, who enlisted at the age of twelve. I interviewed two men who were among these underage sailors; the oral history of one of them appears in this book (chapter 20). Richard Johnson was fourteen when he lied about his age and entered the navy. He survived the war and returned home before he was old enough to vote. How many others went down with their ships before they were old enough to shave may never be known.

Before Pearl Harbor, advancement for enlisted men was slow. For a young sailor in the 1920s or 1930s, it often took several years to advance from seaman to third class petty officer. Those who enlisted in the 1920s might advance no further than second class or first class petty officer after twenty years of service. But within months, or even weeks, after the Japanese attack on Pearl Harbor, advancement was rapid—in some cases extremely rapid. Seamen became petty officers literally overnight. Petty officers found themselves being promoted to chief, warrant officer, or even the rank of ensign. I know of at least one individual who enlisted in 1937 as a seaman. When he finally retired from the navy, he had achieved flag rank. Some men with little more than high school educations became officers.

People who came into the navy after Pearl Harbor often graduated from boot camp as petty officers, depending on how well they did on their aptitude tests and the sort of work experience they had. People who were mechanics, electricians, or metalsmiths in civilian life likewise often graduated from navy boot camp as petty officers in ratings related to what they did as civilians. A man who owned his own tuna boat might find himself the skipper of a small navy ship within weeks or months of being called to serve in the war.

The navy was one of the few options open to young men coming of age during the Depression, but the enlisted men of the U.S. Navy in the 1920s and 1930s were not always well received by their civilian counterparts. In navy towns such as Norfolk, Long Beach, and Honolulu, they were often considered undesirables and limited as to where they could go during their off-duty hours and with whom they could socialize. After Pearl Harbor, when almost every American family had a husband or son serving in the military, everything changed. Overnight, U.S. servicemen of all ranks and ratings were welcomed into the homes and hearts of Americans across the nation, both literally and figuratively.

World War II was also a watershed for various ethnic minorities in the United States. With the sudden need to fill a wartime workforce being depleted by young men called away to fight, black Americans and other minorities moved to where the jobs were, whether in factories to the north or shipyards in California.

In the 1800s and early 1900s the U.S. Navy was not as segregated as it was during the 1920s and early 1930s. Group photographs taken of enlisted men before 1920 show the ranks sprinkled with both black and white sailors. During World War I the navy had over fifteen thousand black sailors. However, under the administration of President Woodrow Wilson, black Americans were discouraged from entering the ranks of the U.S. Navy, and those already in the navy were discouraged or prevented from reenlisting. By the early 1930s, when the nation was well into the Great Depression and many poor American boys looked to the navy as an alternative to poverty and unemployment, there were fewer than five hundred black Americans in the navy.

In the late 1930s the navy started allowing black Americans back into service as the nation began to rebuild its long neglected military. Unfortunately, it allowed them to serve only as messmen and stewards in most cases. However, they did have their battle stations and, like their white counterparts, they passed the ammunition. There were also all-black gun crews. By the time World War II was over, more than eight hundred thousand black men and women had served in all branches of the U.S. military. Close to two hundred thousand served in the Pacific. The navy's segregation policy, however, remained in effect until after World War II, when President Truman desegregated the military.

World War II also opened many doors for women in the military. Before Pearl Harbor, there were only a few hundred women serving in the navy. Most of them were enlisted nurses. (They were given officer status later in the war.) By war's end the navy boasted approximately fourteen thousand nurses (only four of them black) and one hundred thousand others in a variety of ratings, most of them clerical. My mother was one of them.

If the U.S. Navy had few men in uniform before World War II, it had even fewer ships. From shortly after World War I until well into the 1930s no new battleships were built. Several under construction in the early 1920s were scrapped as a result of the Washington Naval Disarmament Treaty. Not until 1933, under the prodding of President Franklin D. Roosevelt, did the United States start to rebuild its neglected armed forces. The first U.S. battleships to be commissioned since the early 1920s were *North Carolina* in April 1941 and *Washington* in May 1941. Even then, the effort was minimal and did not come close to providing the ships, equipment, and men necessary to fight a global conflict against a modern, well-trained, and determined foe.

On the eve of U.S. entry into World War II, the United States had very few aircraft carriers. The first U.S. aircraft carrier, the USS *Langley*, was built on the hull of an old collier in the early 1920s. The next two, *Lexington* and *Saratoga,* were not commissioned until 1927. Both ships were built on cruiser hulls. The USS *Ranger,* the first carrier designed and built as such, was not commissioned until 1934, and was followed by *Enterprise, Yorktown, Wasp,* and *Hornet.* However, when the Japanese attacked Pearl Harbor on 7 December 1941, there were only three U.S. carriers in the Pacific. Fortunately, none was docked at Pearl Harbor on that fateful day, or there would have been none in Pacific waters at the beginning of the war. By war's end, in contrast, the United States had over one hundred aircraft carriers of all types, most of which were in the Pacific.

In addition, a few new cruisers, destroyers, and submarines were added to the fleet during this period just before U.S. entry into the war, but not nearly enough to meet the needs of a nation soon to be fighting for its life. As late as the summer of 1939, just two and a half years before the Japanese attack on Pearl Harbor, the navy was also woefully short of auxiliary ships. It had a limited number of transports, oilers, cargo ships, and ammunition ships, most of which had been commissioned during or right after World War I. It was hardly the sort of navy that would be needed to meet the more modern and better trained navy of imperial Japan. By war's end, however, thousands of ships had been built: ten new battleships, ninety cruisers, six hundred destroyers, and three hundred submarines. Even civilian tugs, tuna boats, luxury yachts, and other civilian-owned ships were purchased or leased and put into commission. Add to that hundreds of amphibious warfare and auxiliary ships, from LCIs and small harbor craft to transports and fleet oilers. With this new and more powerful navy, the United States and its allies fought their way across the Pacific and ended a war that cost tens of millions of lives.

The one compelling reason I have for collecting the oral histories of people who served in wartime is the realization that seemingly ordinary people who might otherwise have lived seemingly ordinary lives did in fact have extraordinary experiences during wartime. In sharing their stories, they add vivid details and unique perspectives to what took place in a war that affected almost every nation and almost every family that lived through it.

On a personal level, I wanted to publish this book about the navy in the

Pacific because my father and one of my uncles served there during the war. During the Vietnam War, I served as an aviation ordnance man aboard the USS *Yorktown* (CVS-10). I spent the better part of two years in Pacific waters, and docked at some of the islands where battles were fought and ships were sunk. My fascination with that area and that era have stayed with me ever since.

More recently, in 1995, my family and I moved to the island of Saipan, where one of the pivotal battles of World War II in the Pacific was fought. My wife worked at the island hospital, while I assumed the role of Mr. Mom and began researching my first book, *Saipan: Oral Histories of the Pacific War.* I not only had the opportunity to meet with and talk to many people from the World War II generation, both American veterans and Pacific Islanders, but I spent a good deal of time physically exploring the island. I climbed mountains, went into many limestone caves, both natural and those dug by the Japanese, and hacked my own trails into the jungle. With books and maps from the war, I retraced the footsteps of U.S. marines and soldiers. I explored the landing beaches where the marines suffered over two thousand casualties the first day of the battle. I explored from the southern tip of Naftan Point to the suicide cliffs at the north end of the island. Five years later, my first book completed, my family and I returned to California. I then started researching this book about the enlisted men and women of the U.S. Navy and the role they played in that magnificent tragedy we all know as World War II.

For many veterans, their wartime experiences have never been far from their thoughts, in spite of productive civilian lives and the energy required to raise families. Many others, since their retirement, have taken a renewed interest in the war and their part in it. They have done their own research in many cases, and have renewed contact with men and women they served with during the war. I also discovered that everybody I interviewed for this book had one thing in common: they all wanted to be remembered for what they did in World War II—not the longest, but surely the bloodiest war yet fought by man.

CHRONOLOGY

1922	Naval Disarmament Treaty signed by United States, Britain, and Japan
1929	Stock market crashes, throwing millions of people out of work
1920s	Cryptanalysts break the Japanese diplomatic code
1933	Franklin D. Roosevelt is elected president of the United States. Congress is prodded into appropriating funds for long neglected military.
1939–40	Both England and United States make inroads into breaking the Japanese Naval Operational codes, JN-25, which proved crucial in shortening the war and saving lives
1941 (September)	President Roosevelt issues a "shoot on sight" order for any ship interfering with American shipping
1941 (December)	Japanese forces attack Pearl Harbor and other U.S Pacific bases in the Philippines and Guam, as well as Dutch and British colonial possessions in Southeast Asia. U.S. Congress votes an additional $10.1 billion post–Pearl Harbor to aid the war effort. Adm. Ernest King is named

commander-in-chief of the U.S. fleet, later to be named chief of naval operations, replacing Adm. Stark. U.S. troops start arriving in Australia. Adm. Chester Nimitz named to take command of the Pacific Fleet, headquartered at Pearl Harbor. U.S submarines ordered to commence unrestricted attacks against enemy shipping.

1942 (January– February)	U.S. carriers begin the first of a series of raids against Japanese islands in Central Pacific. Singapore falls to Japanese forces.
1942 (March– April)	Oil fields of the Dutch East Indies fall to Japanese forces. U.S. Army B-25s launched from deck of carrier *Hornet* bomb Japan (the Doolittle raid).
1942 (May)	Battle of the Coral Sea, the first carrier-against-carrier battle in history. Corregidor in the Philippines finally surrenders.
1942 (June)	Battle of Midway, the second carrier-against-carrier battle in history, and the first decisive victory for the United States in the war against Japan, with Japan losing four carriers, the U.S. one
1942 (August)	Battle of Guadalcanal begins, the first in a long line of counter-offensives begun by U.S. forces against imperial Japan. Numerous naval battles are fought in the waters offshore, resulting in the loss of more sailors than marines by the time the island is secured. General MacArthur begins his long march across Papua New Guinea on his way back to the Philippines.
1942 (September)	Carrier *Wasp* sunk by Japanese submarine
1942 (October)	Admiral Halsey made Allied Commander in the South Pacific. Carrier *Hornet* lost in Battle of Santa Cruz Islands.
1942 (November)	Cruiser *Juneau* lost to multiple torpedo hits from Japanese submarine with loss of most of its crew, includ-

ing the five Sullivan brothers

1943 (February)	Japan evacuates troops from Guadalcanal
1943 (April)	Admiral Yamamoto, architect of Japan's war with the United States, is shot down and killed with the help of U.S. code breakers
1943 (Midyear)	U.S. submarines start making headway in their effort to sink Japanese shipping, with more submarines coming on line (sixty-seven since Pearl Harbor) and problems with defective torpedoes being resolved. Japan goes on the defensive, with island garrisons cut off from supplies. By war's end, many Japanese will have died from disease and starvation. Japan is also losing more ships than can be replaced, especially merchant ships. The United States is building more ships than are being lost (thirty-one new carriers since Pearl Harbor). The tide is turning.
1943 (November)	Admiral Nimitz launches the Central Pacific offensive with marine and army amphibious landings in the Gilbert Islands (Tarawa/Makin). One of many new escort carriers, *Liscome Bay*, torpedoed by Japanese submarine with the loss of over six hundred officers and men.
1944 (January)	U.S. marines and army troops make amphibious landings in the Marshall Islands on the next step to taking the war home to Japan. U.S. Navy ships and airplanes dominate Pacific waters, sinking on average fifty Japanese ships a month.
1944 (May)	Destroyer escort USS *England* sinks six Japanese submarines in twelve days, thanks to help from U.S. code breakers
1944 (June–July)	Mariana Islands: Japan's outer ring of defense is broken with landings on Saipan, Tinian, and Guam. Prime

Minister Tojo and entire cabinet resign in Tokyo. First
Battle of the Philippines Sea. The "Great Marianas
Turkey Shoot" delivers another decisive blow against
Japan's Imperial Navy. Last organized Japanese resistance
on Saipan does not end until December 1945, four
months after official Japanese surrender. Last Japanese
holdout on Guam is captured in the 1970s. U.S. submarines unknowingly kill over four thousand Allied
POWs being transported to Japan by ship over a six-
week period.

1944 (October)   General MacArthur's forces make first landings in the
Philippines at Leyte. Several major naval battles fought,
with the Japanese making the first organized use of
kamikazes to stop Allied advances. Escort carriers
Suwanee and *Santee* hit by kamikazes within minutes of
each other with tremendous loss of life. Japanese super
battleship *Musashi* sunk by U.S. carrier aircraft. Japanese
make first use of kaitans (human torpedoes), sinking the
U.S. oiler *Mississinewa* at Ulithi Atoll.

1944 (November)   First B-29 raids against the Japanese home islands
launched from bases in the Marianas. (The very first
were launched from bases in China.) The U.S. ammunition ship *Mount Hood* blows up off Manus Island in the
Admiralties, killing all aboard with the exception of a
small work party ashore.

1944 (December)   U.S. submarines are running out of Japanese ships to
sink

1945 (February)   Marines assault and take the island of Iwo Jima in the
bloodiest fight in U.S. Marine Corps history

1945 (April)   Okinawa, the last major battle of World War II, and the
bloodiest for U.S. forces in the Pacific. The U.S. Navy
suffers ten thousand casualties and hundreds of ships

sunk or damaged, mostly from aerial attack by kamikazes. President Roosevelt dies. Hitler commits suicide same month.

1945 (August)   USS *Indianapolis,* after delivering parts of first atomic bomb to the island of Tinian in the Marianas, is torpedoed and sunk by a Japanese submarine. Japan surrenders following the dropping of two atomic bombs.

The war is over but thousands of Japanese stranded throughout the Pacific and Asia die of disease and starvation before they can be repatriated. Others refuse to surrender for years, even decades.

Voices from
the Pacific War

CHAPTER I

◆ ◆ ◆ ◆ ◆

Loss of the *Yorktown* (CV-5)
Dwight DeHaven

D wight DeHaven was born in Montana in 1921. His family moved to Oregon after a severe winter killed all of their cattle. He enlisted in the U.S. Navy in 1939 and was discharged as a chief petty officer in November 1945. Like many of his generation, after the war he took advantage of the G.I. Bill, went to college, married, and raised a family. He now lives in San Ramon, California.

The USS *Yorktown* (CV-5) was commissioned in 1937 and was only the second U.S. aircraft carrier to be built from the keel up as such. In her brief career she won three battle stars, two of which were for battles that stopped Japanese advances in the first two naval battles in history between aircraft carriers.

My father bought a small "stump" ranch in Oregon. I helped my mom and dad clear the land in an effort to build a farm. I felt trapped there. You could never do anything if you had cows to milk. You had to do it twice a day, seven days a

Chief Petty Officer Dwight DeHaven, who
survived both the sinking of the USS *Yorktown*
(CV-5) and a kamikaze attack on the USS
England (DE-635) off the coast of Okinawa.
This photo was taken just before his discharge
from the navy at the end of the war.

week. So as soon as I graduated from high school in 1939, I joined the navy. I
signed up for six years, and I got paid off after five years, eleven months, and
twenty-seven days. They let me out three days early.

I went aboard the USS *Yorktown* (CV-5) after my training and went to
Hawaii with the fleet in January 1940. We operated out of Pearl Harbor doing
flight operations. I was in the boiler room, but I wanted to be with a squadron
so bad that I asked for a change in my rating. However, I was told that everybody wanted to be in a squadron and that I should go back where I belonged.
So I resigned myself to being in the engine rooms and boiler rooms. I worked

my way into the boiler repair party, which was responsible for all the steam lines. I worked for a man who was a great engineer. His name was I. J. Klein. He was my mentor and pushed me for all I was worth. He was up for warrant officer and needed to train somebody to take over the boiler repair gang.

In April 1941 we were ordered to the East Coast. We operated out of Bermuda, looking for German raiders in the South Atlantic—ships that were attacking British merchant ships in the area. After that we went to the North Atlantic and convoyed merchant ships to England. German submarines fired torpedoes at us twice during those convoys to England. Our torpedo planes carried 500-pound depth charges and had orders to drop them on German submarines if they saw them. If the *Yorktown* had been sunk by one of those German submarines, I think we would have been in the war earlier than we were.

We were way overdue for an overhaul, so we were sent to Norfolk, Virginia, in December 1941. I got a weekend pass to go to Washington, D.C., and was sitting in a restaurant in Washington on the morning of 7 December 1941 when the Japs attacked Pearl Harbor. I didn't think the Japs could attack Pearl Harbor undetected, but they did. All the time I was at Pearl Harbor PBYs would take off at three or four in the morning, and by daylight they would be several hundred miles out. On 7 December they didn't take off, and I don't know why.

Anyway, we heard the word for all seamen to return to their ships. We got in a taxi and were driving by the Japanese Embassy while trying to get to the train station. We were trapped in the traffic there for about an hour and we could see smoke coming from the Japanese Embassy. They were burning papers.

After the *Yorktown* left dry dock, we went to San Diego and convoyed some ships to Samoa—a contingent of marines. From there we went to Pearl Harbor; I think it was February. Most of the crew was lined up around the flight deck when we came in, and there wasn't a word spoken. It was unbelievable—the battleship *Oklahoma* was upside down. The *California* was on the bottom of the harbor, as were several other battleships.

Later, in May 1942, we were with the *Lexington* at the Battle of the Coral Sea. The Japanese ships were so close to us one night that a Japanese plane tried to land on our flight deck. As he came in, the landing signal officer saw that he was Japanese and waved him off. At the same time he—the landing signal officer—radioed the bridge that the plane was Japanese. The plane went around our bow and back down the starboard side and we shot him down.

During the battle we had several near misses on the after port quarter, and one bomb went down through the main ship passageway and exploded in the ship's service compartment, killing forty-three engineers in that compartment and the compartment next to the one I was in. The shrapnel came through our bulkhead but didn't hit any of us because we were all lying on the deck. The explosion blew out the fires in the after boiler room and I had to go down and reset the "governors." That is when the *Lexington* exploded and sank.

It was dark down in the boiler room, and I had to go down with a battle lantern. When the *Lexington* exploded, I thought we had been hit by a bomb or torpedo. My lantern dropped to the deck and broke, and I was about 14 feet up in the boiler room. That was a fearful experience, being down there with no lights. It made an impression on me that lasted throughout the war. After that, I always had flashlights on me. Even today, I have lots of flashlights around.

Since I was part of the repair party, I didn't have to help retrieve bodies from the compartments next to ours. Just the other day I was talking to a friend of mine in Portland, Oregon. He was on the *Yorktown* and was one of the men who had to bring the bodies out. They were broken up pretty bad, and when he found the body of a close friend, he couldn't touch him. It had such an effect on him.

On our way back to Pearl for repairs we received word to get back at our top speed. We got into the dry dock and worked on the ship for seventy-two hours straight, without any sleep at all—the whole crew. We didn't know it, but we were getting the ship ready for the Battle of Midway. After we cleared the harbor, the captain told us that after the next scrap we were headed for, we would be going back to the States for three months at least.

During the Battle of Midway, being down below, we didn't know what all was happening. The antiaircraft guns started firing and the bombs started dropping. I guess about thirty Jap planes attacked us, and I think about seven got through. We took three bomb hits. One went through the flight deck, forward near the number one elevator and started a fire in the rag locker. We had another that hit between the uptakes and intakes in the forward group of fire rooms. The third bomb was a contact bomb and exploded aft of the island structure, killing fourteen men. We also took a near miss off the fantail, which killed some men back there.

I was in the after boiler cutoff. We had extensions of valves that allowed us to cut off steam to the main steam room below in case of battle damage. We were dead in the water, and it was about an hour before we could get under way again. Then we were attacked again, and I couldn't understand why we couldn't get the combat air patrols from the *Enterprise* and the *Hornet* to help us. We were the only carrier attacked at the Battle of Midway, and we were attacked twice.

During the second attack we got hit by two torpedoes. The *Yorktown* listed to port and was down at the bow. The second torpedo hit about amidships, and my compartment was just aft of amidships. We were listing way over, and all communication on the ship was lost. Our chief said we had better find our way out of there. We had flashlights with us—you bet—and we found the hatch that went up to the second deck. From there, we worked our way up to the hangar deck. The hangar deck was empty except for a fighter that was upside down. The enlisted pilot flying it had flipped it on landing. He had missed the arresting wires and hit the barrier, and that is what flipped him upside down. They had put a dolly under the plane and taken it down to the hangar deck that way.

We got up to the flight deck, and that is when we got the word to abandon ship. There was a chief from my station, and he started taking off his shoes. I told him, "You're going to need those shoes on those hot steel decks on the destroyer." So he put his shoes back on. Everybody was taking their shoes off and putting their watches and cigarette lighters in them as if they were going to come back. The flight deck, when I went back with the salvage crew, was lined with shoes. It was weird. I think the chief and I were the only two with our shoes on when we left the ship.

I started going down the hand line that had knots about every two feet and I saw one guy jump from the flight deck. He landed on a life raft on his back, half in and half out of the water. He folded in half and fell back into the water. It killed him. I started yelling back up to the others, "Don't jump! Don't jump!" Then I looked up, and there was a guy sitting on the side of the ship—sliding down it right at me. This was on the starboard side. I had to push away from the ship to get out of his way.

The ship had a 4-inch steel armored belt right at the waterline, and his heels caught that. His legs broke and his thighbones came right up through his chest and stuck out alongside of his face. His pants ballooned out and the blood gushed out. I was in shock after that. He would have hit me if I hadn't kicked out away from the ship.

I got into a life raft, and then the wounded started coming down. Those of us who could swim and who had lifejackets started swimming to the destroyers to make room for the wounded that were coming down in stretchers. I took off for a destroyer and was about ten feet from a cargo net hanging over the side when it went to general quarters and started backing down. They said more Jap planes were coming back. I figured I could go back to the rafts and take a chance on getting strafed, or I could swim around out there by myself. I figured I was better off by myself.

I was in the water for about an hour or hour and a half before the destroyers came back. I was picked up by the USS *Benham*. They had 720 survivors on the *Benham*, plus their own crew. That night I looked for a place to sleep and found a depth charge rack. I figured under there I was protected by all this angle iron and nobody would run over me at night. I was doing just fine, when in the middle of the night the ship picked up speed and water started coming aboard and woke me up. And about that same time there was an explosion. They thought they had a submarine contact and had fired the "K" gun I was sleeping under.

The next morning we were transferred to the *Portland,* a cruiser. Then the *Hammann,* a destroyer, came alongside. The captain of the *Yorktown,* Elliot Buckmaster, and the guy I worked for, I. J. Klein, were on board. They wanted me to go back to the *Yorktown* with them as part of the salvage crew. I wasn't too enthralled with the idea because I had swallowed so much fuel oil; I was sick to my stomach. So anyway, I went over to the *Hammann,* and then back to the *Yorktown* the next morning.

We went over to the *Yorktown* in a whaleboat from the destroyer. We went around to the port side, and I stepped from the gunwale of the whaleboat onto the hangar deck of the *Yorktown.* The hangar deck is normally 25 feet above the water. The gunwale of the whaleboat was higher than the hangar deck because of the list to port.

We went aboard about six in the morning and had a meeting in the boat shack on the hangar deck. Captain Buckmaster and all the engineering people were there. The captain asked each one of us what we thought could be done to save the ship. The chief water tender said, "Light up the boilers, and get some steam up." I was going to say something in response, but Klein shut me up. I was the lowest in rank, so before I could give them my idea, which was to have the ship towed to Midway, the chief engineer asked me what I would do to counter-flood the ship. I said, "Well, I would fire about three or four well-placed, 5-inch, nonexplosive shells just below the waterline and flood the starboard fuel tanks. That will cause immediate counter-flooding. If that isn't enough, put another shell in there."

One of the officers said he was dead set against that because it would jeopardize the clothing and bedding on the fourth deck. I couldn't believe he said that. Anyway, I never got a chance to offer my idea of towing the ship to Midway. It was then decided to take the tops off the after starboard fuel tanks, which were empty, and pump seawater into them using fire hoses from the *Hammann.* The engine room on the destroyer could put out about 400 gallons a minute. If we had had three or four days, it would have been a great idea but as it was, it was like shoveling against the tide, and we were in enemy waters. We were all worried about Japanese submarines. They were the eyes and ears of the Japanese fleet. They were the first to sortie and the last to leave. We all knew they were out there, and we all knew that they knew our position.

We had five of our destroyers circling us, doing probably 15 knots, but they were not hunting for submarines. I didn't think they could have found a Jap submarine even if one was marching around with them, the water was so riled up from the wakes of all these ships, one right after another.

We worked at saving the *Yorktown* until about two o'clock in the afternoon—dragging fire hoses around and conducting counter-flooding operations. I think it was around then when they brought the whaleboat back over with corned beef sandwiches, with about an inch of corned beef in each one. We were really hungry by that time. Klein and I took our sandwiches and went back to the after boat pocket on the port side. That was on the hangar deck. We were standing there eating our sandwiches when I saw this torpedo wake right at our feet. At the time, I thought the torpedo was coming from the port side. If I had been the captain of that submarine, I would have done just that, fired at the port side because we were already wounded on that side. But as it turned out, the torpedo was going away from us and not at us. It went under the ship.

I was waiting for the next ones to hit. The *Hammann*, which was on the starboard side of the *Yorktown*, was hit by the next torpedo. In fact, some members of our salvage crew jumped over onto the *Hammann*, thinking it would get away. The explosion on the *Hammann* knocked Klein and me off our feet. We got up, then another torpedo hit the *Yorktown*, and that knocked us down again. We got up again, and there was another torpedo hit, and that knocked us down a third time. So the *Hammann* took one, we took two, and one missed out of a flight of four torpedoes. I jumped up after the last torpedo hit and ran over to the starboard side to see what happened. The forepeak of the *Hammann* was just going down, and the stern section was standing straight up and down and the screws were still turning.

There was a kid hanging on the depth charge rack, trying to set the depth charges on safe. They were set to go off at 50 feet. They were also set for quick release from the bridge. I could see he wasn't going to make it; he was back there all by himself. Then the stern section went down, and all those depth charges went off. The sea just opened up with a tremendous explosion.

I think the *Hammann* lost 127 men out of their crew of about 250 people. What the men got in the water when those depth charges went off was a super enema with about 1,200 pounds of pressure and it just exploded their insides.

There certainly were a lot of bodies floating around out there. Later, we went out in a whaleboat, and I helped pick up the survivors. Most of them had blood coming out of their noses from internal bleeding.

We had to abandon ship again. The tug that was towing us came around and took us off, then took us to another destroyer, the *Balch,* and it took us back to Pearl. There they broke up the crew. Half of the engineers went to the battleship *West Virginia,* and half went to the battleship *California.* I spent six months on the *California* helping to get it repaired before it went back to the States. We got it back to Bremerton, then I was sent to "new construction." They were building a new type of ship called "destroyer escorts"—a brand new design. I think they built some 560 [it was closer to 300] of them during the war.

These destroyer escorts were all preassembled. They built sections back in Denver and hauled them out on a train and did the rest of the assembly at the shipyards. I was assigned to one being built in Michigan, and I figured they would sail her down the Mississippi, and out into the Atlantic. I had already been in the North Atlantic in the wintertime, and I thought I would rather go back out to the Pacific. So I put a sign on the board requesting to trade duties. A sailor of equal rating looked me up, and we traded duties because his home was in Michigan. I saw the guy later on out in the Pacific after the war was over in Europe. He came over to the *England* and looked me up. I said, "What did you do in your war since I saw you last?" He said, "We tied up in Naples for six months and supplied light and power to the docks." I said, "You fought a safe war. I haven't been off this ship since I last saw you."

CHAPTER 2

◆ ◆ ◆ ◆ ◆

Flag Allowance

Norman Ulmer

Norman Ulmer was born in 1920 in Burnham, Pennsylvania. He graduated from high school in 1938, but could not go on to college for financial reasons. He then worked on a sailing yacht as a deck hand for the next two years until his enlistment into the U.S. Navy in March 1941. During his time in the navy Ulmer served under several admirals as a member of their enlisted "flag allowance," which consisted of yeomen, radiomen, signalmen, and marines. In this capacity, he served on several fighting ships, including the USS *Enterprise* and the USS *Iowa*. After the surrender of Japan, Ulmer served as part of the flag allowance under Adm. Frederick C. Sherman until his discharge on 30 September 1946, as a signalman first class, after five years and seven months of service. Ulmer is now retired and lives in Lewisburg, Pennsylvania, with his wife of fifty-five years, Margaret Gundy Ulmer.

The first thing I did when I turned twenty-one was to join the navy. So it was on 3 March 1941 that I signed up and repeated the oath of allegiance to the United States of America. After boot camp I reported to the training station in San Diego, California, on 28 June 1941. This was going to be my home for the next four months. After I graduated from the communications school, I was prepared for further training as a signalman and was assigned to a ship that was based in the Hawaiian Islands. What a thrill! I received my orders along with two other shipmates, Doug Fleming and Donald Ruffier. We boarded a navy tanker for passage to Pearl Harbor. Ruffier and I were assigned to the flag allowance of Rear Adm. John H. Newton. He was commander of Cruiser Scouting Force, with his flag flying on the USS *Chicago* (CA-29).

Fleming was assigned to the same ship, but he was assigned to ship's company. Once aboard ship we were all assigned to the same living compartment, and we all stood our watches together on the signal bridge. Since we were the bottom men on the totem pole and had a lot to learn, we didn't qualify as signalmen. Being junior men in our respective watches, we were responsible for recording messages as they were received by other signalmen, and were then responsible for hand-carrying them to the flag bridge, the commanding officer, executive officer, the officer of the deck, the navigator, and so forth.

On 5 December 1941 our task force, under the command of Admiral Newton, in the company of the USS *Lexington,* left Pearl Harbor for the purpose of delivering Marine Corps aircraft to Midway. Since we got under way on a Friday, and Saturday was taken up with gunnery practice, our captain's inspection, which is usually held on Saturday, was postponed until the next day, 7 December 1941. That Sunday, 7 December, I had the twelve midnight to four in the morning watch, and during that watch the admiral's chief of staff, Capt. Spencer Lewis, was on the signal bridge when one of the radiomen came up from the radio shack and said, "Captain, we have just intercepted a radio message—an SOS message. Some ship is in distress. Shall we answer it?" "No! Maintain radio silence. Do not answer it." I might also add that at that time,

Norman Ulmer, signalman first class.

before the bombing of Pearl Harbor, all ships entering and leaving Pearl Harbor at night were under "darken ship." Also, there were antisubmarine nets across the harbor, which had to be opened before you could come in. At that time, there were also orders to maintain radio silence. We learned later that this SOS message was a ruse of the Japanese to see if there were any ships in the area that they might have a problem with.

I came off watch at four in the morning, slept for a while, then got up and shaved and showered to get ready for captain's inspection, which was scheduled for sometime in the morning hours. While I was making preparation for the inspection, a radio flash was received. The following was broadcast over the ship's P.A. system: "THIS IS NO DRILL! THIS IS NO DRILL! PEARL HARBOR IS UNDER ATTACK BY UNIDENTIFIED AIRCRAFT! THIS IS NO DRILL!" This was acknowledged with dismay, as we shined our shoes and polished our brass belt buckles.

The P.A. system came on again: "THIS IS NO DRILL! THIS IS NO DRILL! THE PLANES ATTACKING PEARL HARBOR ARE IDENTIFIED AS JAPANESE! WE ARE AT WAR WITH THE JAPANESE!" As you can imagine, the captain's inspection was postponed, and I never stood another captain's inspection until the war's end.

All ships went immediately to general quarters, and our watches went to four hours on and four hours off. That was probably one of the most strenuous times I ever had aboard ship as far as duty was concerned. We didn't continue that throughout the war, but we did do it during the first part of the war.

The mission to Midway was delayed, and Admiral Newton ordered the task force to return to Pearl Harbor. Search planes from the USS *Lexington* were launched, and a message was sent to the task force by radio. It stated, "Intercept and destroy enemy believed retreating on a course between Pearl and Jaluit [in the Marshall Islands]. Intercept and destroy."

The task force increased speed and headed southward towards the Marshall Islands. The Japanese carriers were, however, retreating to the northwest, and it is possible that we could have intercepted them when they made their withdrawal if we had maintained our position. Fortunately, we headed south, and that was for the better, because otherwise the *Lexington* air group would have had to contend with the air groups of six Japanese carriers.

We were unprepared for the casualties at Pearl Harbor. We saw the mess when we came in about a week later. The water in the harbor was still covered in oil, and the recovery of dead bodies from the ships was ongoing. It was not a pretty sight.

We made at least one more sortie with other ships, then in late December 1941, or early January 1942, the *Chicago* received orders to proceed to Australia and New Zealand. However, I was part of the flag allowance, and we were temporarily transferred to the cruiser USS *Astoria,* to await further assignment with Adm. Jack Fletcher, because he was to become the commander of Cruiser Scouting Force, which he took over on 31 January 1942. He broke his flag on the USS *Yorktown* (CV-5) on 1 February 1942. So the enlisted personnel from the flag allowance of Admiral Newton were reassigned to Admiral Fletcher. This was to be the first of many transfers for me.

On the morning of 16 February 1942, we left Pearl Harbor and proceeded to the South Pacific. The orders to the fleet, or to our task force, were to meet suspected enemy forces. Our task force patrolled the waters, and our air groups kept vigilance in the sky. We made many monotonous patrols until 10 March, at 0545, when we went to general quarters. Planes were launched for a raid on Lae and Salamaua in Papua New Guinea. This action caught the enemy by surprise and, so I'm told, delayed a Japanese move south. The raid also told the Japanese that American carriers were operating in that theater where we were thought not to be, and delayed their attack on Port Moresby. Now, if the Japanese wanted to continue their operations in the southwest Pacific, they would need carriers to support their invasion plans, and it soon became evident that we would be meeting their flattops.

The *Yorktown* had been on a lonely watch in the South Pacific. You might say we had been operating alone. The *Saratoga* had been torpedoed off Oahu on 11 January, and the *Lexington* and *Enterprise* needed repairs. The *Hornet* was en route from the East Coast, and the *Wasp* was sailing to the British Isles. The *Ranger* was in the Atlantic along with an escort carrier, the *Long Island.*

Watchful waiting continued, and the fact that we were practically working alone didn't allow much room for flexibility of deployment. Admiral Fletcher also had a healthy respect for land-based Japanese aircraft, and there were other concerns. The *Yorktown* and her destroyers were running low on fresh provisions. We had been at sea for over a month, and it was predicted that our supply situation would become critical by the first of April.

With no worthwhile objectives south of Rabaul, we continued our zigging and zagging in the Coral Sea. By the second week in April our foodstuffs were in short supply, and bombs were needed for our aircraft. And there was another problem; the self-sealing gas tanks on the F4F fighter planes were deteriorating, and this alarmed Admiral Fletcher. As a result, the number of serviceable F4Fs had been reduced to only a dozen. He radioed the commander in chief, Pacific Fleet [CINCPAC], that if this deterioration continued, it would be necessary for him to retire to Tongatabu in the Tonga Islands. CINCPAC ordered the task force to make for Tongatabu for provisions and upkeep. We arrived in Nukualofa Harbor in Tongatabu on 20 April 1942. We took on lots of provisions, plus ammunition. Liberty was going to be granted, our first in sixty-three days. I was lucky; I went ashore with the first liberty party. The natives lived in grass huts. Bananas, oranges, and coconuts were in abundance, and we were allowed to bring fresh fruit back to the ship with us, since the ship was in short supply. In a few days, it seemed as though every compartment had a stock of bananas, and the *Yorktown* was taking on the odor of a fresh fruit barge.

It was with reluctance that we left this paradise of Tongatabu on 27 April 1942, and in a few days we were going to experience a little bit of hell. We were outbound for the Coral Sea. We probed deeper into the Coral Sea, and our air groups attacked Japanese shipping in and around Tulagi Harbor in the Solomons. This surely alerted the Japs that our carriers were in the area. Subsequently, search planes from our carriers and those from the enemy carriers ended this game of cat and mouse.

As we patrolled the Coral Sea, it became apparent we were going to engage a Japanese carrier force. The Battle of the Coral Sea was fought about three hundred miles east of Papua New Guinea. It was on 7 May 1942 that hostilities began with planes from the USS *Lexington* and the USS *Yorktown* attacking and sinking the Japanese light carrier, *Shoho*. Up to this time I had yet to see a Japanese warplane. That evening, on 7 May, I saw my first one. Three Japanese planes, confused and lost, flew over our bow and joined the landing circle with our planes. It became obvious to them when our ship's guns turned on them that they had made a mistake. Our ship's gunners claimed one of the enemy planes. The other two were frightened off. The *Yorktown* recovered her remaining planes and proceeded to clear the area.

The next morning at 0545 we were awakened with the sound of reveille. It was going to be a long day. On 8 May we had located the Japanese forces, and they had located us. The Japanese planes were picked up on our radar, and our fighters were vectored to intercept and destroy them. It also became evident that we were going to be attacked. There was apprehension and fear when enemy planes started to dive on us. Watching the bombs drop from the Japanese planes, I could determine if they were going to fall short, and contrasted those to the ones that would overshoot our hull. Then there was the reality of the one that was going to hit. For a brief moment, I had the feeling I was going to be killed. I was confronted with my own mortality. I felt it was too late to repent, too late to ask for forgiveness, and too late to ask for mercy. It was too late, because I knew if I were spared I would go on a terrific hoot if I were ever to set foot in the USA again. That all flashed through my mind, and I could not ask God for special favors. Those of us who were topside were looking at the threat and fear of death. It was a fear that I would experience again in other Japanese air attacks while serving aboard the USS *Saratoga* (CV-3), the USS *Bunker Hill* (CV-17), and the USS *Essex* (CV-9).

That day we received one bomb hit that penetrated the flight deck forward of the number two elevator, and about 15 feet inboard of the island structure. Those of us topside were lucky because it was a delayed-action bomb. It passed through the number three ready room, through the hangar deck, and through the second deck. After piercing the third deck, it exploded just before it reached the armored fourth deck. It exploded in a storeroom and expended itself upward. Repair Five, an emergency repair party, was awaiting their call to action in that area. Only two of the party of forty survived the blast. Crewmen were assigned to recover the bloody and blackened bodies, and they were committed to the deep in the early morning hours of 9 May.

The blast did not deter the ship's headway. By early afternoon, the engineering gang had cleared the machinery area of smoke and had nearly all the boilers back on line, and the recovery of our air attack groups had been completed.

The *Lexington*, which had been on our port beam just short of the horizon, suffered bomb and torpedo hits, but everything seemed to be under control. But about mid-afternoon, an explosion rocked her. This touched off fires below decks that were uncontrollable. I watched the *Lexington* inferno from the signal bridge of the *Yorktown*. After assurances that all hands had cleared the hapless ship, orders were given to sink her.

On 15 May 1942 we returned to Tongatabu. A quick assessment was made of the *Yorktown*'s external damage, and no liberty was granted to the crew on this stopover. We were then ordered to Pearl Harbor for repairs. We entered Pearl Harbor on 27 May, 101 days after our departure from there in mid-February. Admiral Nimitz inspected the ship's damage and declared that the *Yorktown* must be ready in three days. The shipyard workers worked around the clock, and the *Yorktown* departed Pearl Harbor on 30 May. When we were well out to sea, Captain Buckmaster made an announcement over the ship's P.A. system. He told us what lay ahead, where we were going, and what would be required of us. To brighten a tense situation, he told us that at the conclusion of this next engagement Admiral Nimitz had ordered the ship to go to Bremerton, Washington, for a complete overhaul. This made me feel better. It made the crew feel better. I did not know at that time, however, that the anticipated return to the States was going to be put on hold.

While we were at the navy yard in Pearl, water-cooled .50-caliber machine guns were mounted on various areas of the ship. This was a jury-rig operation, and there would be no circulating water for the guns. The jackets were filled with water, and the gunners were instructed to fire them until they froze.

We followed the other ships from Task Force 17, namely, the destroyers *Hammann, Morris, Anderson, Russell,* and *Hughes.* Added to this group were the heavy cruisers *Astoria* and *Portland.* We grouped outside Pearl Harbor, and all ships engaged in gunnery practice. That afternoon our air groups came aboard the *Yorktown.* While landing our fighter planes, tragedy struck. Lieutenant Commander Lovelace landed and taxied his plane forward to a position below and abeam of the island structure, just below the signal bridge. The next plane had been given the "cut" to land, and with air speed diminished, the pilot attempted to abort his landing. Without sufficient air speed, he could not get the lift to clear the barrier. Consequently, his tail hook caught the barrier and brought his plane down on Lovelace's plane. The propeller slashed through the cockpit, killing Lovelace almost instantly. This incident on the flight deck just below the signal bridge was gruesome. I'll never forget seeing Lieutenant Commander Lovelace's lifeless body. His head was hanging by threads of flesh and resting on his chest, with blood gushing from his arteries. His plane's engine was running with the throttle open and the propeller whirling at many rpms. A member of the flight deck crew made several attempts to shut down the aircraft, only to be repelled. He was blinded by the blood that was gushing from the dying pilot's body. Sticking his head again into the cockpit, the crewman finally succeeded in shutting down the plane's engine. The remaining planes were brought aboard without further incident.

Ships refueled on the way to Midway, and on 2 June 1942 we rendezvoused with Task Force 16. That same day, scout planes were launched to scout out the enemy and found nothing.

On 4 June we had an early reveille, and on that day I remember taking a message to Admiral Fletcher. With a cool and calm manner he said, "Young man, we're going to get them today." Captain Buckmaster, the commanding officer of *Yorktown,* ordered that our largest ensign [flag] be flown from the mast. It was an inspiring sight for all of us.

Our pilots, flying towards the enemy ships, spotted enemy aircraft heading towards our group. The Japanese planes made the same observation, and each group continued on their missions of destruction. The enemy dive-bombers that made the attack on the *Yorktown* numbered about fifteen. This was at about 1400. At least seven of them were able to get through, and they dove from different directions. This was unlike the action at Coral Sea, when they all dove with the sun at their backs. The *Yorktown* received three hits. One bomb struck forward in the vicinity of the number one elevator, the second aft of the island structure near elevator number two, and the third pierced the stack on the port side. A fourth bomb was a near miss and exploded astern. There were casualties from all the bombs. The direct hits exploded below decks. There was damage to our boilers. The *Yorktown* lost speed and became dead in the water. The flight deck was repaired quickly and would be ready when sufficient speed from the boilers would permit air operations. The emergency force below decks worked feverishly on the damaged boilers, and a breakdown flag was hoisted on our yardarm. This informed the ships in our formation about our condition of readiness. At about 1600 the men in the engine rooms reported that they could give us enough power for about 20 knots. The breakdown flag was then hauled down from the yardarm and replaced with a general information signal, "Mike Speed-five." This was interpreted as, "My speed, 5 knots." This was continually upgraded until we hit the maximum that could be coached from the boilers. As I recall, the final information signal was "My speed, 15 knots." At that speed, we launched fighter aircraft.

While the engine rooms were making their reports, Radar Plot reported a large group of planes about 35 miles away and closing. Our fighter planes were vectored to intercept them. Ruffier and I were directed to take a station atop the signal shelter with orders to report any excessive heat or fire that might emanate from the stack that had been hit from an earlier bomb. From this vantage point, we had an unobstructed view of the approaching Japanese torpedo planes.

We saw two torpedo wakes heading for the ship. No mistaking, they were going to make contact. One of the planes that made the run flew over our flight deck, forward of the island structure. This torpedo plane had three occupants, and they were sitting in tandem. They were the pilot, cameraman, and rear gunner, in that order. I thought surely the rear gunner would strafe us. We were at about eye level with the plane. His armament appeared similar to our .50-caliber machine guns, but the rear gunner did not fire. He was slumped over, and I found out years later that he was wounded.

After we were hit by the two torpedoes, the ship developed about a 30-degree list to port, and orders were given to prepare to abandon ship. When Ruffier and I came down from atop the signal shelter, we proceeded to the storage area for our lifejackets and found it bare. The extra personnel from other divisions on the signal bridge had left us short of lifejackets available to the signal gang.

The *Yorktown* was now dead in the water. I descended to the flight deck in hopes of finding a lifejacket. My search was fruitless, and I walked forward of the island structure, and in the vicinity of the 5-inch guns I found some powder cans. I sealed one with its cap and tied it to my waist. William Foster, a signalman first class, observed my predicament and said he would descend on a line adjacent to mine. We would make an assessment of the buoyancy of the powder can after we reached the water. The can was buoyant and lodged under my left arm. Foster pushed me with his right arm and stroked with his left. I stroked with my right arm, and we cleared the ship.

There were men all around us in the water. Those who had not tied their lifejackets correctly were having trouble keeping them from sliding up over their heads. Some men drowned in their own lifejackets.

For the first time in my life I heard men screaming. My left arm had gone to sleep, and my shoulder ached. Our faces and hands were covered with oil. I had swallowed some of the oil, and I was sick to my stomach. My spirits were low, and I could hear general quarters being sounded on our supporting ships.

A general information signal was flying from their yardarms, PREPARE TO REPEL ENEMY AIR ATTACK! Not a welcome sign. The signal, we soon learned, was false.

Then the USS *Russell* (DD-414) appeared. I reached out and touched her starboard bow. Members of the crew threw me a looped line that was tied with a bowline knot. I stuck it over my head and under my arms, and they fished me aboard. Foster slowly ascended a Jacob's ladder that was hanging over the side. The *Russell* picked up about four hundred survivors. The crewmen of the *Russell* were generous and hospitable. They gave us clothes that literally came off their backs. Just a month earlier, they had done the same when they picked up survivors from the *Lexington* in the Coral Sea. We were given grapefruit to cut the oily taste in our mouths, and hot soup for nourishment.

I'm not sure, but we may have been aboard the *Russell* for two days before being transferred to the sub tender *Fulton* for transport to Pearl Harbor. While aboard the *Fulton,* we were issued new dungarees, underclothes, socks, and shoes. We also had access to lots of soap, shampoo, and hot water. It felt real good to get rid of that oil that covered our bodies.

After arrival in Pearl Harbor we anticipated that we would surely receive orders to go to the States for rest and recuperation with ship's company before being reassigned, but it was not so for members of the admiral's flag allowance. The admiral, his staff, and his enlisted men were transferred to the USS *Saratoga*. The *Saratoga* was in Pearl Harbor, having just returned from the States after being repaired for damages resulting from a torpedo hit earlier in the year. The *Saratoga* was to be our new flagship.

We proceeded west and south, crossing the International Date Line and the equator. We went to sea with plenty of provisions—tons of them—and we were not going to touch any ports for a long time. Our planes flew constant anti-submarine and combat air patrols. June and July passed with no action. In August our air group was spearheading for the marines on Guadalcanal. On 23 August 1942 our combat air patrols shot down a Japanese Zero, and it was believed to be carrier-based. So we armed our torpedo planes with torpedoes, our dive-bombers with armor-piercing bombs, and our fighter planes with all the ammo they could carry.

A situation similar to Midway occurred. The Japanese planes and ours passed each other, but this time at different altitudes. Each group was on the way to destroy the other's carriers. The *Enterprise* bore the brunt of the attack. We were spared because we were hidden by dense cloud cover. That evening we landed our planes and many from the *Enterprise*.

A week later, on 31 August, a destroyer reported four torpedo wakes heading for the *Saratoga*. The ship, under the command of Capt. D. C. Ramsey, skillfully dodged three of them, but the fourth one got us. At that moment, I had just completed sending a message to one of our cruisers in the formation. Fortunately, the torpedo struck a fire room that had been secured, and there were no mortal casualties. A torpedo from a submarine carries a terrific wallop, but this time it wasn't enough to stop the *Saratoga*.

We retired to the Tonga Islands for an assessment of our damage. Temporary repairs enabled the ship to continue on for extensive repairs in the navy yard at Pearl Harbor. While in Pearl, Captain Ramsey was promoted to rear admiral, and Admiral Fletcher was given orders to command the North Pacific. Admiral Fletcher requested that he be allowed to retain his flag personnel. Admiral Nimitz refused his request, stating that our experience was necessary for the flag of Rear Admiral Ramsey, who was now going to make the *Saratoga* his flagship. Admiral Fletcher wanted to keep us on his staff, and we were told that he pleaded with Admiral Nimitz on the grounds that he had told his men "Where I go, you go. If I go to hell, you're going with me." Nimitz did make one concession. He granted us leave on the condition that we be back in Pearl Harbor before the *Saratoga*'s departure. This would be on the completion of yard repairs.

When my leave was over, I returned to Pearl Harbor on one of the old president liners loaded with army troops. The *Saratoga* departed San Francisco on 12 October, and by early December 1942 we were operating out of Nouméa, New Caledonia. In July 1943 Admiral Ramsey informed us that he had received orders and would soon be detached for another assignment. He returned to the States, and Rear Adm. Frederick C. Sherman took his place. Plans were being made to neutralize the Japanese base at Rabaul, and tensions were high on the *Saratoga*. We were with the Third Fleet and were joined by the light carrier *Princeton* in October 1943.

I remember my good friend Harold Probus, signalman second class, coming off watch, and as he entered our living compartment, he said, "I wish my mother had never sent me to Sunday school. I don't want to die and I don't want to go to hell." This about summed it up for all of us. We felt the tensions of the war. We also felt very mortal. From our early religious training, we knew we weren't perfect, and our fear of death was also a fear of condemnation to hell. Yet today I feel we are all comfortable with our lives and certainly don't have the fear of eternal condemnation.

Our forces received a message from JICPOA [Joint Intelligence Center, Pacific Ocean Areas] that the harbor at Rabaul was full of heavy Japanese surface ships and transports that were going to be used to drive our marines off their beachheads at Bougainville. On 25 November 1943 the air group from the *Saratoga*, in company with the air group from the *Princeton*, attacked the shipping at Rabaul on New Britain Island. Many of our planes returned from the strike with heavy damage, some so severe that they were ditched into the sea after landing on the carrier. We wondered how the pilots managed to maneuver these crippled planes. The raid was successful and stalled the Japanese advance.

Shortly after the raid on Rabaul, on 26 November, Admiral Sherman, his staff, and enlisted men were ordered to report aboard the USS *Bunker Hill* (CV-17). Another transfer—another flagship. This transfer was going to be unique. We were going to be transferred at sea via highline to the destroyer, USS *Sterett* (DD-407). The old *Sara* bade us farewell, then proceeded to San Francisco Navy Yard for a long overdue overhaul.

We were aboard the *Sterett* for several days before joining up with our new flagship, the USS *Bunker Hill*. The transfer was effected in the same manner as when we left the *Saratoga*. The *Bunker Hill* would be our home for the next three months. She was a newly commissioned *Essex*-class carrier, and even though we were bitter about staying at sea and not returning home to the States with the *Sara*, we had to admit that this new carrier was the most modern ship upon which we had yet served. This was in contrast to the *Saratoga*, whose interior bulkheads had been stripped of paint and had not been repainted, and had rusty bulkheads, not to mention the damnable water restrictions. So many times I had come off watch and there was no fresh water, and only one scuttlebutt on the mess deck for drinking. It was uncomfortable in the heat of the South Pacific. On the *Bunker Hill* there were no water restrictions. The showers were available twenty-four hours a day.

During our tour of duty on the *Bunker Hill,* it seemed that we were constantly being badgered by Japanese Bettys, our ID for their torpedo bomber planes. So many times an enemy flare would illuminate the task group in the darkness of the Pacific. Thanks to our night fighters, who were specially trained, they kept these enemy planes at bay. Then there were early morning raids that seemed always to happen when we had hotcakes for breakfast. Whenever we were relieved on the 0400 to 0800 watch we would ask, "What's for breakfast?" If the reply was "Hotcakes," we felt reluctant to go below decks. However, I am happy to state that not once did the *Bunker Hill* receive a hit while we were aboard. Near misses, no hits, good gunners.

We finally received some good news. The *Bunker Hill* was ordered to return to Pearl Harbor. The flag was ordered to report aboard the USS *Essex* (CV-9). On 9 March 1944 we reported aboard and departed the following morning for San Francisco and thirty days' leave upon arrival. However, all good things come to an end, and we all reported back to the *Essex* at the termination of leave and departed San Francisco on 16 April 1944. While we were on leave, Admiral Sherman had been replaced by Rear Admiral Harrill. Some of our staff officers had been transferred also. Our old gang was slowly breaking up.

We arrived at Pearl on 20 April and departed on 3 May for our old hunting grounds. In early June 1944 we moved farther west to support the marine landings in the Mariana Islands. Our air group struck Saipan on 12 June, and while the marines were going ashore on 15 June, we struck at the Bonin Islands. Later, we turned south and joined the others of the fast carrier task groups. Intelligence reports indicated the Japanese navy was moving towards the Marianas from their bases in the Philippines, and that there was going to be a showdown.

The Japanese had not committed their carriers since the fall of 1942, and that was off Guadalcanal. At this time the commander in chief of Japanese forces, Admiral Ozawa, was committing his naval air force. This would later be called the Great Marianas Turkey Shoot, officially designated as the First Battle of the Philippine Sea.

Not long after this engagement, Admiral Harrill was stricken with appendicitis and underwent emergency surgery. The flag was ordered to report to Pearl Harbor, and we enlisted men wondered and speculated, what was to be our future. To effect our passage to Pearl Harbor, we were transferred to the USS *Heywood* (APA-6), and our orders were to report to ComFleetAirPac for reassignment. We were the only passengers on board—no troops—just the crew of the ship and the flag personnel.

We reached Pearl Harbor on 10 August 1944 and learned that Admiral Sherman had requested to resume his old command. He further requested that as many as possible of his former enlisted crew be assigned to him. That answered our question about our future—back to sea again. On 13 August we departed with Admiral Sherman on board the USS *Enterprise* (CV-6), with orders to return to our former flagship, the USS *Essex*. Approximately two weeks later we were under way on the *Essex* with Admiral Sherman, now commander of Carrier Division One. Our task group set out to start softening up the Philippines in preparation for landings later in the year.

It was during this time that the Japanese launched their latest and most terrible weapon, the kamikaze. It was a frightening experience to witness these planes boring in through a wall of antiaircraft fire. We did not rely on secondhand accounts of these attacks. We saw it firsthand from the vantage point of the signal bridge.

To date the *Essex* had not experienced any damage from enemy air attacks. Our luck ran out on 25 November 1944. General quarters was sounded, and men scrambled to their battle stations in an effort to defend against two approaching enemy planes. At the sounding of the alarm, I was off watch, in a washroom, preparing to shave and shower before relieving the watch later in the day. You could almost tell the distance of the two approaching planes from the ship by the sound of the antiaircraft fire. First, there was the dull boom of 5-inch guns. That meant the planes were at a distance. Then there was the steady rhythm of the 40-mm mounts: BOOM-BOOM-BOOM-BOOM! Then there was the staccato of the .50-caliber machine guns. That is when you knew they were on top of you.

One of the planes was shot down by our gunners and crashed into the sea. The other one bored in and hit us while I was scrambling to get to the signal bridge. Damage to the ship was not extensive. Within thirty minutes the flames were extinguished and the flight deck was made operational. Regrettably, there were fifteen men killed and forty-four injured. Nine of those killed were black steward's mates. They were killed at their 20-mm gun mount while firing their guns at the incoming planes.

February and March were busy months as the air groups made strikes on Tokyo, Iwo Jima, and Okinawa. Strikes continued through May 1945 on the Ryuku Islands and the island of Kyushu.

On 18 June Rear Adm. Frederick C. Sherman hauled down his flag and was relieved by Rear Adm. G. F. Gauguin, commander, Carrier Division Four. The admiral and his staff were ordered to return to the States, and transportation was provided by the carrier USS *Intrepid*. The *Intrepid* was going to a navy yard for repairs to its damaged flight deck caused by the heavy seas of a typhoon. The *Intrepid* berthed in San Francisco, and within twenty-four hours, with leave papers in order, I was on my way to Pennsylvania.

The atomic bombs were dropped on Hiroshima and Nagasaki while I was home. This brought the Japanese to their knees. However, I was regular navy, and this did not terminate my enlistment obligation. Upon termination of my leave I reported to the West Coast. Hopes for shore duty were negated, and the flag allowance was ordered to Pearl Harbor to await further orders. We were in limbo at Pearl when we learned that our old boss, Admiral Sherman, had entered Pearl Harbor on the USS *Enterprise*. He was returning from Tokyo where he had witnessed the surrender of the Japanese aboard the battleship USS *Missouri*. It occurred to a few of us that possibly we could rejoin the admiral. It was rumored that the *Enterprise* was returning to the East Coast, so a few of us made plans to visit the *Enterprise* with hopes of seeing the admiral. About six of us put on our whites and made our way to dockside. Boarding the *Enterprise,* we found the officer of the deck surprised at our request to see the admiral. A call was made to the admiral's quarters. The admiral's marine orderly answered the phone and inquired our names. After a pause he said, "Send them up." We were escorted to the admiral's quarters by a ship's messenger and were greeted by the marine orderly.

About this time, Lieutenant Morrison, the admiral's communications officer, entered the passageway. There was immediate recognition. We asked if the admiral and the *Enterprise* were going to the States. Then we inquired if it was possible for us to become a part of his flag allowance again. With no hesitation he replied, "Give me your names and service numbers, return to your barracks, pack your sea bags, and await further orders." With elation we returned to our barracks, and while we were packing a jeep pulled up. A messenger dismounted and read our names. He informed us that transportation would be available shortly, and we would be transported to the *Enterprise,* and returned to the States with the admiral.

Recently, 26–30 August 2000, I visited Sand Island, Midway. While there, I met a delegation of twenty people from Japan. They were on the island for the purpose of conducting memorial services in memory of the departed Japanese and American servicemen who were lost in the 1942 Battle of Midway. These services were conducted at the Japanese and American memorials on the island.

The day following these services two Japanese ships docked. They were the JDS *Kashima* (TV-3508) and JDS *Yuugiri* (DD-153). The crews from these ships came ashore, and they also conducted services at the memorials. At the conclusion of the service at the U.S. memorial Rear Adm. Eiji Yoshikawa invited William Surgi and me to join him and others for lunch aboard his flagship. There, the admiral presented Bill and me with baseball caps, compliments of the commanding officers of the two naval vessels.

Before making the trip to the island, we had been told that two of the Japanese airmen who flew over our flight deck during the Battle of Midway would be there. I had hoped to meet these men, and especially wanted to ask why we were not strafed as they passed over the *Yorktown*. My question would go unanswered because neither of the men could make it because of ill health.

The Japanese men we met asked about our postwar feelings. I explained that after all these years we had no animosity, and that we must respect the other's culture and endeavor to live peacefully for the benefit of the generations that follow.

CHAPTER 3

◆ ◆ ◆ ◆ ◆

Photographer's Mate, USS *Suwannee* (CVE-27)

Robert Eustace

Robert Eustace was born in Stockton, California, in 1925. His family moved to San Francisco by way of a paddlewheel steamship in 1932, at the height of the Great Depression. He graduated from Mission High School in San Francisco in 1942 at the age of sixteen and tried to enlist in the U.S. Army, but was rejected because of his age. He then went to work for Eastman Kodak for about ten months until he was seventeen, when he enlisted in the U.S. Navy. The year was 1943. He served most of the war on the USS *Suwannee* (CVE-27). After the war, he went back to work for Eastman Kodak until his retirement. He now lives in Sunnyvale, California.

The *Suwannee* was commissioned in July 1941 as a fleet oiler, but was converted to a *Sangamon*-class escort carrier in September 1942. She fought throughout World War II in both the Atlantic and Pacific, and had thirteen battle stars to her credit by war's end. She was struck from the list of navy ships in 1959 and scrapped in 1962.

On 1 January 1944 I received orders to report aboard the USS *Suwannee* along with Ralph Triggiano, who had gone to navy photo school with me. He was from Chicago, where Al Capone lived just next door. At least that's what he said. He was a cocky little guy—always smoking cigars.

As photographer's mates, we were at the whim of the captain and various division officers on the ship. If somebody wanted pictures of a party in the wardroom, we were there. If some officers wanted pictures of a chart in order to have extra copies, we were there. If the captain wanted all the plane landings monitored, we were there. If the navy wanted publicity photos of a pilot who'd shot down a Jap plane, we were there. Group photos, verification of bomb damage, we were there. We took photos of anything and everything. The only time I did aerial photographs for mapping was over Guam. Photo intelligence was something else, and I never had anything to do with it.

In February 1944 we left for Hawaii. From Hawaii we went to Kwajalein for the invasion of Roi-Namur and some other atolls in the Marshall Islands, where I flew my first mission from the back seat of an SBD, a Douglas Dauntless Dive Bomber. I had an F-56, which was a large 7- by 7-inch negative format camera, in my lap. We also had twin .30-caliber machine guns back there, but in order to use them I would have had to throw the camera overboard. There wasn't enough room in that rear seat for both. But the navy didn't want us to use the guns, so they never taught us. They wanted the cameras back.

Anyway, we took off from the ship and went to about 10,000 feet, then peeled off at an almost vertical dive with our dive brakes on. We dropped our 500-pound bomb at about 2,000 feet and pulled up. We also carried two 100-pound bombs, one under each wing. So we made one run with the 500-pound bomb, then a second run, dropping the two 100-pound bombs. That was my first experience of that, and I thought I would take some pictures as the plane came out of its dive, but I couldn't lift the camera off my lap because of the G-forces. So for the second dive I held a small 8-mm movie camera out alongside the fuselage as we came down. When we pulled out of the dive, the force bent the handle into a *U,* and I almost lost the camera.

I made a number of flights during that operation, then we returned to Hawaii. Our next operation was the invasion of Eniwetok. I almost got my butt

Robert Eustace, photographer's mate, Pensacola, Florida.

busted on that one. We made our diving runs, then I told the pilot that I wanted
to make a low-level run around the island and take some photos. So he went
down to about 200 feet off the water and about 500 feet offshore, and we started
off around the island. All of a sudden the plane banked. I asked the pilot what
that was all about, and he said, "Look!" And these bombs came down past us.
Some planes were making glide bomb runs on the island, and we had flown right
under their pattern. After we got back to the ship, the pilot said, "Don't ever ask
me to do that again. Do you know we were being shot at from the island while
you were taking your pictures?" I didn't notice; I was busy taking pictures.

For our next operation we went to the New Hebrides Islands, then Papua
New Guinea. We were in on the invasions at Hollandia and Aitape, which were
pretty much walk-ins—not much resistance from the enemy. Then we went to
Saipan, Tinian, and Guam in the Marianas. I flew there and did three photo-
graphic runs over Guam at 10,000 feet in a TBM with a twenty-plane fighter

escort. On the *Suwannee,* we had twenty-one F6F Hellcats and nine SBD dive-bombers at one time, but they were later replaced with TBFs. We had planes that would go out and not come back, and we had a lot of plane crashes on the ship, but most of the time the guys survived those. And you know, unless you knew the guys you don't remember them. I didn't like to fly in the TBFs at all because there was no way out of them.

When the Great Marianas Turkey Shoot (First Battle of the Philippine Sea) took place, all of the "big boys"—the attack carriers—went west to meet the Japanese coming our way, and we were left behind to take care of the troops on shore. They would call in our planes to bomb and strafe the enemy, and make things a little easier for them.

After the Marianas, we went back to the New Hebrides, then on to Peleliu. Our activity there didn't impress me one way or another, but the marines sure took a beating. Then we went to the Philippines for the invasion of Leyte.

On 20 October 1944 we went on station at Leyte Gulf. We had three escort carrier groups there under Vice Admiral Kincaid. We were in Taffy 1, and there was Taffy 2 and Taffy 3. Taffy 3 was about 60 miles from us, then there was Taffy 2, and Taffy 1, which included the *Suwannee.* We were the closest to Leyte Gulf. On the twentieth we were attacked by two enemy planes that were going after our sister ship, the USS *Sangamon* (CVE-26). They came in real low, and we fired on them as they were coming through, and I took pictures of them. By looking at the splashes in the water on those photos, I think we put more shells into our sister ship than we did into the Jap planes. You could see the tracers going right into her. It happened all the time; you just didn't hear about it. We got hit on the *Suwannee* by shells fired by other ships all the time, too.

On 25 October my photo position was on the bridge, near the lookouts. I had a little platform about 30 inches or 40 inches around, with no railing, and it was about 40 feet off the flight deck. I had only a 4-inch by 4-inch steel beam to hold onto if I had to. I was up there and watched as a kamikaze came in at the USS *Santee,* another escort carrier. We had a 5-inch gun on our stern, and it fired on the Jap plane as it made its dive for the *Santee.* One of the shells blew up just underneath the kamikaze and deflected it enough so that it missed the flight deck and hit alongside the ship, but it still killed a few people. Then about five or ten minutes later I looked back and saw two planes coming across our stern. One was an F6F Hellcat, and the other was a Jap plane, but I couldn't make out what kind. All the ships in the area started firing at it. The F6F in pursuit of the Jap plane was taking hits from our fire. We were knocking pieces off the Jap plane, but it kept coming. Then it made a roll toward us, and I was taking pictures of it the whole time. Then I saw flashes coming from its wings. He looked like he was shooting at me, so I ducked behind this 4-inch by 4-inch steel beam. I know I should have stayed out there; I know I should have kept taking pictures, but I was scared. He was a kamikaze, and he came down and hit us on the flight deck, aft of the island. The plane hit about 30 feet forward of the hole that went down to the magazines. The engine and the pilot's head went on through the hangar deck to the main deck. The rest of the plane went right through the middle of the flight deck, shed its wings, and exploded on the hangar deck, killing approximately one hundred fifty to two hundred guys right there, because that is where all of the ordnancemen and ammunition handlers were stationed during general quarters. By then, I had started taking pictures again.

The plane hit near the elevator on the after part of the ship, so the elevator was inoperable. However, at the time, most of our planes were in the air attacking the Jap fleet that was engaging Taffy 3. Some steel plates were brought up on the forward elevator and were used to patch the hole in the flight deck. Within a half hour we were bringing aboard planes, even though we were wiped out pretty good below decks.

Meanwhile, we got the fires under control on the *Suwannee,* and the dead and wounded were being taken care of. We had a lot of wounded with burns, and a lot of them didn't live very long. About all we could do was put boric acid on the wounds and give them morphine.

The next morning, 26 October, I was down in the lab, which had a lot of holes from shrapnel. I was getting ready to develop my pictures from the day before, when I heard there was another bogie coming in. I grabbed my helmet and camera, left the lab, and went to the ladder that led up to the gun tub that was just off the flight deck. That was about 200 feet or 300 feet back from the

U.S. aircraft carriers in the Pacific, taken from the
USS *Suwannee*. Photo by Robert Eustace

bridge. I remembered I had left my lifejacket back in the lab, so I turned around
to go back and get it. I lost about thirty seconds doing that, just enough so that
when I got back to the gun tub, the guns started going off. I looked up, and here
was another kamikaze coming down at us. He looked like he was coming right
at me. I took one picture of him, then I could see that he was veering forward
of where I was standing. I managed to get three pictures off before he hit. He
hit about 100 feet away, near the forward elevator, and wiped out most of the
people on the bridge. Anybody who was exposed got killed, and if I had been
on my camera platform, I would have been killed too, because it was only about
25 feet from where the plane hit.

The bomb exploded on the flight deck and knocked the forward elevator
out, and wiped out CIC [Combat Information Control]. We were taking
aboard aircraft at the time, and the kamikaze landed right on top of a TBF that
had just landed. The rear seat gunner on the TBF fired up at the kamikaze until
it hit on top of him. We were wiped out forward. We had a lot of planes parked
up there. They all caught fire, and stuff was exploding. It was just a mess.

Dead American sailor awaiting burial at sea in the torpedo room aboard the escort carrier USS *Suwannee*, 1944.

I was on the starboard side of the ship, and the wind was such that all the smoke was coming right back at me, so I couldn't get any pictures. I then went back down the ladder, through officers' country, through the pilots' ready room, and then up another ladder that went back up to the flight deck. I was about 200 feet away and had just put one foot on the flight deck when—BOOM!—I went flying through the air and landed on the catwalk, and broke the camera. I thought we had been hit by another kamikaze. I didn't know it at the time, but we had taken back aboard a TBM with depth charges in its bomb bay and they had cooked off, causing the third explosion and more deaths.

I looked down, and there was a piece of metal in my leg. I reached down and pulled it out. It was no big deal. Then I thought, "Well, I'll go back to the lab and get another camera." I tried to slide down this ladder by officers' country, but a piece of shrapnel had gone through the railing and it hung me up like a piece of beef. There was smoke everywhere, and I was scared. I had to get down on my hands and knees to get below the smoke. I went back to the fantail until I could get myself together. There were guys floating by in the water. Some of them said, "Come on in; the water is fine." But a lot of those guys didn't make it because there were a lot of sharks in those waters.

I could still hear things exploding, so I crawled on my hands and knees to the lab. It was dark inside—no lights—and we were dead in the water. I could hear screaming and hollering all over the place, but I found another camera and started loading it with film when Lieutenant Mahan, my division officer, came in with a lantern and fogged all the film. He was in damage control, and when he saw me, he said, "Bob, I thought you were dead," because he knew I was supposed to be on the bridge. I said, "No. I'm trying to get another camera ready." He said, "Forget about that. We need help with the fires. Get up there and help out."

I went up on the flight deck, and it was a mess. Things were still exploding, so I helped with a fire hose. We had lost water pressure, but some chief who knew the system figured out where the damage was and how to bypass it. That gave us water back to the system, and we were able to fight the fires. That chief won a medal for that.

I did that for about twenty minutes and by that time we had knocked the fires down and washed the gasoline over the side. But we had so many wounded, so many guys badly burned. It was the flash burns and the flames that killed so many men. People were cooked completely through, right where they stood. You could pull on a man's arm and it would come off. I remember one guy by the name of Tino. He said, "Bob, how bad am I hurt?" He looked all right to me. Then he said, "What's the matter with my back?" He turned his back to me, and it was just one big, massive blister. It stuck out about 2 inches, so I took him down to sick bay, and it was a mess down there, too.

We had a photographer's mate "striker" in the lab by the name of Kenneth Nelson, and he was in the photo lab on the second day when we got hit by the second kamikaze, and he got a concussion. He told me he was going to die if

A 100-pound bomb explodes in the bomb bay of a TBF aboard the carrier *Suwannee,* killing the pilot and radioman, and wounding several others, 1945.
Photo by Robert Eustace

he didn't get some oxygen, so I got another guy and went to the forward part of the ship where I knew we could find some oxygen bottles. Now mind you, the ship is dark, and there were body parts all over the place. We crawled on our hands and knees, feeling our way along, skirting the edge of the hole where the bomb went through, and we didn't know what our hands were getting into. We finally got some oxygen, and coming back was a little easier. We brought four bottles back, and I think it saved Nelson's life.

The ship's medical personnel had taken over the wardroom and the pilots' ready room. The ship's commanding officer, Captain Johnson, was down there. He had been burned pretty bad. We even had wounded in the passageways. Everybody who wasn't hurt was helping out. I was put to work sticking guys with morphine. What else could I do? A lot of guys were in shock and died, just like that. During that two-day period, out of a crew of about 900 we had 553 killed, wounded, or missing. That's a lot for a small carrier.

Taffy 3, to the north of us, got shot to pieces. They had a lot of casualties in the water, and they weren't picked up for two or three days. Hundreds could have been saved if the navy had searched properly.

Some tin cans pulled alongside, and we started offloading some of the badly wounded so they could be taken to a hospital ship. That was a very slow process, and we only sent the ones who we thought might have a chance of living.

We were effectively knocked out of action. We had no forward elevator, no aft elevator, and our flight deck was damaged, so we couldn't handle planes. All of our planes were gone. They had either been shot down or landed at Tacloban, so we headed for Peleliu. There was a hospital ship there. We dropped off the major part of our wounded there, then went back to Pearl Harbor. The bridge personnel had been pretty much wiped out. The captain survived, but he was badly burned. Our executive officer, I'll never forget his name. It was Shimerhorn Van Mater. He conned the ship from the aft steering station, down by where the landing signal officer stood during flight operations. Then after we cleaned up the bridge, we were able to steer the ship from there, but we had lost most of the boatswain's mates and the personnel who handled the wheel watch.

We were still taking pictures, but only of the damage done to the ship. We had six photographers on board, and all of them survived. I was the only one who had been wounded. When we got to Pearl, we dropped off a few more wounded, then headed for Bremerton, Washington. We arrived there in November 1944. We pulled up to the dry dock, and all the crew were taken off and put in floating barracks. The yard workers came aboard the ship that night and broke open all of our lockers and stole all of our valuables. Welcome home! Here we had just come back from the war and we were all beat up, and we expected a welcome, but not like that.

I was given casualty leave and went home to San Francisco, but nobody seemed to give a damn about what I had just been through. The civilians I met were more worried about rationing. They were worried about gasoline stamps, and getting tires for their cars, and putting enough meat on the table. They didn't seem to give a damn about the war. Or maybe it was just me. Maybe I was wiped out mentally, or maybe I expected more when I got home. Anyway, I borrowed my stepfather's car and went to my uncle's farm in Lodi, California.

I had to get away, so I spent the next two weeks at my uncle's. I took his dog with me and roamed the fields, and went down to the river. I just had to get away for a while, and it made me feel better.

After my leave was up I went back to Bremerton. They got us patched up and out of dry dock in ninety days. What happened was, all those pictures we took of damage to the ship were flown to Bremerton from Hawaii by the first officer of the *Suwannee,* and the shipyard prefabricated all the parts and sections we needed, based on the pictures. So the damaged sections were just cut out and the new ones were welded in, and we were on our way back to the war.

We left Bremerton and stopped somewhere near there to pick up ammo, then went on down to Alameda Naval Air Station to pick up planes. We dropped off the planes in Hawaii. We missed Iwo Jima, but went to Ulithi, then to Okinawa on 1 April 1945, where we provided air support for the troops. We did that for a number of days, then were shifted to the island of Ishigaki, near Formosa. A lot of suicide planes were coming out of there. They would fly from Formosa to Ishigaki to refuel, then head for our ships off Okinawa. We were there for eighty-seven days straight, and sending out strikes every day. We lost a lot of planes and pilots. We had a lot of planes that came back damaged, and we would just shove them over the side. We threw dozens over the side, because we didn't have the facilities to repair them.

We also operated with some British carriers, and boy, did we envy them. They had armored flight decks. I saw suicide planes come in and bounce off their flight decks and go over the side. Kamikazes didn't bother them a bit.

Every so often we had to go into Kerama Retto for supplies. We could carry a lot of fuel, but we did need to get ammo and food. We would go in right after sunrise, and there was almost always a smoke screen in there, but our flight deck always seemed to be just above it, so it would protect the smaller ships but not us. However, we were never attacked while we were in there. I guess we just picked the right days to go in. But our sister ship, the *Sangamon,* got hit right in the photo lab on its way out one day. A friend of mine from navy photo school was killed—a guy by the name of White.

After two and a half months off Ishigaki we were all worn out. Our pilots

A 40-mm antiaircraft battery aboard the USS *Suwannee* (CVE-27), somewhere in the Pacific, 1944 or 1945. Photo by Robert Eustace

were worn out. They were dropping a lot of 100-pound antipersonnel bombs around the airport on Ishigaki. These bombs had arming vanes—little propellers—on the fuse in the nose, and arming wires going through them to keep them from arming before they were dropped. Our TBFs carried twenty 100-pound bombs in their bomb bays, and after the bombs were dropped, the radioman was supposed to look through a little window into the bomb bay to see if there was anything hung up on the bomb racks. Well, this one time the radioman looked and reported the bomb bay was clean. But what happened was one of the 100-pound bombs was hung up, and when the pilot closed his bomb bay doors it fell free of the arming wire and armed itself. When the pilot landed his plane he caught number six wire. I was not on my platform that day, but on the bridge where the captain was. I thought the plane might hit the barrier so I started cranking off photographs, and about that time the plane blew up right in front of my face. This was maybe 75 feet from me. The explosion blew me back into the bridge, and when I looked up the plane's engine was flying through the air. My ears were ringing, and I couldn't hear anything for three days. I looked over at the captain, and he was on his knees, looking at me, and we were both wondering what the hell had happened. Then I jumped up and started taking more pictures of the flames and the wreckage. I have a lot of hearing loss to this day because of that, but I never reported it.

When the bomb went off, it blew the engine off the plane, and the pilot was still sitting there, holding the stick in his hand, but the top of his head was gone. The radioman was also killed. The gunner ran over and jumped off the side of the ship, but was rescued. The landing signal officer was riddled with shrapnel, but I think he lived. The guy running up to take off the tail hook was blown over the side, but lived. A destroyer picked him up.

We were at Buckner Bay, Okinawa, when the first atomic bomb was dropped. After the second bomb was dropped and the war was over, we were told that we were going up to Nagasaki. I was called up to the flight deck and was told to take a flight over the city and take some pictures before we went in. They had a TBM on the catapult, so I jumped in. I didn't have a parachute; I didn't have anything except a camera. We were catapulted off and flew into the bay at Nagasaki. The weather was crappy, so we came in at low altitude at the harbor entrance, then climbed to about 1,000 feet. We were looking for a POW camp. We didn't find it in the valley, but we did go over a hill behind the city and found it there, and it hadn't been damaged by the atomic bomb, so the navy sent the hospital ship USS *Mercy* in to pick up the POWs. I took the first aerial photos of Nagasaki after the bombing, and I gave most of them to the museum at Los Alamos.

The weather closed in on us, and we couldn't find the entrance to the harbor. It was raining and there was lightning and everything else. Here we were: the war was over, and I was wondering if I was ever going to get home. But we finally found the harbor entrance, got out, and found our way back to the ship.

Some of the officers wanted to go ashore to ground zero at Nagasaki, and of course they wanted a photographer's mate to go along to take pictures. This was two or three weeks after the bomb was dropped, and most of the streets had been cleared so that cars and trucks could get through, but the city of Nagasaki was flattened. None of us knew anything about radiation at that time, and to this day there is no official record of the *Suwannee* from the time she was at Okinawa until we left Japanese waters after the final surrender. The navy has no record of her ever having been at Nagasaki. Some of the guys thought they might have been exposed to radiation, and when they tried to find out more, they discovered there was no record of them having been at Nagasaki. I mean, six weeks of the ship's history just disappeared from official U.S. Navy records.

After we left Japan, we took the air group back to the States and dropped them off. Then the navy put bunks on the *Suwannee* and made a troopship out of us. We made two trips to Okinawa to bring troops back to Long Beach and Bremerton. That was in September, October, and November 1945. By then I was the only one left in the photo lab. I was twenty years old and single. All of the guys who were getting out hadn't been in the navy as long as I had, but they were older and had more points.

I was a first class photographer's mate by the end of the war, and one day I was called in by some officer and asked if I would like to stay in the navy. I said, "No, sir!" I could have stayed in and retired when I was thirty-seven, but I decided not to. See, when you are in combat, the relationship between officers and enlisted men is much different than during peacetime. Everybody's ass is on the line. During the war, if somebody wasn't liked he could fall down a ladder, or even off the ship, so people made a point of getting along, including the officers. But the day the war ended, everything reverted to the way the navy was before the war. For example, I had to start eating in the first class mess. I could no longer eat with the lower ranking men I worked with. It was a caste system, and I didn't like it. And the officers started getting on you if you didn't salute them. During the war it was much more casual. I didn't know what a guy's rank was and I didn't care. We all had a job to do, and that was the only thing that mattered.

Anyway, I didn't have enough points to get out until 15 March 1946. I got off the ship in Bremerton, Washington, and went back to San Francisco. The war was finally over for me. I didn't go back to work at Eastman Kodak for a while. I was kind of messed up. Loud noises would bother me, and I didn't like being around people because I felt that people didn't understand what I had been through. I was carrying my heart on my sleeve. Some people get over it and go back to civilian life, and some people never get over it. I had a few bucks, so I bought a motorcycle and just traveled around for a while. Then one day I ran into Ernie McCarra, my old boss from Eastman Kodak. He said, "Hey, Bob, when are you coming back to work?" I said, "Ernie, I'll be in on Monday."

CHAPTER 4

◆ ◆ ◆ ◆ ◆

Crew Six of the "Boomerang"

William Sheehan, USNR (Ret.)

William Sheehan was born in Oakland, California, in 1922. He graduated from high school in 1941 and went into the navy in October 1942. Sheehan served out most of his active duty years during World War II in VPB-16, which was a squadron of PBM3D Mariners, a seaplane built by Martin Aircraft Company. The PBM Mariners were first designed and tested in the late 1930s and went through numerous modifications before and during World War II. The PBM3D went into production in 1943 and that was the model flown by the crews of VPB-16, which was commissioned in December 1943 and headed for the Pacific theater of war shortly thereafter. Sheehan left the regular navy at war's end but remained in the Naval Air Reserves until his retirement from the active reserves in 1966. He now lives in Vacaville, California.

I wanted to enlist in the navy because the army didn't look like anything I wanted to do, but I wasn't twenty-one and my mother wouldn't sign for me.

Crew of the "Boomerang," a PBM-3D. Taken in Kaneohe, Hawaii, June 1944. *Top row, left to right:* Bill Sheehan, Lieutenant Isringhausen, Kermit Hotvdt, Robert Lindstrom, George Kirsch, Tom Conway. *Bottom row:* Gerald Rivard, Joe Kushner, Delmar May, Richard Hansen, Eugine Brewer.

Then I received a letter from the Draft Board, and that's when my mother let me join the navy. That is when she went to San Francisco and signed the papers.

My navy experience was kind of unique. I went to boot camp in Farragut, Idaho, and it was a very cold environment. I did well on the aptitude tests and was allowed to select the school I wanted, and I selected aviation machinist school, which was located in Norman, Oklahoma. I was there for thirteen weeks, then went to Pensacola, Florida, for gunnery school. I was then transferred to Air Wing Five in Norfolk, Virginia, and from there transferred again to Banana River, Florida, which is now Cape Canaveral, to PBM School. Each man in the crew had an assignment, and I was assigned to be a flight engineer.

A few months later, in December 1943, Navy Patrol Squadron Sixteen (VP-16), later to be designated Navy Patrol Bombing Squadron Sixteen (VPB-16) once we arrived in the forward areas, was formed at Harvey Point, North Carolina. Lt. K. O. Hotvedt was my patrol plane commander [PPC]. He was an officer whom I was fortunate to meet and fly with.

The squadron was formed under the command of Lt. William Scarpino, and the executive officer was Lt. Ralph John. We received brand-new airplanes, the PBM3D, and they had R 2600-22 engines in them. The bureau number on my plane was 48198. It was like the plane's social security number. I flew in that plane the whole time I was in that squadron. In fact, when we came back to the States after our tour in the Pacific, I flew with her right into Alameda Naval Air Station in California, where she was disassembled and overhauled. I don't know what happened to her after that, but that was many, many months later.

Our training really started at Banana River, Florida, and continued at Harvey Point. We did antisubmarine warfare training, dropping live depth charges. We flew combat air patrols, actually guarding ships that went up and down the East Coast. There were German raiders—ships that were disguised as freighters that would slip in among stragglers from convoys and sink them. However, only once did we make a challenge where there was no response. Our PPC, Lieutenant Hotvedt, ordered us to general quarters. The PBM was armed with .50-caliber machine guns from bow to stern. We manned our guns and test-fired them. As flight engineer, my general quarters station was the port waist gun. When we started our run, people on the ship must have heard our guns being test-fired because somebody scrambled up the quarterdeck and raised the signal flags that signaled to us that they were a friendly ship, and the attack was called off at the last moment. That was quite a thrilling thing for a young guy like me.

We left Harvey Point in early April 1944. As enlisted men we didn't know where we were going, and neither did a lot of the officers. We deployed in small groups. In the group that I was in, we flew from Harvey Point to Eagle Mountain Lake in Texas. The airplanes were very slow. We cruised at a speed of around 115–120 knots, depending on how much weight we carried. And right from the beginning we had problems with these Wright R 2600-22 engines. My plane didn't have any problems on the way out, but some of the others did. We stayed at Eagle Mountain Lake one or two days before flying on to San Diego, and then on up to Alameda.

There were three or four planes in our group that left Eagle Mountain Lake for San Diego. We weren't in the air more than four or five hours when our executive officer, Lt. Ralph John, called our flight leader, Lieutenant Arle, and said he was having engine trouble, and that he was going to have to go on single engine. I think there were twelve men aboard that plane, and they started throwing out all of their gear to lighten the plane. They jettisoned everything they possibly could, but still couldn't maintain altitude. Within five minutes of going on single engine he had crashed and was burning. Everybody on board was killed.

We circled around for awhile. The plane captain, George Kirsch, and I volunteered to bail out to go down and see if we could help, but Lieutenant Hotvedt ordered us to stay aboard. He said, "All hands are dead." So we flew on to San Diego.

In San Diego, we discovered more problems with the engines. We had a lot of oil leaks, and spent a day or two getting those fixed, then flew up to Alameda. And by that time, there had been two PBMs that had attempted to fly from Alameda to Kaneohe, Hawaii. One went in the drink, and one had to come back on single engine. The crew from the PBM that went in the drink spent several days in a life raft before being rescued. Navy Intelligence suspected sabotage, not engine problems, so there was a big investigation. No proof of sabotage was uncovered, but there was evidence pointing to engine valve seat problems, so they decided to change all the cylinders on the engines at Alameda, which took several days.

From Alameda to Kaneohe, we flew by the seat of our pants. It was dead reckoning, watching a compass, and using a handheld sextant. The weather was awful on the east side of the Pacific, and we had to fly above the clouds if we wanted to shoot the sun. If we could see the water, we would drop smoke bombs and take a drift reading of the wind. So our navigation was hit and miss.

However, on the other side of the point of no return, where we had no choice but to keep on going, the weather was much better, and we were able to get some good sun shots with our sextant. Then we started to have problems with one of the engines. It was in really bad shape, but we were able to keep it going, and we did make it to Kaneohe. It took us 16.6 hours to make the crossing, according to my logbook. One of the later planes in our squadron actually missed the islands to the south. By the time they found their bearings and turned north, they ran out of gas and had to land in the ocean. They were then towed in to Hawaii.

When we got to Kaneohe, George Kirsch, the plane captain, and I looked at the engine we had the problem with and discovered that the maintenance people at Alameda had failed to tighten the nuts on the rocker arms. That changed the valve clearance on the valves and made the engine run rough.

The whole time we flew those PBM3Ds we had nothing but trouble with those R 2600-22 engines. One of the biggest problems was with the valve seats on the cylinders. They had a way of coming loose and snapping the valves off, which would cause the engine to quit. And if it wasn't that, it was something else.

Corrosion was another problem. We fought corrosion constantly. Normally, after you fly a seaplane, you would land at a base. The plane was pulled up a ramp and out of the water, and hosed down with fresh water. But when we operated at sea, there was no base and no fresh water to hose the planes down with. The salt water would eat up the electrical connections, the control cables—everything.

We spent approximately a month at Kaneohe, flying antisubmarine patrols, and doing more training. There was a lot of camaraderie in that squadron. We were just a bunch of friends. It was really great. We had baseball games between the officers and men, and there was a big luau with a roast pig before we left for the forward areas.

In late May or early June 1944 we left Hawaii and flew to Palmyra Island. We spent a night there, then flew to Canton Island on our way to Eniwetok Atoll in the Marshall Islands. In the meantime, another PBM on another flight lost an engine and crash-landed in the water near Howland Island. Everybody aboard survived and was rescued, but the plane had to be burned because it couldn't be flown out.

On Eniwetok, we lived in tents. The island had been taken by the marines several months earlier, and there were still the remains of Japanese soldiers lying around in the sand—mostly bones by that time. We spent a couple of weeks there, then received orders to move our operations to Saipan, but we were having propeller problems on our plane, the "Boomerang," and had to stay behind until we could fix it.

Admiral Spruance, in charge of the Fifth Fleet at that time, wanted some seaplanes up there to help him locate the Japanese fleet he knew was out there someplace. Five planes from our squadron flew up to Saipan. When they arrived, our squadron commander, Lieutenant Commander Scarpino, met with Admiral Spruance right away. The admiral told Scarpino he wanted his five planes fueled and ready to go immediately to help search out the Japanese fleet.

They took off at night in very rough seas, and all five made it off. One of our pilots from VPB-16, Lieutenant Arle, made radar contact with the Japanese fleet, but his radio operator, Chief Petty Officer Tibbets, was unable to make radio contact with our task force to let the admiral know. According to Tibbets, the problem was "skip distance"—bouncing the message off the ionosphere. The message was sent in code and was picked up in places like Pearl Harbor and even Washington, D.C., but Admiral Spruance never got it. Part of the goof-up, too, was that the people who did receive the message didn't relay it back to Admiral Spruance. They couldn't read the code, but they had the address and didn't relay it. So there was more than one goof-up there.

Then, out of desperation, Lieutenant Arle had Tibbets send the message in the clear—that is, not in code—and it still didn't get to Spruance until seven hours later. After they landed, Lieutenant Commander Scarpino and Chief Tibbets had to face Admiral Spruance and were chastised. The admiral was very angry, because if the task force had had the information earlier, it could have made a significant difference, and we probably would have been able to sink a significant number of the Japanese ships without having to launch our carrier planes from such a great distance.

My crew, on Lieutenant Hotvedt's plane, the "Boomerang," left for Saipan on 24 June, after we received our new propeller. After we joined the other planes in our squadron at Saipan, we learned that one of the other planes in our squadron had been attacked by friendly F6F fighters and one of the crew, Gilbert Person, was killed.

When we first arrived off Saipan, the Japanese were still sending their planes over. In fact, when Lieutenant Commander Scarpino and the first five aircraft arrived, the fleet was under attack. When we on the "Boomerang" arrived, it was at night under the same conditions. Our radar screen lit up with ships—I mean hundreds of ships. I remember later being in the air during the day and seeing ships from one horizon to the other. There were no lights set out for us, and Lieutenant Hotvedt had a hell of a time finding a place to land. He just took a shot at it, and we bounced in for a landing. Then ships started laying smoke, and we came under enemy air attack. That was our first taste of being in a forward area.

Our orders were to carry depth charges set for 50 feet and to patrol for submarines. We had five sectors around the Mariana Islands that we patrolled. The routine was, patrol one night, spend one night on our seaplane tender, the USS *Pocomoke,* around which the planes were buoyed, and one night on a buoy watch. The buoy watch was mostly a maintenance thing—fighting the corrosion, and keeping the bilges empty of water. After a couple of months, the hulls leaked badly from the beating they were taking, and from the growth on the sides and bottoms of the planes. We had algae and barnacles growing on the hull, and they would work their way into the rivets and pop them out, so that we had water trickling into the bilges of the planes. And before we could fly, we had to pump the bilges, and during take-off more water would be forced back into the bilges, and we had to pump them again once we got into the air. We were constantly pumping bilges. By the time our deployment was over, those airplanes had just about had it. They all needed major overhauls.

Other than that, buoy watches were pretty monotonous. We slept a lot, and I wrote a lot of letters home. Sometimes we went swimming, but we had to watch out for sharks, so one of the guys would sit up on the wing with a gun.

And before the island was secured, we took incoming fire from the Japanese on shore, and one day our plane, the "Boomerang," was hit. We were about 4 miles out when shells started hitting around us. The thing is, the flashes from the Japanese guns usually gave them away, and our ships would return fire and put them out of business. But still, they were able to get off a few rounds. I was on watch, along with Dick Hansen, Joe Kushner, and Delmar May. The officer in charge was Ensign Lindstrom. The other half of the crew was on the *Pocomoke*. I was inside the plane when they started shelling, and some of the shells were pretty close, so everybody stayed below. But pretty soon it stopped because our ships opened up on the enemy guns and put them out of commission. Then, all of a sudden, the airplane started to list to one side. A piece of shrapnel had gone through one of the floats, and it started to take on water. It was the port float that got hit, so we all ran up on the starboard wing and bounced on it until the port float came up out of the water. Then the radioman went below and signaled the *Pocomoke* to send out a repair party with a new float, which they did.

We had another airplane that was badly damaged, and that was just before Saipan was declared secure. It was just after the Japanese made their banzai charge on the island, and we had to haul this plane of ours out of the water in Tanapag where the Japanese had a seaplane ramp, and several of us from crew six were sent ashore to guard it until it could be cannibalized for spare parts. There were a lot of Japanese planes lying around there, and an American TBM, a Navy torpedo bomber that had been shot down sometime during the fighting. There were also quite a number of dead Japanese soldiers that hadn't been buried yet, and others that were floating in the lagoon. Even when I was on the *Pocomoke*, bodies would float by the ship, and you could smell them when they were still several hundred yards away. Some of them were U.S. Marines, and they would be picked out of the water. But if they weren't marines, they were left in the water. Eventually, however, all of the dead Japanese were buried in mass graves.

While I was ashore on Saipan, there was still a lot of shooting going on, and I did get to know some of the marines who guarded our perimeter. I met one marine who was a bazooka man. His name was Frank Zark. He told me how when he first landed, he stopped a Japanese tank with his bazooka. He was hungry and couldn't sleep at night because he was afraid he would get his throat slit by Japanese, so I let him sleep in the damaged PBM, and I stood watch all night so he could sleep. But he snored so loud I was afraid he was going to bring Japanese soldiers in on us. I'll never forget him. He said he was going to go back to Australia and marry a girl he was engaged to down there. I only knew Frank Zark for the few days I was on Saipan. I never saw him again after that.

As I said, I was only on the island for a couple of days, but I saw American marines do things I won't repeat. I didn't like what I saw them do, and I just won't talk about it. However, I will tell you that one morning I heard a lot of shooting. There was an aircraft that had crashed across a ditch, and a Japanese soldier was hiding under it. I guess he thought the coast was clear that morning, but when he tried to clear out, he was spotted, and the marines killed him. The only time I was on the island after that was after the island had been secured and the squadron had a beer party. We were each given three cans of beer to drink, then we went back to the *Pocomoke*.

Most of our patrols were routine. Many times planes in our squadron detected submarines, but the ones that were sunk were sunk by surface ships. As far as I know, VPB-16 never sank a submarine. However, one night while crew six was on patrol, a large group of American ships was crossing our patrol sector, but about three or four miles from this convoy our radar picked up a disappearing blip. It was what we called a "sinker." The blip would show up only every two or three sweeps on the radar screen, especially at long range. But then we closed in on it. We figured that it was a Japanese submarine running on the surface at conning tower depth. But when he saw us inbound on him—I'm making an assumption here—he went to periscope depth. We lost him on radar but had a pretty good fix on where he was and dropped a smoke flare on the last place we saw him on radar. Then we laid a standard sono-buoy pattern and picked him up again that way. He was twisting and turning, and we could pick up his propeller cavitations. We had this guy cold.

I wondered why Lieutenant Hotvedt didn't drop any ordnance on this guy. We had a FIDO, a sound-seeking torpedo, on board that goes for cavitation or any other kind of underwater sound. He didn't want to do it because he was afraid the submarine would shut down his engine when he heard the FIDO go into the water. Then the FIDO might go after one of our ships, which were only a few miles away. He was a very cautious man, so we notified the convoy, and one of the escorts sank it the next day. Other planes in our squadron had similar experiences.

In late August 1944 we were sent to Ebeye Island, Kwajalein Atoll, for engine changes, and to get the planes out of the water to clean the corrosion from our guns and the rest of the plane. Following that, we received orders to go to the Kossol Passage, Palau. This was the one occasion when the whole squadron took off at the same time.

In November 1944 we received word of a typhoon heading our way. Our task group commander ordered our planes to fly out. We were given several possible destinations, and I believe Saipan was one of them, and several of our planes did fly to Saipan to avoid the typhoon. Then the waves started getting very high, and the wind got stronger. One plane crashed trying to take off and was a complete loss. By the time our turn came to take off, the wind was blowing at 70 knots, and the task group commander called off all the flights and told us to stay put, so we weathered the storm on the water. I was on the plane, and we buttoned down all the hatches. Pretty soon we started all of the engines because we were dragging our anchor. One of the men down below in the galley came rushing up to the flight deck and said the bulkhead had collapsed and water was coming in. The bow compartment was flooded and the galley was flooded, so we had to pull up all the decking and start a bucket brigade, and we did that all night long.

The storm finally passed, and we had sustained some damage to the plane. The plane was underwater half the time during the storm. It's amazing those engines kept going. God had been with us. We didn't lose any planes or men from our squadron, but I think other squadrons did.

It wasn't long after the typhoon that we received orders to return to the United States. I think that was late November 1944. Our airplanes just couldn't fly any more. They had holes in them, barnacles and algae growing on the hulls, and all of the engines needed to be overhauled. They were worn out. We had been out there for six months or longer. Our aircrews had flown anywhere from 60 to 120 hours a month. That's a lot of flying.

We flew back the same way we had come out—Canton Island, Palmyra Island, and Kaneohe. Lieutenant Hotvedt's wife had delivered a baby, and he was anxious to get back. From Kaneohe we got our orders to fly back to Alameda Naval Air Station in California. We were almost at the point of no return when the starboard engine started to sputter. Only half of the magneto was working, so we had to turn around and go back to Kaneohe. We repaired that problem and took off again the next morning. This time the port engine started having problems. Again, we were only about forty or fifty miles from the point of no return, and had to turn around and go back. On our third attempt we made it all the way to Alameda. I spent the rest of the war at Alameda, and when it was over, I was discharged right away. That was in November 1945.

There is not a day that goes by that I don't think of the men I served with in VPB-16. I have great affection for those men. I was in other squadrons after we returned to Alameda, and in reserve squadrons after the war, but I never felt the same towards them as I did for VPB-16 and the men I served with in that squadron. I'm sure the feeling is mutual, because when we go to reunions they talk about it—the friendship and the caring they feel for each other.

It wasn't until 1990 that I started looking for my old squadron. They started having reunions around 1986. Lieutenant (jg) Isringhausen, the copilot on "Boomerang," died shortly after that first reunion in 1986. Of the eleven members of crew six from the "Boomerang," only three of us are left that I know of. Some of the others I have never been able to locate.

CHAPTER 5

◆ ◆ ◆ ◆ ◆

Aboard the
USS *Pennsylvania* (BB-38)

Jim McDavid

Jim McDavid was born in 1921, in Waco, Texas. He graduated from high school in Fort Worth, Texas, in 1938, and worked at various jobs until 1941, when he enlisted in the U.S. Navy. He served aboard the USS *Pennsylvania* (BB-38) from before the Japanese attack on Pearl Harbor until the end of the war. Since he was regular navy, he had to stay on active duty until his six-year enlistment was up in 1947. He then went to work as a civilian at the naval shipyard at Hunter's Point, San Francisco, and retired from there after twenty-seven years. He and his wife now live in Sacramento, California.

The battleship *Pennsylvania* was commissioned in 1916, and was one of the battleships at Pearl Harbor that was damaged but not sunk during the Japanese attack that took place on 7 December 1941. She served throughout the Pacific theater of war until she was torpedoed off the coast of Okinawa just days before the Japanese surrender in

August 1945. She was later used as a target ship during the atomic bomb tests conducted at Bikini Atoll in 1946. In 1948 she was sunk off the coast of Kwajalein Atoll.

My grandfather, father, and uncle bought a ranch in Kopperl, Texas, sometime during the 1920s. They raised a lot of cattle and cotton down there, and it was a pretty good-sized ranch, but the Depression hit and the price of beef went down. They couldn't sell the beef, and on top of that we had a drought. So basically they went broke; they lost their shirts and had to give up the ranch. When I graduated from high school in 1938, my mother and father told me, "You know, we have had a tough time and can't afford to send you to college." So from 1938 until 1941, when I joined the navy, I worked. The government had the Civilian Conservation Corps, but they also had some technical camps that people could go to. There was one of these south of Waco, and I went down there. I had a real good teacher who taught me drafting, and I worked a couple of jobs after that as a draftsman.

One day I told my dad, "I need more education." I had seen these navy recruiting posters that said, "Uncle Sam Needs You," so I went to a recruiting office and talked to them, then went back and talked to my mom and dad about joining the navy. My dad said, "I don't mind you joining the navy, but I don't want you ever coming home with a tattoo." So I joined the navy, but I never got a tattoo.

I was nineteen years old and had never seen the ocean, or even a ship. I took a train to San Diego, where I went to boot camp. After boot camp, I was assigned to the USS *Pennsylvania,* and it was at anchor in Long Beach Harbor. I was sent up to Long Beach on an old four-stack destroyer. I had never been to sea before, and I was one sick cookie.

When I went aboard the *Pennsylvania* I was assigned to 6-A Division, which was a gunnery division. In those days we slept in hammocks, and there were

Jim McDavid aboard the USS *Pennsylvania* (BB-38),
taken sometime during World War II.

about three or four of us who came aboard together. A coxswain took me up
to my division, and I asked him where I was going to sleep. He told me to take
any pair of billet hooks, secure my hammock, and go to bed. I did that, and
about 0200 men started coming back off liberty—the old-timers of the division. This first class boatswain's mate, named Ferlow McNellie, came in and
found me right where I shouldn't have been, where he put his hammock. He
was in charge of the enlisted men in that division and took his knife and cut
down my hammock, and I ended up sleeping on the deck my first night.

I was a "hot-shell man" on one of the 5-inch guns. When they fired the gun,
my job was to catch the shell casings when they came out. I wore asbestos

gloves and an asbestos apron because the shell casings were hot when they came out. I would stack them up, and they would be sent back to the manufacturer for recycling. Now, if we had a "hang-fire"—in other words, if the shell didn't go off—I had to catch it and throw it overboard. The shells were heavy for a guy who only weighed about 140 pounds. If the shell did hang-fire, we waited a bit before taking it out just in case it fired late, but we didn't wait too long, and they told me they could go off once they were removed from the gun. That's why we threw them over the side as soon as they came out.

So I started off in a gunnery division, but I didn't stay there. I wanted to get into electronics. Back then they were called radiomen; now they are called electronics technicians. Before the war we didn't have any radar on our ships. The only electronics they had on board were radio transmitters and receivers, direction finders, fathometers, and things like that.

There was a Mr. Kline who came aboard ship about the same time I did. Mr. Kline was an ensign then, and I was getting tired of catching those hot shells. So one day, after gunnery exercises, he walked by, and I said, "Mr. Kline, I joined the navy to learn a trade and I'm on a list for the electrical shop, but if I don't get in I'll wind up as a hot-shell man on a 5-inch gun for six years, and when I get out and look for a job, all I'll be able to say is I was a hot-shell man on a 5-inch gun. I don't think there's much employment for hot-shell men on the outside." Mr. Kline said, "I agree with you. I have an opening in sky lookout forward." That's up in the crow's nest. We had a tripod mast, and up in sky lookout forward there was a place for about eight people—an officer, a chief petty officer, and some enlisted men. They were plane spotters. We didn't have any radar; everything was visual. He said, "You can go up there, and that will be your new battle station." I said, "Well, that will be better than catching hot shells." This happened one week before the Japanese attacked Pearl Harbor, and the guy who took my place on the 5-inch gun got killed. In fact, the whole gun crew got killed.

The officer in charge of sky lookout forward told me, "You're pretty articulate, so I want you to be a sound-power telephone talker with damage control." And he said, "If we get a bomb hit anywhere on the ship I'll tell you to tell them our observation of where the damage is. Then they can send a repair crew."

The Japanese attack came on a Sunday, and we came back into Pearl on the Thursday or Friday before. We were the flagship of the Pacific Fleet, and our sister ship was the USS *Arizona*. The week before, the *Arizona* had been in dry dock, and it was customary to take everything off the ship that they could to make it lighter. Now, when we pulled back into Pearl Harbor that day, it was our turn to go into dry dock. We pumped all of our fuel oil over to the *Arizona*, and transferred all of our bag-powder for the 14-inch guns to the *Arizona*, and anything else that would lighten the ship. I've always felt kind of guilty about that, because I was part of the working party that took all that stuff over to the *Arizona*.

In those days the shipyard just provided the dry dock; they didn't do any of the chipping and painting. Practically the whole crew had to go over the side of the ship and scrape off barnacles and old paint, then prime it with red-lead, and paint it. We had to do the whole bottom of the ship in a couple of days, and the lower your rate, the dirtier the job. Two destroyers also went into dry dock with us, the *Cassin* and the *Downs*. They were a part of our task group, and were forward of us in the dry dock.

On Saturday, the night before the Japanese attacked Pearl Harbor, the navy had a thing over at the Enlisted Men's Club, called the Battle of the Bands. All the battleships had bands, and they were all over there playing that night. I had two friends on the *Arizona*, Don and R. L. Boydson. We played football together in high school. We went over to the Enlisted Men's Club together by liberty boat, and enjoyed ourselves listening to the bands. After it was all over, I told Don and R. L. we should go on liberty together on Sunday. We made plans to meet at the fleet landing, then go to church. After that we planned to go to Waikiki. They never made it. They were both killed when the *Arizona* blew up on Sunday morning.

When the Japanese attacked on Sunday morning, 7 December 1941, I ran up the tripod mast to my battle station in the crow's nest. The Japs must have gone for the battleships at Ford Island first, because by the time I got to my battle station, all hell had broken loose over on Ford Island. The *Arizona* had been hit, and the *Oklahoma* had been hit and had about a 45-degree list. I had a front-row seat at Pearl Harbor. The planes were flying by, and I could see those big red meatballs on their sides. The destroyer *Shaw* was in another dry dock. I saw her get hit and go up like the Fourth of July. Then the two destroyers that were dry-docked with us both got hit. I looked down at one of them, and there was a sailor manning a .50-caliber machine gun, shooting at the Japanese, and he was barefooted. There was a fire on the ship below decks, and he was dancing from one foot to the other because of the heat, but he refused to leave that gun. I said to the chief petty officer standing next to me, "How would you like to be down there next to him?" The chief said, "That guy is doomed."

The bomb that hit us was 500 pounds and had a delayed fuse on it. We had guns one, three, and five on the starboard side, and gun number five is the one where I had been hot-shell man. The bomb went through the main deck and the casement deck, and hit the armored deck, which was made of 4 inches of steel and ran the whole length of the ship to protect its vital parts—engine rooms, fuel tanks, and things like that. When the bomb hit the armored deck, it rolled around down there for awhile before exploding. There was a musician down there on an ammunition-handling party for a 3-inch gun. He had brains enough to jump behind the hammock netting where all the hammocks for that deck were stowed when not being used. The hammocks absorbed all the shrapnel from the bomb, but when he came out he was in shock. I think the explosion scrambled his brains. I remember seeing him standing there because I had to go down with a working party to clean up all the body parts. He was standing there like a statue. We put the dead in piles—heads here, arms and legs there—and the rest we cleaned up with a broom and a dustpan.

Now, the bomb killed all those guys down there, but the concussion went back up the hole and killed the gun crew on the number five 5-inch gun. The hot-shell man was blown backwards, and he was sitting there with his back to one of the boats on deck. When I first saw him there, I thought his head was inside the boat, but he didn't have any head.

There was another hot-shell man on one of the other guns by the name of Cord, and he was told not to throw any hang-fires over the side because there wasn't any water in the dry dock and they might explode and damage the ship.

So when we secured from battle stations later that day, Cord had about a half-dozen hang-fires stacked up underneath one of the boats. When he asked Mr. Kline what he should do with all the hang-fires, everybody looked at them, then got the hell out of there. Hang-fires were quite common back then because the ammunition was so old—probably from World War I.

I had a friend by the name of Jack Smith on the ship, whom I'd gone to school with back in Texas. Later that day I said to him, "Let's request permission to go over on the beach. I saw where one of those Japanese planes landed over by the hospital. If we can get off this ship, we'll go over there and get a souvenir off that Japanese plane." They let us off the ship, and when we stepped onto the dock, there was a dead guy lying there. He was a doctor off our ship, or maybe he was a pharmacist's mate. He had been killed by a strafing plane while trying to evacuate the dead and wounded from the ship. Anyway, the pilot from that Japanese plane survived, and he could speak English. I took a plate off the engine that said it was made by Pratt and Whitney.

I think there were two other battleships at Pearl Harbor that had been bombed but not torpedoed, and the navy wanted to get us out of there because we were all that was left out of nine battleships. I can't remember what day it was we left Pearl Harbor, but we arrived in San Francisco on 29 December. The other two battleships—I think they were the *West Virginia* and the *Maryland*—went up to Bremerton, Washington. I didn't have liberty that first night in San Francisco, but I did on New Year's Eve, and the liberty boat let us off over by the Ferry Building. I had only been in the navy for six months, and three months of it had been in boot camp. But I'll never forget the people of San Francisco. They opened their hearts up to us. People were waiting for us on the dock, and they wanted to take us home and feed us. I will always love San Francisco and the people who live there for that. They couldn't do enough for us. Of course, being a seaman second class I couldn't afford to go to the bars, and I wasn't old enough anyway.

Later, we went over to Hunter's Point for repairs. Besides the bomb damage, they had to replace our 5-inch guns. All the rifling was gone. Some men from Mare Island were brought down to help, and while we were there, I was made part of a working party to go down to radio one to help install some new radio receivers with the yard workers. There was a first class radioman down there—a reservist—who took a liking to me. His name was Ken Steiner. In civilian life he had been a ham radio operator, and the navy needed men with those skills because the navy was starting to install radar on some of their ships. He said he was going to talk to his division officer and get me transferred down there with him. "But," he said, "you have to learn Morse code." I said, "Where am I going to learn that?" And he said, "You're going over to the *Delta Queen*." The *Delta Queen* and the *Delta King* were ferry boats that used to run from San Francisco to Sacramento. They were paddlewheel riverboats. Steiner said they were going to bring them down and use them for barracks and have a code school on one of them. So I lived aboard the *Delta Queen* for about two months and went to code school.

Then one day Steiner and I went on liberty together, and he said we were going to a bookstore. He bought me a book that was two inches thick, and it was all electronics. He said, "By the time I'm through with you, you will know every problem in that book." I said, "But I'm not even a seaman yet." He said, "You take the test for seaman, then we'll start studying for third class." I went all through the rest of the war with Steiner, and he gave me a college education. He pounded it into me; he made me study, and that's how I made my living when I got out of the navy, as an electrician.

When I made second class petty officer, Steiner said, "You are going to be in charge of all electronics above the main deck." John Hunter was the other second class petty officer, and he was going to be in charge of all electronics below the main deck. I said, "Ken, that's fine with me. My battle station has always been topside. I don't like going below decks." If I was going to get killed, I didn't want to drown below decks. I preferred to get it topside. See, when the *Oklahoma* rolled over at Pearl Harbor, there were a bunch of guys trapped inside the hull, and they had to cut them out. One of the men they cut out was Bob Fellamey, and he was transferred aboard the *Pennsylvania*. When they pulled him out of the *Oklahoma*, his hair had turned as white as a sheet of paper.

In October 1942 we were back to San Francisco, and there was a yard worker working on the ship. His name was Al Weddle. One day he said, "McDavid, I want you to come up to the house tonight, and my wife is going to make you a chicken dinner." He lived down in Pacifica with his wife Nellie. I went down there with a shipmate, and after dinner the family next door came over to meet some sailors who were at Pearl Harbor. They brought their sixteen-year-old daughter with them and I married her in April 1945, the same day President Roosevelt died.

I spent the rest of the war in the Pacific. We were in the Aleutians, the Gilberts, the Marshalls, and the Marianas. We would come up on some of those atolls, and they looked so calm and peaceful, with palm trees swaying, and when we got through with them we had knocked down all the trees. We tried to kill as many Japanese as we could to make it easy for the marines. Our job was to support the amphibious landings, because the *Pennsylvania* was a World War I battleship and too slow to travel with the newer battleships like the *Iowa* and the *Missouri*. We couldn't keep up with them. There were six of these World War I battleships, and we made up a task force and were always assigned to amphibious landings, whereas the fast battleships—the new ones—were in a task group all their own.

After the Marianas were taken, we went to the Admiralty Islands, where they had a floating dry dock. We pulled into it because we were having problems with one of our propeller shafts. Another ship also came in because it had picked up a bunch of Japanese from a freighter that had been sunk, and they had them all back on the quarterdeck. They came in so they could get them off the ship—put them in a stockade.

While the ship was at anchor, a Japanese plane came in at sunset. They liked to come in at that time of day and get between the ship and the setting sun because they were hard to see that way, and they couldn't be picked up on radar. Anyway, this ship had just set anchor when she took a torpedo in the bow.

The *Pennsylvania* got hit at Pearl Harbor but went throughout the rest of the war without getting hit again until we got to Okinawa, just before the war ended on 12 August 1945. And we got hit the same way this other ship got hit.

A Japanese plane got between us and the sun, and his torpedo hit us in the stern and killed a bunch of quartermasters. That's where their living compartment was. That torpedo almost sank us. Our stern was only a couple of feet above the water, and if it hadn't been for two fleet tugs, we would have sunk. They tied up beside us and sent divers down to close all the watertight doors and pump water out of all the flooded compartments.

The *Pennsylvania* had two rudders and four screws. I think the torpedo knocked off one or two screws and jammed one of the rudders, so we couldn't navigate the ship on our own. Those two tugs had to tow us back to Guam, where we went back into another floating dry dock. I'll never forget when the *Pennsylvania* was raised out of the water, I looked at the big hole in the stern of the ship, and there was a guy's leg hanging out, but it was just bones because the fish had eaten all the flesh off.

At Guam we were patched up as best they could. Two of the screws were fixed up, and I think one of the rudders was fixed also. We could move after that, but not very fast, so these two tugs towed us from Guam back to Bremerton. About halfway back one of the propellers hung down and impeded our progress, so divers were sent down to cut it loose. While they were doing that, sharks showed up, and the divers had to get out of the water. But we had to cut that screw off, so what they did was take meat and mutton, and the cooks threw it off the front of the ship. They fed the sharks off the front of the ship so the divers could go back down on the stern and finish cutting the screw off.

The war was over, and when we got back to Bremerton, all the reservists got off the ship, including Steiner. I was regular navy and still had two more years left in my enlistment, so me and one other guy were the only ones left in the department. Eventually they took all of us off the ship, and I was given leave. When I had only about a week left in my enlistment, I was offered chief if I would reenlist for four years, but I turned it down. My wife had had a baby by then and I had spent most of my six years in the navy at sea, and four years of that had been in the Pacific, so I was ready to get out. But I really liked the navy, and if I hadn't gotten married, I would have stayed in.

CHAPTER 6

◆ ◆ ◆ ◆ ◆

Repair Four aboard the USS *Maryland* (BB-46)

Lawrence Dibb

Lawrence Dibb was born and raised in San Diego, California, and enlisted in the U.S. Navy in 1941, while still in high school. He was supposed to report for duty in February 1942, upon graduation from high school, but because of the Japanese attack on Pearl Harbor on 7 December 1941, he found himself at the Naval Training Center in San Diego on 8 December 1941. After only about two weeks of boot camp, he was headed by train for Bremerton, Washington, with orders to report aboard the USS *Maryland* (BB-46), then in dry dock where she was being repaired after having been damaged during the attack at Pearl Harbor. He went aboard as a seaman apprentice and was eventually assigned to the carpenter's shop, which was part of what was called R Division. R Division consisted of painters, carpenters, shipfitters, patternmakers, and sailmakers, with responsibility for ship repair, boat repair, fire and rescue, and damage control, among other things.

The *Maryland* was commissioned in 1921, and when Dibb went aboard there were men who had served on her since she was first commissioned. Some of these men were still aboard when the war ended. The ship had been their home for most of their adult lives. Dibb left the *Maryland* shortly after the ship was hit by a kamikaze off Okinawa. He left the navy at war's end as a carpenter's mate first class. He is now retired and lives in Vacaville, California.

I was in boot camp long enough to get my sea bag and some shots. Then I was put on a train with a couple of hundred other guys, and we were sent to Bremerton, Washington. When we arrived on 31 December 1941, we were all marched to our ship, the USS *Maryland*. She had left Pearl Harbor with some temporary patches along with the USS *Pennsylvania* after the Japanese attack on Pearl Harbor. When we got aboard, we were all lined up and asked, "Who wants to shoot Japs?" Well, about 60 percent of the men stepped forward, and they were made part of the deck crew that manned the guns. I ended up as a compartment cleaner and mess attendant. That is how I started out, but later ended up in R Division as a carpenter's mate, and that's because I had taken wood shop in high school and had worked after school and on weekends as an auto mechanic apprentice.

The carpenter's shop was on the port side between turrets numbers one and two. The shipfitter's shop was amidships with a passage between it and the carpenter's shop. That was home. That is where we worked and slept. That was R Division.

The *Maryland* left dry dock somewhere around February or March with almost a whole new crew, and we went up to the Aleutians to bombard some islands where the Japanese had gone ashore. One of my duties at that time was fire watch on one of the catapults the floatplanes were launched from. Those floatplanes were launched from the catapult by firing a 5-inch shell casing. The explosive charge is what shot them off. So whenever the planes were being

Lawrence Dibb, carpenter's mate 3/c. Photo taken in front of the Royal Hawaiian Hotel in Honolulu, Hawaii.

launched or recovered, I had to be back there. We had fire hoses and fire extinguishers. As a matter of fact, later, at Tarawa, the flash of flames coming from the exhaust from the floatplanes allowed the Japanese to sight in on the *Maryland* with their 8-inch guns. They didn't hit us, but there were some near misses.

After leaving the Aleutians, we went to San Francisco and up and down the coast of California for quite awhile. We didn't have much of a navy at that time, and the entire West Coast was declared a military zone. There was also concern about Japanese spy networks among the Japanese American population, and there were spies; I don't care what the revisionists say. If the Japanese packed up and moved inland, they were fine, and many did. But the ones who didn't were sent to camps.

I remember when I was living in San Diego, there were these big radio towers inland—military radio towers—and that ground around them would not grow anything. I mean sagebrush had to struggle; it was just rocks in that area, and yet there were Japanese farms all around those towers. My father, a member of the San Diego police force, told me that many Japanese were caught with shortwave radio sets, and detailed maps of North Island, the U.S. Navy Training

Center, aircraft factories, the Marine Training Center, and Fort Rosecrans on Point Loma. None of these things were needed to grow corn and tomatoes.

We went to Pearl Harbor in the spring of 1942 and were backup at the Battle of Midway in June 1942, but we didn't do anything there. Our maximum speed was only about 21 knots, so we made up a task force separate from the carrier task force, and were in a line between the carriers and their escorts, and the West Coast. We were just far enough back that we could get into the action if it turned into a surface battle.

After that we went back to San Francisco for awhile, then back out to Pearl Harbor and down to Fiji. We went down there to help stop the Japanese from invading Australia. We were always out at sea, but we never made contact with the enemy until our forces made landings at Tarawa in November 1943. So we had about a year where we just roamed around the Pacific. The reason we did that was because we didn't have any supplies. We didn't have the ships. We didn't even have very many oilers. We had to refuel out of Fiji and carry enough to refuel the destroyers that were with us. Basically, we weren't ready for the war. On top of that, most of our ships were being sent to help England and Russia, at least during the first year of the war.

At Tarawa we fired on the island before our troops landed and knocked out some of the big guns the Japanese had there. I mean, we are talking about a little piece of island. We were throwing in 16-inch shells, and a lot of them would hit and ricochet off. Then we started firing armor-piercing shells at a higher trajectory, and that did the job. There was no high ground there; it was like shooting at a pool table.

You know, when I first went aboard ship, some of the officers we had could hardly get up a ladder. These guys were so old and had been in the navy so long, I think some of them had been born in a hammock. They needed all that gold braid to hold themselves together. But that changed after the war started. The navy retired some of them, or sent them to shore duty, and replaced them with younger officers.

We didn't have too many problems with the crew. If there was anybody who didn't get along with the others, he was gone, and when the navy needed experienced men for "new construction," we didn't send our best men. We kept the best, and the deadwood got transferred. We were always training. Our lives depended on it, and your life depended on the other guy doing his job. If somebody didn't do his job, we got rid of him real quick. We had a pretty good bunch of guys in all the divisions; there were very few guys who wanted to leave the ship. I don't think I knew of anyone who left the *Maryland* who didn't want to come back. It was that kind of a ship.

After Tarawa, we went to Kwajalein, and that wasn't too bad. Then we went to Saipan. That is when we got torpedoed. I was up on deck, and it was just as the sun was going down. I was with a buddy, "Horse" Matthews, and he was fishing with the line tied around one of his toes when this plane flew right over our bow. I said, "Hey, that ain't one of ours!" Then, the torpedo it dropped hit our bow and we were less than 100 feet from where it exploded. Two men below decks were killed, but neither me nor my buddy was hurt. I was also trained as a diver, and I had to go down and lace the bow together with cables so that we could get the ship back to Pearl for repairs.

After repairs were made, we went to Peleliu in support of the landing there, then on to Leyte and the Battle of Surigao Strait in October 1944. All of our battleships were ones the Japanese thought they had sunk at Pearl Harbor. That was a classic battle between surface ships, and I think it only lasted about eleven minutes.

After that we went back to Leyte, where we took a hit from a suicide plane. I was below decks when it hit between the 16-inch gun turrets, number one and number two. It actually hit turret number two and skidded, and hit under the overhang of turret number one. The shipfitter's shop was between and below the two turrets. The bomb that the plane was carrying went through the shipfitter's shop, penetrated that deck, and hit on top of the hatch cover on the armored deck, and put that hatch cover through its own hole. If that hatch had not been closed, we would have ended up like the *Arizona* when it was hit at Pearl Harbor. That bomb would have hit the magazine that was below it. Instead the bomb exploded upward.

We had four repair parties on the *Maryland,* and my battle station was repair four in the after part of the ship, between turret number three and turret number four. Repair one was on the main deck between turrets number one and number two. A lot of the men in repair one were wiped out when the plane hit, along with some gunner's mates who were manning the 20-mm guns.

As soon as that plane hit, the loudspeaker called, "Dibb and ten men go forward. We can't get any answer from anybody up there." I took my line tender, who was a musician, and some other men and went forward. I had on an RBA [rescue breathing apparatus], and we went up the starboard side, through the officers' quarters, and up onto the quarterdeck, to turret number one and turret number two. There was a ladder that went down to the shipfitter's shop, and there were probably about six guys working around this ladder, so I went between the two turrets and walked right over where that bomb went through the deck and didn't even see it; it was that dark with all the smoke and everything. I missed stepping into it by sheer luck.

Like I said, the carpenter's shop was on the port side, and all my buddies were in the carpenter's shop and the shipfitter's shop. I started down the ladder to the carpenter's shop, but my line tender wouldn't let me go down. I had a rope tied around me, and if I got into trouble, I could give it a couple of yanks and he could pull me back. He said, "Don't go down there!" I think he was spooked—shook up. So I unhooked my line and went down by myself with a battle lantern. The ladder came out in a passage between the carpenter's shop and the shipfitter's shop. There was nobody in the carpenter's shop, and no damage to speak of. My purpose for going down there was so I could report any damage to damage control.

The sick bay was just forward of R Division and on the second deck, and I had a buddy who was down there. I opened a hatch to go down the ladder. The first and second steps were in place, but the third step wasn't, and when I hit bottom, I landed on top of a dead guy. I was in a berthing space, and just forward of that was the sick bay. There was a lot of smoke down there and no lights, so I crawled along the deck toward the sick bay. When I got into the sick bay, I entered the part that was the dispensary, and in there was a pharmacist's mate. He was lying face down. I grabbed the back of his head to turn him over, and it felt like a beanbag. He had bought the farm, so I went past him and into the sick bay itself, and in there were a whole bunch of guys lying on the deck. They were all alive, but had covered themselves with wet blankets. One guy was sitting up, and also covered with a blanket. I pulled the blanket off and shined my battle lantern on him, and it was my buddy, Lou Berry.

He had been operated on for a cyst in his rectum the day before, and it was all packed with gauze. After the bomb went off, he had gotten all the guys out of their bunks and into the showers. They wet a bunch of blankets, and covered themselves with them. They had tried to get out the other side, but couldn't. Then they tried to get out the port side and couldn't.

I asked Lou if he could walk, and he said he couldn't. I got a stretcher off the bulkhead and threw it down. I said, "Get in the stretcher and I'll drag you out of here." I told him to lie down, but he said, "I can't; I'll die!" I said, "If you don't lie down, we're both going to die. We have to get out of here!" But I had no idea how we were going to get out of there, because the ladder I had come down was missing.

I turned to the others in the sick bay and said, "If any of you can walk, come on. If you can't, I'll get some help down to you. I can only take one out at a time." Then I started dragging Berry out, and my RBA stopped working, and the compartment was still full of smoke. That's why I told Berry we had to get out of there or we were both going to die.

We got out past the dead pharmacist's mate and into the next compartment, and about that time a battle lantern showed up on the other side. I hollered in that direction. They had come down from the starboard side and opened another hatch. With their help we got all the other men out of the sick bay.

Later, I went into the shipfitter's shop and helped clean up the mess. There were no bodies, just parts of bodies. This was after we had transferred all the wounded and dead off the ship. Another carpenter's mate by the name of Mally was helping clean up, and he found an arm. This was maybe three or four days afterwards, and he came up to me with this arm and said, "What am I going to do with this?" I said, "Throw it over the side; the guy will never miss it." And that is what he did.

I think we had thirty or forty dead from that. I had two friends, Chief Turret Captain Charles Evens and Chief Boatswain's Mate Vernon Zoller. They both died during the attack. Zoller was just going through the hatch on turret number one, and the hatch wasn't closed when the plane hit right underneath it, and he got badly burned. I talked to him before they took him off the ship, but he died on the way to the hospital ship.

Sick bay was destroyed, so all the guys who were wounded were moved into junior officers' country, and all the junior officers had to find someplace else to sleep. I talked to everybody back there—all the wounded—before they left the ship.

When the plane hit, there was this steward's mate, a huge black guy, coming down the port side, right between the carpenter's shop and the shipfitter's shop. He was lying there on the deck, but I didn't see him because they got him out of there quick. I knew him pretty well, and he would come to me and tell me about this "ninety-day wonder" from the South who was always giving him trouble. He would say, "This guy is from the South, and he is giving me all kinds of trouble. I can't make the guy happy. One of these days I'm going to get really upset," or something like that. I said, "Don't do anything. You have no chance of winning. If you want to get even with him, spit in his food. Spit in his coffee, mix it up, and hand it to him." He did, and he felt good about it, and I don't blame him. But anyway, when this steward got wounded, he had flash burns and was put in the bunk of this ninety-day wonder from the South down in junior officers' country, and that just tickled the tar out of me.

I went back to see him and said, "How you doing?" His black skin had peeled off, and he was pink underneath. He said, "The doctor checked me over and said not to worry, that I would probably end up being as black as I ever was."

After we left Leyte, we went back to Pearl for repairs and missed going to Iwo Jima, but Okinawa was the next big one, and we went through some heavy action there. We took another suicide plane at Okinawa. It was in the evening, and again I was right in the middle of it. I was on the third deck, aft, and just underneath turret number three. This made it easy for me to leave the ship when the opportunity was offered. Being close to getting killed three times was enough for me.

We took the hit, and the loudspeaker came on, "Dibb and ten men go aft!" I was already aft. We went up on deck, and we were fighting fires as soon as we got there. We were supposed to keep the fire ahead of us, but it got all around us. The kamikaze hit right on top of turret number three, and my battle station was right underneath it, below decks. We were fighting the fires, and ammunition was exploding all around us—20-mm ammunition—because on top of turret number three were four 20-mm gun mounts. There were three men to a mount, plus a couple of talkers who communicated between the gunners and fire control. All of them were killed but one. His name is Justin David, and he comes to our reunions. David was coming down the ladder from the turret as we were fighting the fire. He was on fire, and we sprayed him with water as he was coming down and put it out. I said, "Is there anybody else up there alive?" He said, "I don't think so." Then I went up the ladder to the top of the turret, and there was nothing up there but twisted wreckage and bodies. Those guys fired their guns right up until the moment that plane hit.

Right behind the turret were big radar screens, and after we had the fires out, we were able to account for all the dead except for a couple. Then they found one of them spread-eagle, stuck to one of the radar screens. A surgeon had to go up and cut him off. He was nailed to the spike in the middle of the radar screen.

After Okinawa, I was given a choice of either shore duty until I could be assigned to new construction, or promotion to chief, which would have meant a transfer. Either way, I wasn't going to be able to stay on the *Maryland*. By then I had been made first class. They knew I wasn't going to take the exam for promotion, so they just gave it to me. This was in May 1945, after President Roosevelt died, and after the war in Europe was over.

While I was on the *Maryland*, I turned down advancement to chief, warrant officer, and ensign, because as a second class I was one of the only guys who didn't have to stand watch except when we were at general quarters. As a second class, I was in charge of the fresh water hole for over two and a half years. After I was made first class carpenter's mate, I lost the fresh water hole.

We made all of our fresh water from evaporators, and it was for the boilers on the ship. If we were under way and we had enough left over, then we could provide some for the crew for bathing. We also kept an emergency supply, because when the destroyers pulled alongside to refuel, they also took on fresh water.

All I had to do was check the fresh water supply for salt every day, turn in a report as to how much water was on board, and turn the fresh water on or off, depending on how much we had. If we were running short on fresh water, I switched over to salt water, and it wasn't heated.

After Okinawa was over, I knew we were going to be sent back to the States to be "regunned" for the invasion of Japan. That is when they put on new 5-inch/38s and changed the rifling on the 16-inch guns. We burned out the rifling on the 16-inch guns a couple of times.

I was in San Diego when the war ended. I actually got to pick where I wanted to go while I waited for orders to new construction, and the *Maryland* never went to sea again while the war was going on.

The old crew of the USS *Maryland* started having reunions in the early 1970s. I started going to them after I retired. The newest USS *Maryland* is a submarine. The old *Maryland* was scrapped at Mare Island, California, after the war was over.

CHAPTER 7

◆ ◆ ◆ ◆ ◆

The USS *Astoria* (CA-34) and the Battle of Savo Island

Abe Santos

A be Santos was born in Santa Clara, California, in 1921, and enlisted in the U.S. Navy in 1939. After completing boot camp, he was assigned to the USS *Astoria* (CA-34), a heavy cruiser. He was first assigned to the deck force, but was later reassigned to the engineering division at his own request. The *Astoria* was one of four U.S. cruisers lost in the Solomon Islands during the Battle of Savo Island in August 1942. Santos left the navy after World War II as a machinist mate first class, but was recalled to active duty for the Korean War. He is now retired and lives in Capitola, California.

The USS *Astoria* was commissioned in 1934, and had three battle stars to her credit before going down in 1942.

The *Astoria* left Pearl Harbor a day or two before the Japanese attack on 7 December 1941. We were taking replacement civilian workers to Midway Island to relieve the ones that were there. All we had on board was target ammunition—no armor-piercing shells. The captain of our ship at that time was P. B. Haines. He had taken over command of the ship from Richmond Kelly Turner, who later became an admiral with the amphibious forces. We heard later that Captain Haines had a son who had just graduated from the Naval Academy and was aboard a destroyer at Pearl Harbor, and the captain was so happy because he was going to see his son at Pearl Harbor after our return from Midway. However, while we were on our way to Midway, the Japanese attacked Pearl Harbor and his son was killed. Captain Haines left the ship after that, and the word was that he had an emotional breakdown. Capt. William Greenman replaced him. He was the last skipper of the *Astoria*.

I was standing in the chow line on the *Astoria* on the morning of 7 December when it came over the ship's loudspeaker that the Japs had bombed Pearl Harbor. Everybody thought, "Why are they having a drill on a Sunday morning?" Nobody thought it was real. But after that we were ordered to "strip ship." That meant throw everything overboard that might go flying around if we got in a fight—chairs and things like that.

We never reached Midway. We turned around because Midway was under attack too. I was a fireman third class at that time and spent much of my time below decks, so I didn't get to see much, and much of what I heard was scuttlebutt.

We didn't go directly back to Pearl Harbor. We stayed out for several days and returned on the following Thursday. There were still fires burning, and there were still bodies coming up. I don't remember how long we stayed at Pearl Harbor, but our first battle after that was the Battle of the Coral Sea. We were there when the *Lexington* got sunk, and we picked up a lot of survivors out of the water. We also picked up a lot of pilots who didn't have a carrier to go back to. They would land alongside us, and we had boats in the water that would pick them up.

After the Battle of the Coral Sea we went back to Pearl Harbor, then headed for Midway. When I wasn't on watch during the Battle of Midway, I liked to stay topside. I made the excuse that I couldn't get below decks before they secured all the hatches. A lot of us did that when we weren't on watch so that

Abe Santos, survivor of the sinking of the
USS *Astoria* (CA-34) at the Battle of Savo
Island, one of the worst defeats in U.S.
naval history.

we could see what was going on. I saw a lot of dogfights that way between our fighters and the Japanese.

After the Battle of Midway we headed for the Solomon Islands. We got out there on 7 August 1942, and were sunk on 9 August 1942. The marines hadn't landed on Guadalcanal when we arrived, and we were firing broadsides onto the island in preparation for their landing. I think the Battle of Savo Island started around midnight on 9 August 1942, and we didn't have any experience at fighting at night. I think we were in the battle for only twelve minutes before we lost power. I was in the after engine room when we lost power, and water from the boilers and superheated steam started coming in. It was hot! We tried to get out of there, but the hatch was sprung and we couldn't get it open from the inside. But then a damage control party, topside, opened it; otherwise we never would have made it out.

We made it up into the after mess hall above the engine room, and there must have been about fourteen of us in there when we took a hell of a hit from an enemy shell. All I saw was a big flash. I was standing next to a metal countertop, and the force of the blast threw me against it and dented it down by about 10 inches. When I came to, all I had on were my pants. My shoes were blown off, my lifejacket was blown off, and my wristwatch was blown off. I heard guys screaming. One guy was screaming that his arm was blown off. Only about four of us survived that hit.

Everybody in the number two fire room was killed. There were several sets of brothers on board, and there was one guy who was looking for his brother, but his brother was in the fire room that nobody came out of. All of us made it out of my engine room, but a lot were killed in the mess hall.

I had one really good friend in the engine room by the name of Harry Lee McCann, from Norfolk, Virginia. I weighed 118 pounds, and he weighed about 190 pounds. He had been hit in the leg, and he told me, "Don't let me die!" Then we took another hit, and he was split wide open and killed. Water was coming into the mess decks, and I went up a ladder through what is called a "trunk" to the fantail. The water was coming into the trunk, too, and I had to push bodies and parts of bodies out of my way to get out of there. To this day, I don't know how I did it, but I got McCann's body topside. The next morning I sewed him up in canvas and loaded him down with weights. But he went down with the ship before we could give him a proper burial at sea.

There were so many holes in the ship that when I got up onto the fantail I could look down into the mess hall that I had just come out of and see a lot of my friends lying there dead. One of them had his head split open like a watermelon. There was fire everywhere, and ammunition in the ready boxes was going off. We were burning from stem to stern. I found a lifejacket and put it on, but felt something rubbing my neck, so I took it off and found a jawbone with some teeth in it. I peeled that right off and got rid of it.

One of our division officers was split open right down his back. He was a tall, handsome guy from Texas. When I bent over to see how he was doing, he asked me for some water. I can't tell you where I found it, but I did find some water, and when I held him up to give it to him I became covered with his blood. He was still alive when the ship sank, but we couldn't get him off. You know, it bothers you if you see one dead person, but if you see a bunch of dead people, it doesn't bother you as much. I don't know why. Before the ship went down, I found some canned pineapple, and I sat there on a box and ate pineapple with dead guys and parts of bodies all around me. I can still see this warrant officer by the name of Carpenter lying there with a piece of canvas over him and one leg sticking out.

I was still aboard when it started to get light. Ships had come alongside and started pumping water into us to put out the fires, but no water was being pumped out. Then about 11:15 in the morning there was a big explosion forward on the port side. I think one of the magazines blew up. Exactly one hour later we sank. I was standing right next to Captain Greenman, and he had shrapnel holes all over him, and I did too. I said to him, "Captain, aren't you going to give the word to abandon ship?" And he said, "Well, we aren't down yet." I can still hear him saying that.

We had a chaplain on board who was wounded pretty bad. He didn't want to leave the ship, so a couple of us put a lifejacket on him and threw him overboard, but I never saw him again after that.

I walked over the ship as it rolled, and jumped off near the propeller shaft. The water was full of oil and my skin started to burn from all the shrapnel cuts I had in my skin. For weeks after that, whenever I would comb my hair, pieces of shrapnel would come out.

I was trying to get away from the ship, and people were jumping on top of me. I didn't have a lifejacket on and grabbed hold of a guy who did. He almost went berserk. He started hollering, "Turn me loose! Turn me loose!"

There was a guy named Smittie from Chicago; he had a lifejacket on, and he grabbed me by the hand and pulled me out about nine or ten feet away from the ship. Then I said, "Okay, I can make it now," and I never saw him again after that.

We still had wounded lying around the ship when she went down, and they went down with her. And even with all the noise and commotion I could hear

Captain Greenman yell, "Turn around, men, and watch your ship go down!" She rolled, the bow went up, and the ship went down by the stern. Right after she went under a big geyser of water shot up.

I was in the water for six hours without a lifejacket before I was picked up. I stayed afloat by doing backstrokes and then just floating on my back. After a while I started hallucinating. I heard a choir singing, and even today, if I am under stress, I will hear that choir again.

I was just about ready to give up and let myself go under when I saw something about 20 feet away. I swam over to it, and it was a 5-inch ammo canister. I held it under my right arm to stay afloat until I was picked up.

We lost a lot of guys to sharks. I heard one guy in the water near me say that something bit him, then I never saw him again. Another man who was picked up had half of one foot bitten off by a shark.

Finally, a whaleboat off a destroyer came by, and the officer in charge told me to let go of the ammo canister and swim over, but I told him I couldn't. So he said, "I'll pick you up on the next run." Boy, did I cuss him out, so he told the coxswain to pick me up, and they had to pry the ammo canister out from under my arm.

The whaleboat took me alongside a tin can that had a cargo net hanging over the side. I made three or four tries at climbing up it, but couldn't make it. I was so tired after all that time in the water. They ended up pulling me aboard with a boat hook. I was sitting between the two stacks of the destroyer, all covered with oil, and somebody gave me a bowl of soup to eat. Then all of a sudden the destroyer shuddered. Somebody said we had taken a torpedo in the stern. Then a big cargo ship pulled up alongside and lowered a cargo net over the side so we could climb aboard. I don't know how long I was on the tin can, and I don't know how long it took the cargo ship to pull up alongside us. There was so much going on, and so much confusion.

Guys were trying to climb up the cargo net to get aboard the cargo ship, and some fell between the two ships. Guys were just climbing over the top of each other, trying to get off that destroyer. Some were caught in the screws and chopped up, and others were crushed between the two ships.

I got aboard, and there were men from other ships that had been sunk during the battle. After I had been aboard for awhile, I started helping the corpsmen with some of the wounded. There was one kid, I can't remember his name, but he didn't have any ears, nose, or lips. They were all burned off. I never saw him after that, and I doubt that he survived.

We had another guy from off the *Astoria* who was a first class water tender in the engine rooms. He said he was running along the deck after the ship got hit, and he thought he was stepping in holes, but what happened was, he had one of his feet blown off and he was stomping along on the stump. Captain Greenman was all over the rescue ship, looking after his men, and I was standing right there when he came by and asked the water tender how he was doing. He said, "You know, Captain, I always wanted to be a chief in the navy, but now I guess I never will." Just then a chief petty officer was walking by, and Captain Greenman said, "Come here, chief." The captain reached over and took the chief's hat and put it on this guy's head, and said, "You are a chief petty officer," and the guy went to tears.

I don't remember the name of the ship, but it took us all to Espiritu Santo. We were there for about three or four days, and then went on to New Caledonia with an old three-stack cruiser, the USS *Raleigh,* as an escort.

The USS *Chicago* (CA-29) was there, and a friend of mine from school, Anthony Ornellis, was on board. He was a gunner's mate and gave me a toothbrush and a bar of soap. The *Chicago* was later sunk, but he survived and was picked up by the light cruiser *Helena,* but was killed later when the *Helena* was sunk at the Battle of Kula Gulf. I had another friend from school who was also on the *Helena* when it was sunk. His name was Paul Beaggi, but he survived and lives in Santa Clara, California.

In New Caledonia, I was put aboard the USS *Wharton* (AP-7), a troop transport. There were so many people on board that you had to find a place to sit down, and stay there. I still didn't have any shoes, and my feet were burning up on those steel decks. We had some Red Cross personnel on board, and I asked one of them if I could get a pair of shoes. He told me, "Well, the officers haven't been tended to yet." I was so mad when he said that, I took off after him. If I had caught him, I would have thrown him over the side.

Captain Greenman was aboard, as well as some of the other survivors from the *Astoria,* and we were having burials at sea almost every day. Some of the wounded who got off the ship were dying.

I don't remember how long it took us to get back to Pearl Harbor, but it took us quite a while for some reason. I started having migraine headaches after that, and the doctors said it was from a concussion I received on the ship, and that I would just have to live with them. I still get them today, but not as bad. And I still have nightmares—I still see my dead friends. My wife told me that I used to call out their names in my sleep.

CHAPTER 8

◆ ◆ ◆ ◆ ◆

The USS *Indianapolis* (CA-35): A Survivor's Story

Donald Shown

Donald Shown was born in 1920, in a farmhouse in eastern Oregon. His father worked on the family sheep ranch until the farm went bust during the Depression. The family of three girls and two boys then moved to Olympia, Washington, where Shown lived until he graduated from high school. With jobs hard to find, especially for young men just out of school, he felt lucky to be accepted into the armed forces. He enlisted in the U.S. Navy in 1939, and upon completion of boot camp in San Diego, went aboard the USS *Indianapolis* (CA-35). He served aboard the *Indianapolis* from then until she was sunk by a Japanese submarine in the summer of 1945, after having delivered parts for the first atomic bomb to the island of Tinian in the Marianas. The *Indianapolis* was traveling unescorted between Guam and the Philippines when she was sunk with the loss of most of her crew. The *Indianapolis* was commissioned in 1932 and had ten battle stars to her credit before she was sunk.

Shown left the navy in 1945 and worked at various civil service jobs until his retirement in 1975. He lives in Vallejo, California.

During the Depression there weren't many jobs available, even for men who had families, so I decided to go into the navy with a high school buddy of mine by the name of Kenneth Sullens. We went in, in September 1939. After boot camp Kenneth and I wanted to stay together, so we requested the same duty assignment. There were ten of us out of boot camp who were in the same draft to go to the *Indianapolis,* and at the time the *Indianapolis* was in dry dock at Mare Island.

We were sent up to Mare Island aboard the *McDougal,* a destroyer. After gunnery practice off San Clemente Island, the *McDougal* pulled into number one dry dock at Mare Island, and the *Indianapolis* was in number two dry dock. We weren't transferred right away to the *Indianapolis.* First, they made us go over the side and help scrape the bottom of the *McDougal,* then they transferred us and we had to do the same thing on the *Indianapolis.* In those days they didn't have all this fancy equipment, sandblasting equipment and paint sprayers. It was what they called an "all hands evolution." Practically everybody but the captain had to go over the side and scrape and paint the bottom of the ship.

When I first went aboard the *Indianapolis,* I was put in the Fourth Division—a deck division. I was a swabbie and stayed there for two years. We had eight 5-inch/25 antiaircraft guns. Actually, they were used for both surface targets and antiaircraft defense. They were open mounts, and my first battle station was as a "loader"—taking shells coming up from the magazine and putting them in the fuse pot. Eventually, somebody got the idea that I might make a good "pointer," so I became a "pointer" on one of the 5-inch/25s. We used to have what they called "short-range battle practice." A target was pulled by another ship in the opposite direction at 1,000 yards. There was no automatic control in those days. It was all manual, cranking those guns up and down and back and forth. Each gun had a "pointer" and a "trainer." The pointer controlled the elevation, and the trainer controlled the azimuth. During those short-range battle practices I earned an E for efficiency for our gun, and as a first class pointer I earned an extra $5 a month. That was enough for one liberty in those days.

Eventually, they thought I might make a good rangefinder operator. Before radar the navy had rangefinders—optical rangefinders. I was sent to school in San Diego for three months for that—fire control and rangefinder school. That was before the Japanese attacked Pearl Harbor.

After the *Indianapolis* was through in the yard, we went south to San Pedro, where the fleet was at that time. We stayed there overnight, and the next day got under way for the Hawaiian Islands. We operated out of Hawaii for two years before the Pearl Harbor attack. We were at sea when that happened. We had left the week before. We were taking a detachment of marines down to Johnston Island, where we had a radio station.

My friend, Kenneth Sullens, stayed on the ship with me for two years. Then he took this test for what they called the V-12 program, an officers' training program they had during the war. I don't know what the hell happened, if he just didn't like the program or what, but he got out of it. The next time I saw him, we were down in the South Pacific at one of the atolls the fleet used to operate out of. He came aboard the *Indianapolis* in fatigues, like a marine. He was in the Seabees. I didn't see him again after that until the war was over.

We stayed at sea for quite awhile after Pearl Harbor was attacked. We went back in eventually, then went on different missions. We convoyed troop transports from San Francisco to Melbourne, Australia. That was during the first six months of the war. Then we operated with the *Lexington* and the *Yorktown* around New Guinea. After escorting some more troops to Australia, we came back to Pearl and took aboard foul weather gear and headed up to the North Pacific—the Aleutian Islands. The Japanese had taken two islands in the Aleutian chain, Kiska and Attu. We intercepted one of their ships and sank it. We stayed up there and went on patrol for fifty-five days, I think it was. That was rough duty, let me tell you! Waves would break over the bow of the *Indianapolis,* and the water would splash right up on the bridge, and that was 100 feet from the waterline. That is a pretty good size wave. In fact, we had to go back to Mare

Chief Petty Officer Donald Shown, one
of the few men to survive the sinking of
the USS *Indianapolis,* sunk by a
Japanese submarine just weeks before
Japan's surrender.

Island for repairs after that patrol. I was standing in one of the passageways waiting to go to chow. The deck there was two or three inches thick because it was
just over the fire rooms and boiler rooms, and when we hit a big wave, the seams
where the deck was welded opened right up. Seams also opened up in the hull;
we had to go back to Mare Island to be put back together.

Admiral Spruance took command of the Fifth Fleet, and the *Indianapolis*
was his flagship. He took over for Admiral Halsey for the Battle of Midway
because Halsey was in the hospital with shingles. We covered the landings at
Tarawa with our main batteries—our 8-inch guns. By then I was a pointer on
one of the 8-inch guns. And one of the things that we did that was unusual was
to use our 8-inch batteries to shoot down planes, particularly the torpedo

planes. When one of those projectiles hit the water in front of a plane, it put up a spout of water that might go 100 feet up in the air. I have seen torpedo planes hit one of those spouts, and the torpedo would go one way and the plane another way. It worked! I fired the guns myself.

What I remember most about Saipan was all the Japanese civilians. We were off the island waiting to be called in for fire support, and we would see all these bodies floating by the ship, and they were all tied together—civilians. They were dead. They jumped off the cliffs—babies, children, and women—all tied together.

Okinawa was the last operation we were in. We got hit there by a kamikaze. I had just come up out of the mess hall. I had the 0800 to 1200 watch on the forward antiaircraft director and was heading up there. I looked up, and there was this damn airplane coming straight down. He looked like he was right over my head. He hit back by the number three turret on the port side, where the garbage grinder was. Some chief—I don't know who the hell he was—came running across the quarterdeck. I said, "Hey, chief, where the hell did he hit?" He just pointed back and kept running in the other direction and said, "Back there. Aft, aft!" He was going south as fast as he could go.

Before the plane crashed, he dropped a bomb that went down through the ship—through the mess hall, through a berthing space, through a fuel tank, through the bottom of the ship—and exploded underneath it. The Fourth Division berthing space was down there with about half a dozen guys asleep in their bunks. It killed all of them and blew the deck up until it was about a foot from the overhead. It destroyed our evaporators, so we couldn't make fresh water anymore. Some of the crew pushed the plane over the side. It was just hanging there. I know one of the men who helped do that. He lives right down here in Hayward, California.

We limped into Kerama Retto, a small island near Okinawa. We had a hole in the side of the ship below the waterline. A soft patch was put over the hole, and we got back to the States like that. We couldn't make fresh water, so we had to fill our tanks at Kerama Retto before leaving, but that water was for the boilers and drinking. We had to take seawater showers until we got back to the

States. You might just as well forget about seawater showers. You felt just as dirty afterwards as you did before you took one.

We stopped at Pearl and took on some more water, enough to get back to the States—to Mare Island. The ship was repaired at Mare Island, and all of our guns, communications equipment, and fire control equipment were upgraded. While we were in the yard, there was a building at the north end of Mare Island that was so secure that nobody knew what was in it. The stuff that was in that building was put on board the *Indianapolis.* Then we went over to Hunter's Point, where some army officers came aboard with satchels or briefcases strapped to their wrists. A canister was welded to the deck up in officers' country, and it was guarded by marines twenty-four hours a day. You couldn't get anywhere near it. When we got to Tinian, we pulled up to the end of one of the runways and anchored. An LST came out with all these admirals and generals and took all this stuff off. It was in a big crate.

From Tinian we went to Guam. We stayed overnight, then left for the Philippines the next day. We had orders to join up with some battleships and other cruisers for the invasion of Japan. At fifteen minutes after midnight on 30 July, we were hit by a Japanese torpedo and sank.

I was in the chief petty officers' quarters, about as far away from where the torpedoes hit as you could get. The chief petty officers' quarters were on the second deck at the stern of the ship, right below the after turret. I was in my bunk, and there were two other chief petty officers in bunks above me. When the torpedoes hit the ship, the bunks above me came down on top of me. I had a hell of a time getting out from under there. I lifted those goddamn bunks up and crawled out. I got dressed and headed forward to the number three mess hall. The ship was starting to list, and that was just a few minutes after it was hit. A Marine Corps officer, Captain Parks, was saying, "Get topside! Get topside!"

I went up the ladder to the boat deck, which was just above the mess hall. When I got to the boat deck, everybody was just standing around looking dumb. Most of those people had never been on a ship before. Some of them had just come out of boot camp. Better than 50 percent of the crew had been replaced while we were at Mare Island. There is a guy over here in Benicia, California, who was a seventeen-year-old kid, fresh out of boot camp. He had never been to sea before. A few weeks later, he was swimming in the water.

I had been in a lot of rough water on the *Indianapolis,* and I knew when the ship rolled if it was going to come back up or not. I knew when that ship started to roll, it wasn't going to come back up. And when she went down, she was upside down, with her stern sticking out of the water, and the screws still turning.

Some of the men had lifejackets and some didn't. I had a lifejacket and went off by the garbage grinder. There was a boat davit there. I grabbed one of the ropes and swung out as far as I could and dropped into the water. I missed hitting one of the propeller shafts by about a foot. There were no rafts. We had what were called "floater nets." They were cargo nets, and every so far there was a cork disk to keep it afloat, and that is all we had to hang on to, other than our lifejackets. I stayed with a group and hung onto that so I wouldn't drift off. I think there were about 100 in my group who were picked up. There were maybe 150 when we started that first night.

These float nets had survival packets on them, with flares and things to eat like crackers, but no water. I didn't care about anything to eat. Water was what I wanted. And with those lifejackets, you couldn't let your head drop down. In other words, you could not go to sleep or you would have drowned. So I couldn't sleep during those four days and five nights.

A lot of guys, especially near the end, just gave up and died. Some of them started hallucinating and seeing all sorts of damn things. Some hallucinated about diving down to a drinking fountain and getting a drink of water. Some thought they saw an island and swam off to find it. But I made up my mind that if anybody was going to survive, it was going to be me. But I think if we had stayed out there another twelve hours, none of us would have survived.

There were sharks there, too—damn right there were. You could look down in the water and see those bastards right under your feet—hundreds of them. There was one guy—I don't know if he was hallucinating or what, but he said, "I'm standing on one." But as long as we stayed in a group, they left us alone. They only attacked you if you swam away from the group. When I was a kid and used to go fishing, we would put a cork on the fishing line. If we saw the cork go under we knew we had a fish. When a guy got hit by a shark, it was just like that. The shark would hit him, and he would go under. When he came back up, there was nothing below his lifejacket. Yep, it was a rough deal, I'll tell you.

There was a guy, Chuck Gwinn. He was a pilot on antisubmarine patrol out of Ulithi, and he was the one who spotted us in the water. Ships were contacted and sent to pick us up. The USS *Basset*, an attack transport, picked up the group I was in and took us to the island of Samar. I faintly remember being picked up. The ship put a landing craft in the water. The landing craft had a cargo net over the side, and I remember trying to climb up it, but I don't remember making it up. All I remember is landing in the bottom of the landing craft. Somebody must have reached down and pulled me in. The next thing I remember is being in a bunk on the *Basset*. Some guy asked me, "What would you like?" I said, "A glass of water." Shit, I hadn't had a glass of water in five days. That glass of water was the most delicious thing I ever had in my life.

I was in a hospital on Samar for a few weeks. Then I was flown to Base Eighteen Hospital in Guam. I was there about a month, I guess it was. The navy brought a bunch of us back to San Diego on the *Hollandia*, a baby flattop. From there the navy gave us all thirty days' survivors' leave. When my thirty days' leave was up, I reported to Bremerton Navy Yard. My enlistment was up 15 September 1945. I waited around and waited around, and they put me on a goddamn watch detail. I kept going down to the personnel office—the separation center—and asking where my records were. The personnel man said, "See that stack over there? Those are all records. If you can find your records, I'll process you out." I went through that pile in no time. I found my records and said, "Here, get me out of this chickenshit outfit! My enlistment is up." I had had it by then. I didn't want no part of the navy after that. The navy didn't even come looking for us. If it hadn't been for Chuck Gwinn, flying that antisubmarine patrol, I wouldn't be here today.

CHAPTER 9

◆ ◆ ◆ ◆ ◆

S-Boat Sailor
Edward Damour, USN (Ret.)

Edward Damour was born in Detroit, Michigan, in 1921. He enlisted in the U.S. Navy in 1939, right out of high school, and served throughout World War II in submarines, first in vintage S-boats dating back to World War I, then in the newer, more modern fleet boats that eventually replaced the aging S-boats. He stayed in the navy after the war and retired in 1959. He now lives in Vacaville, California.

The old S-boats that Damour first went to war in were large by World War I standards. However, by the time the United States declared war on Japan, following the Japanese attack on Pearl Harbor, most of them were at least twenty years old, and many were not fit for combat. The USS *Pargo,* which Damour served on later in the war, was what was referred to at the time as a fleet boat, and served as the backbone of the U.S. submarine navy that helped bring the war with Japan to an end.

After boot camp, about November or early December 1939, I went aboard my first ship, a beautiful cruiser called the *Chester* (CA-27). I loved that big ship, and shortly after I boarded her, we left for the East Coast by way of the Panama Canal—my first trip through the canal. We took part in some activities in the Caribbean with the British, so we got used to the idea of war long before the Japanese introduced us to it.

In February 1941 they sent us back to the West Coast, then out to Pearl Harbor. At that time the navy needed submarine people very badly, especially in certain ratings, but there weren't enough people volunteering. Normally, if you volunteered for subs, they would send you to the submarine school in New London, Connecticut, for a period of approximately one year. I didn't do that because they needed people right away.

Physical exams were given to several of us on the cruiser, and only two of us passed. The other fellow who passed was married and didn't want to go, so I went as a nonvolunteer. I didn't oppose it, and it was just as well. But I did like that big ship, the USS *Chester*. My joy was to be on that ship.

I started off as a seaman apprentice, and after ten months I was a radioman third class, and that's why I was being urged to go into the submarine service. I was quite pleased with it after I got there. The submarine base at Pearl Harbor was a beautiful place—big screened-in barracks, swimming pool, movies, a chapel everything. They even asked me which submarine squadron I wanted to go into. I think one of them was Squadron Six. These were fleet boats. The other squadron was made up of S-boats, old submarines with 900-ton displacement. They were small and crowded—very uncomfortable. Anyway, I asked, "Who gets to live in this beautiful barracks? Who gets to use this big pool?" I was told the people from the S-boats, because there was no room for everybody to live aboard at one time. Only the duty section stayed aboard.

These old S-boats were built right around the time of World War I, maybe the early 1920s. The level of development was not the greatest. They were worn out. The squadron I could have gone to, Squadron Six, went to the Philippines, and they were almost all wiped out when the Japanese attacked in December

Chief Petty Officer Edward Damour, S-boat sailor.

1941. There may have been one or two that survived. The first one to be sunk was the USS *Sealion*.

My first assignment was on the USS *S-34*. The old S-boats didn't have names, just numbers. When I went aboard, they said, "We're going to promote you. We like the looks of you." And they did. They made me captain of the head. But that was only one of my jobs. My other job was to assist the electrician in watering the batteries. That might seem like a small task, but those submarine batteries were quite large. There were sixty cells in each battery, and there were two batteries, and each cell weighed one ton. And when you topped off these cells with water, parts of the deck had to be taken up. It was an enormous amount of work.

When I started out in the navy, I was making $21 a month—pay grade one. Actually, I didn't get that much because they took out $3.50 for life insurance. When I went into subs, I got an extra $10 a month. Six months later, after taking an extensive exam, I qualified as a submariner, demonstrating the ability to handle almost any task on board. If I had gone to submarine school and had had the advantage of a whole year of training before coming aboard that boat, I still would have had to wait six months before attempting to qualify. So without the submarine school I did it in a minimum of time. At the same time, I made second class. I was making big money. As a second class I was making $72 a month, plus $25 more for having qualified as a submariner. I was rich—$97 a month!

Shortly after I went aboard the *S-34*, the skipper asked me if I would like to go to the Naval Academy, and of course I said I would. They gave me the physical, and at that time you had to be near perfect to get into the academy. I had no problem with the eyes, but they noticed I squinted a little bit. They examined me a little further and noticed that I had some astigmatism, and that wiped me out. I didn't go to the Naval Academy.

Shortly after I made second class, the S-boats got transferred to San Diego, where we provided services to the Submarine Sonar School. That was where the navy trained sonar men to operate the equipment, which we practically inherited from the British. We provided the submarine target for the destroyers to practice on. At the same time, I gained a lot of experience in tracking destroyers that were trying to kill us. Of course, later on a lot of Japanese destroyers did try to kill us, and some American destroyers tried to do the same thing. One of our best submarines, the *Seawolf*, was sunk by an American destroyer escort in spite of every attempt made to identify itself as friendly. At any rate, I did gain a lot of experience. My ears were unbelievably good. I could pick up the slightest sound that a ship might make from as far away as 35 miles, depending on the conditions.

While we were in San Diego, 7 December 1941 rolled around. A friend of mine and I were at a movie, and they stopped the film and told everybody to go to their place of duty. When we got back to the submarine base, they were already loading torpedoes and stores aboard. We went to sea within a couple of days and were strung out in a line with the idea of intercepting Japanese moving towards the Panama Canal, but that never occurred. That was our first patrol, and it was uneventful.

Not too long thereafter, we were sent to the Aleutians. They were sending these old S-boats up there two at a time. I think it was the *S-23* that lost a bow plane on the way up. It just fell off. I mean these old boats were falling apart. Unsafe mechanisms are what they were. When we got up to the Aleutians, the *S-35* had lost its radioman because of a bad back. I was then transferred to the *S-35,* and was to be returned to the *S-34* once a relief was found for the radioman who hurt his back. I never saw the *S-34* again. She got terribly beat up. The Japanese depth-charged her. She barely survived and was sent to Bremerton, Washington. They gave my buddy, Melvin Lars "Pete" Petersen, the Silver Star for his performance in saving the boat. Later on he died on another boat, the USS *Golet,* when it went down. I named one of my boys after him. He was a mighty fine guy. I talked to Pete just before he went to sea on the *Golet.* He said, "We won't be back. We hardly have any qualified men on board." They only had five men qualified for subs on board, and as he said, they didn't come back.

The *S-35* was my home for the next three war patrols. We made our first run out past the Aleutians. The Aleutians are just east of the Kamchatka Peninsula, and near there was a big Japanese naval base, Paramashiro. We got caught on the surface one night by a Japanese destroyer and submarine, and they attacked us. We were just sitting there big, dumb, and happy. We didn't know what the hell we were doing; we were neophytes. I heard the alert come down from the bridge, "Captain to the bridge! Captain to the bridge!" The captain went charging up to the bridge, but meanwhile I secured everything in the radio shack and headed for the forward torpedo room, where my listening equipment was. I got it fired up and going, and I could hear a goddamn torpedo coming toward us. The Japanese sub had fired it at us. We estimated that it must have passed between the conning tower and the gun mount while we were going down. Then the destroyer depth-charged the living shit out of us. He didn't kill us, but he damaged us. We didn't know we had been damaged until we tried to make another dive the following morning. We stayed down for twenty hours before we felt it was safe to come back up. Plus, we had no air left. We were starting to become slow-witted from the foul air.

When we surfaced, we charged our batteries as well as we could and as fast as we could. Then that morning we went down again. That is when we discovered we couldn't close the conning tower hatch. The water came in like gangbusters, and we caught fire. Fortunately, it was a routine dive; we weren't being forced down. We had electric heaters all over the place, to keep us warm. They had sent us to sea with no foul-weather clothing. We had nothing in the early days of the war. We had soldiers with no guns. We had destroyers left over from World War I—old four-stackers—and old S-boats like us, all falling apart. This nation was woefully unprepared for war. We were a stripped, helpless nation. Anyway, the sea-water came in and shorted out all these electric heaters, and that's what started the fire on board. We were lucky we survived; I don't know how we did.

I never smoked until after that happened. After that I had a smoke every once in awhile. I did it in part to make the air taste better. The air was so foul on those old S-boats. It was a small boat with about thirty-five people on board.

After a couple more patrols on the *S-35*, the Japanese hit Midway. At the same time, they hit us at Dutch Harbor. We knew they were going to attack, but we didn't know precisely when. So we went to sea as quickly as we could. We were out of the harbor and on patrol when one of their planes machine-gunned the hell out of our conning tower while we were going down.

I did a total of three patrols on the *S-35*, which were memorable if for no other reason than the weather. The weather in Alaska—the Aleutians—was terrible, and we had men badly injured by being washed down from the bridge into the conning tower. They smashed their faces on the ladder, and things like that. It was a mean place to be. It was cold and there were rocks, with visibility almost zilch. The *S-27* had run aground that way and was lost. The crew was saved by PBYs.

Some time after that an experienced first class radioman became available, and it was decided they would rather have him on board than a little old second class, so he went to the *S-35*, and I started standing watches at the Dutch Harbor radio shack.

When the *S-35* came back from its next patrol and was approaching the dock, one of the crewmen fell over the side and was crushed by the boat closing in on the pilings on the pier. He got caught from just below the chest on down. When they pulled him out, he looked like a broken doll. I have never forgotten his screams. I dream about it even today.

A couple of nights later the captain of the *S-35,* James Stevens, was having quite a party at the officers' barracks. He was feeling pretty good, and the boat was leaving in the morning for San Diego. They were pulling the S-boats out of there. So I said, "I'd like to go back with you," and he said, "Be aboard." I didn't say anything to anybody, because I knew I was pulling a fast one. After we had been under way for a few hours, I made my appearance, and Captain Stevens said, "What are you doing here?" I said, "You told me to be aboard."

When we got to San Diego, they put me in sonar school, and that's when I met my wife. I went up to Long Beach one weekend, met this little lady, and two weeks later we were married. After twenty-eight years of marriage we were divorced. You see, I spent twenty years in the navy, and that's rough on a marriage. And at the time I didn't think I was going to live very long and didn't think in terms of long-term planning. We were losing submarines fast in those days. We lost fifty-two during the entire war—almost 23 percent of our entire force. We had about sixteen thousand men who actually made patrols. Of those, we lost thirty-five hundred. The army lost about one percent of its people, which is a big number but a small percentage. The marines lost 10 percent. The German submarine force lost even more. They lost 66 percent of their people. There is an international organization of submarine people. We all have something in common. We were not killed.

It was in late 1942, that I got orders to go to the submarine USS *Pargo* (SS-264), a brand-new boat in New London, Connecticut. I went there as a first class radioman and served on her till the end of the war except for when I was sent back to school for some advanced training.

We had a lot of qualified men on board. We had a picked crew. Our skipper, Ira Dye, was very much an Errol Flynn type, tall and heavily built. Our executive officer was Dave Claggett, and he was fantastic. One time, we were making a surface attack on some Japanese ships at night. Dave Claggett was on the periscope down in the conning tower. We were running at full power towards the ships, and Claggett told the captain, "A little closer, Captain, a little closer." The captain was on the bridge, and he yelled, "Dave, I can see the goddamn people walking around on the deck!" "Just a little bit closer, Captain," Claggett said. Then we started firing our torpedoes. We sank a few ships that way. They gave Captain Dye the Navy Cross for that. The captain always gets the medals.

We made our first war patrol off Nagasaki, and there was lots of Japanese shipping off there. We made lots of night surface attacks with radar. The radar was beautiful. The old S-boats had nothing like that. During the entire war the *Pargo* made eight war patrols and torpedoed twenty-seven enemy ships. I made the first three, and then was sent off for more schooling.

When I finished my advanced courses at Treasure Island, the *Pargo* was at Mare Island. I called the captain, and in about an hour I was on my way back to the *Pargo* and made the eighth and last war patrol with it. I was on the bridge with the captain off the coast of Japan one day, and I felt a concussion. I mentioned it to the captain. I said, "Did you feel that?" He said, "Yes." As we found out later, it was the first atomic bomb, the one they dropped on Hiroshima.

That night, or the next night, we went through the minefields that separated Tsushima, the lower part of Korea, from Japan. There were moored mines everywhere. The chain to one of them dragged along the hull before it let go. Anyway, we did get into the Sea of Japan and sank three ships while we were there. We made one last attack on a Japanese ship and missed. The escort that was with it came roaring over us, dropped some depth charges, and went right on. We never saw that before. They would usually come back around and try to get us.

About one o'clock that afternoon we ran up the periscope with the antenna on it and found out the war had ended. Until then we had been submerged and didn't know it had ended. That probably explained why the escort made only one run on us.

The problem for us was that we were in the Sea of Japan, and the only way out was through the minefields, and we didn't want to do that. We didn't think it was too smart. So we were in there for another month. Finally, our people got the dope as to where a clear path out was, and we went back to Pearl Harbor. That was the end of the war for me.

◆ ◆ ◆ ◆ ◆

CHAPTER 10

Quartermaster aboard the USS *Buchanan* (DD-484)

Joe C. Tacker

Joe C. Tacker was born in 1924 in Corinth, Mississippi. He enlisted in the U.S. Navy in January 1943, with the idea of becoming a navy aviator. However, he ended up going to quartermaster school out of boot camp before being assigned to the USS *Buchanan* (DD-484). Nineteen months later, on the day the war ended, he received orders for naval flight training, which he successfully completed. Tacker remained in the navy as a pilot until 1950, when he went to work for Hawaiian Airlines. He retired from Hawaiian Airlines in 1979. Tacker lives in Monterey, California, where he still flies a friend's plane.

The USS *Buchanan* (DD-484) was commissioned in March 1942 and fought throughout the desperate early months of the war in the Solomon Islands. She suffered battle damage on numerous occasions, but survived the war to sail into Tokyo Bay in August 1945. She had sixteen battle stars to her credit by war's end. In 1949 she was turned over to the Turkish Navy.

The reason I enlisted in the navy was because I wanted to be an aviator. I graduated from high school in May 1942, and got a job with Glenn L. Martin Aircraft Company in Baltimore, Maryland. My wage was sixty-one cents an hour. I enjoyed working in Baltimore, but most of my co-workers seemed to be intent on nothing but dodging the draft. That was all they wanted to do. But that wasn't my purpose for being there, so I went home at Christmastime, 1942, and told my folks I wanted to join the navy and become a naval aviator. When I went to the navy recruiter, he told me there were three thousand people in line for the program ahead of me—the V-5 program, I think it was called. He told me if I really wanted to get into the navy aviation program, I should enlist in the regular navy, because it would be easier to get in from the inside than from the outside. I bit on that, and it wasn't long before I found myself in the middle of the war in the waters around Guadalcanal.

I went to San Diego for basic training, and the navy had all these schools we could sign up for. We were given tests to see what schools we might qualify for, and I had to figure out which school would be useful to me as an aviator even though it was the surface navy I was fooling with at the time. I selected quartermaster school and got it. I was a company commander in quartermaster school, and in another company at the same time there was a young recruit by the name of Henry Fonda. I selected quartermaster school because that involved navigation and the piloting of ships. I found it to be very interesting and eventually came to be an expert navigator.

From quartermaster school, the navy sent a bunch of us to New Orleans, and the next thing we knew we were on *LST-1133* for transportation to the South Pacific. I went up on the bridge and told the captain I had just gotten out of quartermaster school. I was only a third class, but they asked me to help correct their navigation charts. So me and a guy who had worked for Rand McNally, the map company, went to work correcting all the charts on the ship. Then we started taking over the navigation of the ship and ended up navigating it all the way across the Pacific. We went through the Panama Canal and on to New Caledonia. The quartermaster who was assigned to the LST hadn't had any schooling as a quartermaster and was glad to have us. He was learning on the job.

We went all the way by ourselves. We weren't part of a convoy. On the way over, somebody said, "Here comes a torpedo!" I didn't see it, but whoever did said that we had such a shallow draft that the torpedo went right under us.

We arrived in New Caledonia at night, and I was transferred right away to the destroyer *Buchanan* (DD-484). That's how much of New Caledonia I got to see. The next morning we were under way. The ship had just come from Sydney, Australia, where it had been on R & R. We went from New Caledonia to Pervis Bay on Tulagi Island, across the strait from Guadalcanal. By that time, it was August 1943.

The captain of the *Buchanan* when I arrived aboard was R. E. Wilson, and the executive officer was Commander Morey. Walter Hoffman was our communications officer, and he became the executive officer after Morey left the ship. Hoffman and I have remained friends to this day. He was also interested in becoming a navy aviator but never did while he was in the navy. However, after the war he bought his own airplane and learned to fly.

Not too long after I came aboard, Captain Wilson was relieved by a Captain Curtis, who stayed with us for as long as I was on the *Buchanan.* The senior yeoman aboard the *Buchanan,* Harold Bizzner, became a good friend of mine, and still is. He became a successful architect in southern California after the war. Harold's general quarters station was on the "annunciators" on the bridge. That is what you send signals down to the engine room with: forward full-speed, left engine, right engine, and so forth. That was Harold's job, and I was on the helm, so we spent a lot of time up there together.

We never had any desertions while I was on the *Buchanan,* but we did have a radioman who went berserk, and we had to put him in a straitjacket. I don't remember exactly where we were at the time, but he could take five-letter code at a fantastic speed, and he was an excellent radioman. As good as he was and as fast as he could take code, he almost had to be a savant. I remember our communications officer being quite upset about losing him. After we got him in a straitjacket, we put him in a boatswain's chair for transfer to an oiler, and the way he was thrashing around I thought for sure he was going to fall into the ocean. I never heard what happened to him after that.

In the Solomons, we did mostly patrols up the "Slot," antisubmarine patrols, and shore bombardment. I can't remember for sure, but I think my destroyer squadron was DESRON-12, and we had a mission one night to go into Rabaul—to make a raid on Rabaul Harbor. The whole squadron went into the harbor, and we fired everything we had, including torpedoes. I was on the helm and watched the whole thing like a movie. I thought it was a pretty dangerous thing to do, but we got away with it. I saw fires on some of our ships. I thought they got hit by some airplanes that were strafing us. We went in, shot up the place, got out, and got back to Tulagi. As it turned out, none of our ships got hit.

We then went into Bougainville—I think it was late 1944—and I think just two or three destroyers from our squadron were there for that raid. We weren't steaming very fast as we fired at some Japanese shore batteries, and we could see them firing back at us. Some of their shells hit in the water around us, then one hit us in the fantail on the starboard side, right about where the deck meets the hull. It hit right by where our depth charges were, and we were very lucky that none of them went off.

Quite a few guys were hurt. I had just been relieved on the helm and was back by one of the signal bags when we got hit. One of the officers in gun control just above the wheelhouse took some shrapnel in the gut and was hurt pretty bad. A couple of us grabbed him and took him down to the wardroom. Another kid who was back closer to where the shell hit got his leg all mangled, and the doctor down in the wardroom was in the process of taking the lower part of his leg off when we arrived with the wounded officer. The doctor said, "I need some help!" I told him I was needed up on deck, because I'm the sort of person that if you stub your toe and it bleeds, I have to lie down and catch my breath. But he said, "No, you stay right here!" There were three or four wounded men down there, as I remember. So I stayed down there for quite awhile and helped him while he took this guy's leg off.

The next thing I remember is when we came back to Pearl Harbor. We were presented with the Presidential Unit Citation. Some admiral came aboard, and we had to get all dressed up. We were pretty proud of that, plus we were going home for some leave. We pulled into Mare Island in California for an overhaul and repair of battle damage. The entire ship's company was moved into a barracks, and when we had liberty we went into San Francisco religiously.

After we left Mare Island, we went back out to Pearl, then on to Ulithi Atoll. That was a sight. I never saw so many ships in one place, and there never have been so many ships in one place since. That's when we started being assigned to various carrier task forces, Task Force 38 and Task Force 58, depending on which admiral was in charge.

I remember the Philippines because that is where we got into a big typhoon. That's the one where we lost three destroyers, the *Spence,* the *Hull,* and the *Monaghan.* Before the typhoon hit us, the *Buchanan* had been out on what was called the "cat's eye." During carrier air strikes, one destroyer would be sent out about 50 miles from the task force, and planes coming back from a mission had to circle us to get clearance before continuing on back to the carriers. That was to keep our ships from shooting down our own planes. They would get clearance from us, and we would radio back that a certain number of our planes were on the way.

While we were coming back from that station, I was watching the barometer, and it was going down like mad. I knew from quartermaster school that when the barometer dropped like that we were heading into a storm, a real storm. We were talking about it on the bridge when we got orders to refuel and take on supplies. The position we were given for refueling was right in the middle of this storm. We kept waiting for a change in orders, but they never came, so we went on in.

On a destroyer, as you use up your fuel, you replace it with seawater in order to keep ballast. But before you refuel, you have to get rid of the seawater. That is called "blowing your tanks." Well, we got orders to blow tanks, but by that time we were rolling from the high seas. Our skipper said, "No way! We're not ready to hook up yet." The seas got so bad that they had to tie me to the helm, and my friend, Bizzner, was tied to the annunciator. Everybody else was being thrown from one side of the bridge to the other, and seawater was actually coming into the bridge. Everybody was all banged up, bruised, and cut. I thought we were going down, I really did.

The skipper thought the radar was out, and he was screaming for the radar technician to come up and fix it. He came up and said the radar was okay. The captain said it wasn't and made the technician take it apart. What had happened was, we were keeping station with the rest of the ships by tracking them on our radar. The three ships we were tracking were the *Spence, Hull,* and the *Monaghan,* and they had capsized and gone down. That is why the captain thought our radar had gone out. It wasn't the radar, it was our references, the destroyers; they were gone!

We didn't lose anybody, but we did lose a lot of equipment. It was a miserable time, and as I recall, we didn't eat for seventy-two hours. I was really disgusted with Admiral Halsey, because you didn't have to be a well-educated meteorologist, or aerologist as we called them in the navy, to know we were sailing into a dangerous situation. There were never any orders for us to change course. And the terrible thing was, six months later, Halsey did it again—got us right into another one off Okinawa.

While we were doing radar picket duty off Okinawa, the *Hazelwood* (DD-531) got hit by a kamikaze, and Commander Morey went over to take temporary command of her. I went with him to be his quartermaster and helmsman. The captain and everybody on the bridge on the *Hazelwood* got wiped out when they were hit by the kamikaze. They lost all of their control people—all of their quartermasters.

When we got aboard, we couldn't steer the ship from the bridge; I had to steer it from the emergency steering station, which was back on one of the stacks. There was one body in the rigging, hanging upside down, and they couldn't get it down, at least not at that time, and I had to stand there and look at that body the whole time I was steering the ship. I was probably on the *Hazelwood* for five or six days, and every day we had burials at sea. After awhile, we got a tug to take us under tow, and they took us to Ulithi.

I developed a method for watching the kamikazes and could tell if they were coming for us. I would point at one with my index finger. Once I had it blanked out, I would count to three. If I didn't see it after the count of three, I knew he was heading for us. If he came out from behind my finger, I knew he was going for somebody else. When I did that, the other guys would say to me, "What the hell are you doing?" I just told them I was seeing which way the plane was going.

On the day the war ended I was on the *Buchanan,* somewhere between Okinawa and Japan, and that's the day my orders for flight school came in. I left the *Buchanan* not knowing what great things lay ahead for the ship. While I was trying to hitchhike my way to Pensacola, Florida, for flight training, the *Buchanan* was selected to transport Gen. Douglas MacArthur to the USS *Missouri* for the signing of the official Japanese surrender. She also transported Admiral Nimitz and Admiral Halsey from their flagships to Yokohama. I thought that was a fitting end for a great fighting ship. I went on to do my flight training, became carrier qualified, and flew as a navy pilot until I got out and went to work for Hawaiian Airlines in 1950.

◆ ◆ ◆ ◆ ◆

Aboard the USS *Porterfield* (DD-682)

John Sheehan

John Sheehan was born in 1925 in Omaha, Nebraska. He enlisted in the U.S. Navy in June 1943, a month after he graduated from high school. He served on the USS *Porterfield* (DD-682) throughout his time in the navy during World War II and was also trained in UDT as a frogman. Sheehan left the navy after the war and went to college, where he played football. He now lives in Santa Cruz, California.

The *Porterfield* won ten battle stars in World War II and remained a part of the Pacific Fleet well into the 1970s, serving in the Korean War and the Vietnam War.

Originally, I was going to go into the Marine Corps with four of my buddies from high school, but I had a friend, Carl Samuelson, who was in the navy and just out of boot camp. He convinced me that the best thing to do was go into the navy. He survived the war, and as a matter of fact I played college football against him after the war. The four friends of mine from high school who went into the marines were all killed, either on Iwo Jima or Okinawa.

After boot camp I went to quartermaster school, then to Treasure Island in San Francisco Bay, where I received orders to a destroyer being built in San Pedro. It was the USS *Porterfield* (DD-682) and was commissioned on 30 October 1943. Our captain was Cdr. J. C. Woefel. After our shakedown, which was in November and December, we left for Kwajalein Island with Task Force 53 and arrived there on 31 January 1944. After our arrival in the Marshalls, Lieutenant Commander Walzen took over as skipper of the ship, and he was a wonderful officer to serve under. He retired after World War II as a vice admiral. Commander Walzen was regular navy. Most of the other officers were reservists, although later on we received some academy graduates on board.

We were also the flagship for Destroyer Squadron 55. We had a commodore on board, Commodore Todd, who was in command of the squadron. I had a good rapport with him. Sometimes he would sit in the captain's chair on the bridge, and if I was on the helm, he would chat with me. He had been an enlisted man and had come up through the ranks. He made admiral before the war was over, and was on Guam as part of the staff making up plans for the future invasion of Japan.

Commodore Todd was highly respected. I remember one time, when the *Porterfield* pulled up alongside the USS *New Jersey,* and Admiral Halsey came aboard to pay his respects to Commodore Todd. Admiral Halsey was on the bridge, leaning over the chart desk with Commodore Todd, when I came in, in my white hat and undress blues. Admiral Halsey looked at me and said, "What are you all dressed up for?" I said, "For you, sir." Then he said, "Pass the word for the crew to get comfortable. Tell them to put on their dungarees. I don't want them to dunk me when I'm on my way back to the *New Jersey.*"

The Marshalls was where we first saw combat. We did some shore bombardment, but it wasn't too rough. However, while we were anchored in the lagoon at Enewetak, we had trouble with Japanese trying to swim out to the ship with explosives. At night we were especially vulnerable to this sort of thing. The smallest armaments we had on board were some 20-mms, so we had to get some .30-caliber and .50-caliber machine guns and place them all up and down the port and starboard sides of the ship in order to protect ourselves. And we did kill lots of Japanese trying to swim out to our ship.

After the Marshalls campaign we went to the Admiralty Islands to support landings down there. I remember that while we were down there, the captain let us go swimming off the ship, but we had a lot of problems with sharks. Some people were attacked, and one man was killed. The one who was killed was trying to climb up on the screw guard of the ship when a shark bit his leg off. We had boats out with men in them with rifles, but that didn't help.

After that we had a little break at Pearl Harbor, then went to the Marianas for the invasions of Saipan, Tinian, and Guam in June and July 1944. Again, we were there for shore bombardment. There was one situation at Saipan where we were trying to lob 5-inch projectiles down the top of the smokestack on the sugar refinery on Saipan, because we were told that there was a Japanese observer in the top of it. We weren't successful in lobbing any shells down the smokestack, but we did destroy the sugarcane refinery.

We also took a hit from an enemy shell while we were off Saipan. It hit fire control, just above the bridge. Several people were killed, and a signalman on the bridge was wounded. I happened to be on one of the 5-inch guns when that happened.

For the landings at Leyte in October 1944 we were reassigned from the Fifth Fleet, which was under Admiral Spruance, to the Third Fleet, which was under Admiral Halsey. On 24 October 1944 the light carrier *Princeton* was hit by an aerial bomb. We were part of the destroyer screen for her and getting ready to go alongside after a huge explosion rocked her aft of the island. I saw the explosion and remember seeing ten or fifteen bodies fly through the air. The *Princeton* began smoking heavily, and several more explosions followed. However, the *Cassin Young* (DD-793) went in instead and picked up survivors. I think she was also damaged by the explosion, as was the *Birmingham,* which was on the other side of the *Princeton.* Some of the bodies flew over the *Cassin Young* and landed in the water. We went to see if there were any survivors, but couldn't find any. I guess they were just blown to pieces. While picking up survivors from both the *Princeton* and the *Birmingham,* we were busy fighting off fifteen or twenty enemy planes, which had broken through our fighter screen. We picked up 130 officers and men from the *Princeton* and 4 from the *Birmingham.*

We continued to hang around in the area until another destroyer sank what was left of the *Princeton.*

In December 1944 we found ourselves off the Philippines when we were hit by a typhoon. We lost three destroyers, the *Hull,* the *Spence,* and the *Monaghan.* We were heading into the storm, and the waves were so high that once we got to the top of one, we would roar down the other side and hit the trough with a terrific crash. It felt as though the ship was going to explode. Then every once in a while we would get hit on the beam and roll over. At one point we rolled 10 degrees beyond the point at which we should have capsized, but didn't. It was horrendous! We were like a cork, just bouncing around. We had some people from the deck force who had to go forward to secure some equipment that had come loose, and one of them was swept overboard.

If you know anything about a *Fletcher*-class destroyer, you know that the one deck that runs forward to aft is the main deck, and it is exposed to the outside. The only way you could get from the crews' quarters to the bridge was to go up to the main deck, which was very difficult during a typhoon, with water washing over the main deck. I had to do that, and it was a devastating experience. There was no way to reach the bridge from the crews' quarters below decks. The 21-ton *Fletcher*-class destroyers were the backbone of the destroyer navy in World War II.

The whole time we were in the Philippines we were pretty much under attack. That is where we first encountered kamikazes, but they seemed to go mainly after the bigger ships. We never got hit, although we were under attack a lot. And we never got any relief from those attacks until we went to Ulithi.

One time I was on the 1200 to 0400 watch on the bridge. We were to the east of Luzon. It was a moonlit night, and I heard something. I looked low on the horizon, and here came a Betty bomber right above the water, and he was coming right at us. I think he must have seen us at about the same time I saw him. I hit the deck because I thought he was going to hit us. He pulled up at about the same time and knocked off our radar screen. That's how close he was to us. He circled around to come back at us, and one of our 5-inch guns shot him down. We always had two 5-inch guns at the ready, even when we weren't at general quarters.

In January 1944 we sailed between Luzon and Formosa, and towards the waters off French Indochina. On the way we encountered two Japanese transports with troops on board. We sank them with shellfire, then continued on to French Indochina, where we did some shore bombardment. On the way back to the Philippines we passed through the area where we had sunk the two transports five days earlier, and there were bodies and debris everywhere. The captain decided we should pick up some of the bodies to see if there was anything that might identify the units that were aboard the transport. The bodies were so decomposed that the people who pulled them aboard had to wear gas masks. I was standing on the bridge and saw two of our men with pliers trying to pull the gold teeth out of one of the bodies. I was at a reunion a couple of years ago and was talking about that to one of the fellows, and he said, "That was me."

Shortly after that I left the ship and went back to Pearl Harbor for a one-month training program in UDT, underwater demolition team. I volunteered for it. I stayed one night at the Royal Hawaiian Hotel in Honolulu, then went to the island of Kauai for the training. When I started the training I weighed 193 pounds, and when I was finished I weighed 173 pounds. The training was intense and involved a lot of swimming and learning how to set off explosives. I was also trained as a "call fire." That is when you go into an area in the water near the beach before the marines land and direct the shellfire of the bombardment fleet. After that, my job was to direct the landing craft in, using colored smoke.

After the training I was sent back to the *Porterfield*, and our next operation was Iwo Jima. As a UDT man, I went into Blue Beach one day ahead of the marines. We went in to make sure there were no obstacles in the way, and no electric cables leading into the water where the marines would land. The Japanese had done that before. We didn't find any manmade obstacles, but we did have to blow up a few coral heads that were in the way.

I was in the water off the beach when the landing craft started coming in, and I signaled to them with colored smoke where to land. Afterwards, I swam out and was picked up by an LCVP. That was all I did at Iwo before I went back to my ship. We stayed in the area of Iwo for awhile after that and did some shore bombardment, then went to Ulithi and prepared for the landings on Okinawa.

During the month of March 1945 we were on patrol off the coast of Japan. We had encountered several Japanese gunboats, which were on patrol along the coast. They were small but heavily armed, and in rough seas they were hard to see. On two occasions we were hit by their gunfire before we were able to sink them. We were told by fleet headquarters that we would probably encounter hundreds of these small Japanese patrol boats before we reached Tokyo Bay for a permanent stay.

During the course of many of the operations that we took part in, we were able to save the lives of many pilots and crewmen who had to ditch in the water. On one occasion, a badly damaged F4F Wildcat from the USS *Langley* had to ditch close to our ship. It was seen from our ship that the pilot was having trouble getting out of the cockpit. We were trying to lower the whaleboat to rescue him, but his plane was sinking fast with a Lieutenant Sanders still in it. Two men from the *Porterfield* jumped in the water to help him. I had a line around my waist and was prepared to go in and also help in case they weren't successful. But they did their job well, and I wasn't needed. Both men were awarded medals for their bravery.

On 26 March we landed troops on Kerama Retto. Again, I went in as UDT, but there was not much to do there. The Japanese didn't put up much resistance. Then, on 27 March, we started our operation at Haguchi Anchorage, Okinawa. This was an altogether different situation from what I had experienced on Iwo Jima. The Japanese had taken telephone poles and pounded them into the beach, underwater, so that no landing craft could get in. It took about one hundred of us two days to remove all the obstacles. And near the beaches the Japanese had all sorts of catacombs in the sides of the cliffs, and they were shooting at us from there the whole time. We had to call in fire support from our destroyers, but these catacombs were reinforced with concrete, and the ships had to use armor-piercing shells. Removing the obstacles was all manual labor. We had some sub chasers, and we secured cables around the telephone poles. Then the boats would pull them out.

After the obstacles were removed, I went back to the *Porterfield,* and we went out to the radar picket line. Early on, the kamikazes were going after the bigger ships, then they changed their strategy and started coming after the destroyers. It was sheer hell! Hundreds of kamikazes were coming in after the destroyers. We were sitting ducks. We saw other ships get hit, and we shot down lots of planes, but we were never hit. However, we did have a close call one time. I was on the bridge when it happened. The kamikaze was at about 500 feet and dove right at us. It just missed the fantail, and nobody was hurt.

On 6 April, while we were on picket duty, we came under heavy attack, and the USS *Newcome* was severely damaged by kamikazes. We picked up twenty survivors, many of whom were badly burned. The USS *Leutze* was also damaged. Darkness came, and by 2015 the USS *Defense* had the *Leutze* under tow. A fleet tug took the *Newcome* in tow, and both were taken to Kerama Retto. We screened them until they made the anchorage. We then went alongside a hospital ship and transferred the wounded we had aboard. Then we went to an ammo ship and took on fresh stocks of much needed ammunition.

We started having some engine problems as a result of the near miss from the kamikaze and were sent to Ulithi to a floating dry dock for repairs. They couldn't repair the problem there, so we were sent back to Pearl Harbor, then to Bremerton, Washington. While the *Porterfield* was at Bremerton, she was being refitted for the invasion of Japan. All of the torpedo tubes were taken off, and rocket launchers were put on. I was at home on leave in Nebraska when the war ended, and my leave was extended for thirty days.

I had no problems getting to sleep after the war. I was more interested in going to college and playing football. I never gave any more thought about my time in the service until I started going to reunions, and that was in 1985. Before that I was more interested in my family and my job.

CHAPTER 12

◆ ◆ ◆ ◆ ◆

Aboard the USS *England* (DE-635)

Dwight DeHaven

After the loss of the *Yorktown* (CV-5) at the Battle of Midway (see chapter 1), Dwight DeHaven was transferred to "new construction" aboard the USS *England* (DE-635). Destroyer escorts were a new class of ship. They were first introduced to the U.S. Navy during World War II and were smaller than destroyers. During the last two weeks of May 1944, the *England* sank six Japanese submarines in twelve days, a record that stands to this day in the annals of antisubmarine warfare. The *England* was later hit and severely damaged by a kamikaze while on picket duty off the coast of Okinawa in 1945. She was sailed back to the East Coast of the United States, where she was scrapped at war's end. Another *England* was commissioned after World War II and is now a part of the mothball fleet in Suisun Bay, California.

The crew for the ship assembled at Mare Island in California and went aboard for the first time there. I think only a half-dozen of us had ever been to sea before. Capt. W. B. Pendleton was the captain of the USS *England* when it was commissioned in December 1943. He was from the Asiatic Fleet, as I remember, and was a crusty kind of a character—very businesslike. My guess is he was about fifty-five years old at the time. I remember he liked to go ashore whenever possible. Once we had to change the fuel pump on the whaleboat when we were anchored at Ulithi, which was a huge lagoon. It was like being anchored at sea. The lagoon was choppy that day, and we were standing on our heads trying to work on the engine in the whaleboat. I had two or three men helping me with it, but they were getting seasick, and Captain Pendleton was pacing back and forth. He wanted to go ashore bad. We finally got the engine fired up, but it wasn't adjusted, and black smoke was just rolling out of it. The captain said, "That's good enough for me," and he jumped in and told the coxswain to take him to the navy landing. All you could see was his head sticking out above this cloud of black smoke as they headed for shore. He wanted to get to the officers' club so he could have a drink.

Lieutenant Commander Williamson was our executive officer at that time, and he and Captain Pendleton worked quite well together. Williamson was not as brusque as Captain Pendleton, and he was more open and accessible to the men. He had empathy for the white hats—the sailors. I think he was a reserve officer and came to the *England* from the Submarine Chasing Center in Florida. He was training inexperienced ensigns to become deck officers. It was from his experience at the Submarine Chasing Center that he developed a method for rescuing men at sea that the navy still calls the "Williamson Turn." It's a method of rescuing a man overboard by turning the ship out and away from him so that the stern doesn't run over him.

When I came aboard the *England,* I was the junior chief petty officer, so I was put in charge of the auxiliary machinery. I was later moved up to the forward fire room. I had responsibility for the whaleboats, the ice machine, evaporators for boiling salt water to fresh water, the auxiliary piping system, after steering, and the anchor windlass. I had to check out all the equipment before we went to sea, and I found out that someone had stolen all the injectors from the engine on the whaleboat—injectors for injecting fuel to the pistons. This was for a diesel engine, and we were supposed to go to sea the next day. I had a midnight working party go over to another destroyer escort and steal the injectors out of her whaleboat.

Before we left I also discovered we had no welding machine on the ship. I told the chief engineer, Mr. Peterson, that going to sea on an iron ship without a welding machine was like going to sea on a sailing ship without spare lumber. So again, we had a midnight raiding party. I stole a welding machine off one of the finger piers on Treasure Island and got caught hoisting it aboard by Mr. Peterson. He said, "Put it back on the dock or you'll have me in jail by the time we reach Pearl Harbor." I said, "Yes sir, I'll do that." As soon as he went to the wardroom, I hoisted it back aboard and he caught me again. He said, "I thought I told you to put it back on the dock." I said, "I did, but you didn't tell me to leave it there." So we went to sea without a welding machine.

We hadn't been in the Pacific very long when we received an assignment to an antisubmarine picket line to intercept some Japanese submarines sailing between Manus Island and Truk Island in the Carolines. This was in late May 1944, just before the Marianas operation, and the Japanese submarines were sent out to see where the American fleet was going to go, whether it was going to the Philippines or the Marianas.

When we got on station, everything seemed to work magically. Pendleton went into CIC—Combat Information Control—and took over control of plotting the course of the submarines, and Williamson handled the ship from the bridge. It was a combination that worked very well.

I was in the forward engine room when the first sub we hit blew up. It knocked us all off our feet, and all the glass in our gauges broke, the explosion was so violent. We sank six subs in twelve days, and for every submarine we sank, I ran around the engine room yelling, "Another blow struck for the *Yorktown!*" I was giving everybody high-fives when nobody knew what a high-five was. By the time we got the sixth submarine, I thought they were going to give me a section eight—I was just going crazy. I was yelling, "How do you like it now, you bastards?" The crew really thought I was going psycho. As a result of our sinking those six Japanese submarines, we were given two weeks of liberty in Sydney, Australia.

After that we were involved in the Philippines operations. That is when the Japanese started using kamikazes. We escorted some marine raiders to Leyte thirty days before the actual landings. We dropped them off on the beach so they could contact the guerrillas, let them know about the coming invasion, and get their people organized. During the invasion I saw Major Dick Bong shoot down his first enemy plane. The plane he shot down blew up, and it looked like he flew right through it. He came out doing a vertical victory roll.

In August 1944 Captain Pendleton was made a commodore, and I believe he was sent back to the States. I never heard anything about him afterwards. Lieutenant Commander Williamson took over as captain of the ship, and I think the crew was delighted. He was well liked.

For me, the toughest part of the war was off Okinawa. We were out there for nineteen days on what they called the "Ping Line," looking for submarines. We were actually a radar picket ship. We didn't have any problems with submarines, but there were a lot of suicide planes out there—kamikazes. The Japs sent out 320 planes on one raid. They were all over the place. Our captain liked to turn the stern of the ship to the kamikazes as soon as one made a dive at us, and try to turn out from under it.

One made a dive on us within a few days of our first going on station. He came down at about a 70-degree angle. Just before he got to us, the captain turned, sidestepping him, and only a wheel, a wing, and a few gallons of gasoline hit us. The kamikaze had a delayed-action bomb, but by the time it went off, he was in the water and well astern of us.

Every day we would change stations, and every day the ship that relieved us got hit by a kamikaze. We would spend two days on the Ping Line doing radar picket duty, then we would get a day in the transport area, but you could hardly breathe in that area because of the smoke screen that was laid down. That was supposed to give us a night of rest.

Every time we got into a situation where there were suicide planes coming in, and we could hear the antiaircraft fire, I would designate one man to each ladder in the engineering spaces to turn on the flashlights I had taped to the ladders in case we lost power. That's when the men started calling me "Flashlight Dwight." I was fearful of being down there in the dark after my *Yorktown* experience.

During general quarters we had way too many people down in the engine room—people who really weren't needed to operate the machines. To give them as much protection as I could during these kamikaze raids, I had them lie down on the floor plates between the main motor and the main alternator, which were two pieces of heavy machinery. I laid them out like cordwood, figuring that would be their best protection from shrapnel. The only thing they wouldn't be protected from would be superheated steam if the steam lines were ruptured.

We were on station for nineteen days before we finally got hit. The kamikaze that did hit us almost missed us. We were in a high-speed turn to port. The captain had just called for full astern on the port screw. The kamikaze caught a wing on the boat divot on the starboard side, and that turned the plane into the side of the ship—into the superstructure. The men on the 20-mm guns back there, and the crew of the 3-inch gun, were all killed.

The plane had a delayed-action bomb on board that entered the wardroom area. It exploded and killed everyone in the number one repair party that was in the forward mess hall, which was just below the wardroom. The shrapnel came down on them from above. The chief radioman, Schindler, was a good friend of mine, and he got trapped in the radio shack. All the men in the radio shack were burned to death. They didn't have an escape route. We lost 34 men out of 180–200 men on the ship.

There were men on the bridge who couldn't get down because they were surrounded by fire. A lot of them ended up jumping into the water. One of them, Max Hawk, jumped off on the starboard side, which was a no-no because the ship passed right over him, and he passed between both screws. How he survived, I'll never know. The others jumped off the port side, while we were still in a high-speed turn. The ship just kept going in circles, and we ran down some of our men who were in the water.

The chief engineer, Mr. Hieler, who had taken over when Mr. Peterson was transferred, was under the pile of men on the deck plates. I pulled him out and told him that it looked like we had been hit in the superstructure, and that he might end up being captain of the ship, although I found out later that the captain and everybody on the bridge had survived. He couldn't get up the ladder on the side where the superstructure was because there was fire up there, so I helped him up another ladder and told him that we had communications throughout the whole ship and that he could con it from any engine space. I told him that if he wanted to change course or stop, or whatever he wanted, to just let us know and we could do it. That was the last I saw of him until we were in the "bone yard" at Kerama Retto, one of the little islands off Okinawa where they took all the wounded ships. There were so many badly damaged ships there. We came by the *Aaron Ward,* I believe it was. The decks were gone, the superstructure was gone. You could look down and see the engine rooms and pieces of machinery. It only had about 6 inches of freeboard.

When Mr. Hieler first came aboard, he took me aside and told me he had checked out my service record and had read about my adventures on the *Yorktown.* He said he hoped to see some similar action before the war was over. I said to him, "If we live through this war, I hope to someday remind you of this conversation." While we were at Kerama Retto we went out to the fantail of the ship where fifteen to twenty bodies of our shipmates were laid out, and I said to Hieler, "Do you remember that conversation we had?" And he said, "Oh yeah! I think I've seen enough action. I was ready to go home a long time ago."

◆ ◆ ◆ ◆ ◆

CHAPTER 13

Aboard the USS *Emmons* (DD-457/DMS-22)

Claude Eaton, USN (Ret.)

Claude Eaton was born in 1917 in Henderson, North Carolina. He attended one year of college before running out of money and then was forced to get a job. His intention was to make enough money to go back and finish his education. However, as a result of the Great Depression he lost his job, and he enlisted in the U.S. Navy in 1937. After basic training he was sent to San Diego, California, to attend Hospital Corps School and was stationed there for the next two years. Before and after Pearl Harbor he served on a variety of ships and at various shore stations. After his participation in the Normandy landings in June 1944, he received orders to the USS *Emmons* (DMS-22), which had only recently been converted to a fast destroyer minesweeper. He served out the rest of the war aboard the *Emmons* until she was hit by five kamikazes in April 1945, off the coast of Okinawa. Eaton is now fully retired and lives in Vallejo, California

The USS *Emmons* was commissioned on 5 December 1941 as a destroyer, DD-457.

Even though I had four years in the navy as a pharmacist's mate, by the end of my enlistment in 1941 my draft board was looking for me. In those days your military obligation was not considered complete if you hadn't served three years in the U.S. Army. Even if you had spent ten years in the Marine Corps, the draft could still get you. That rule was changed three months after I reenlisted in the navy. I wasn't planning to make a career out of the navy. I was saving my money from my four years in the navy to go back to college, and I had enough but couldn't get a student deferment because my enlistment ended between semesters. So to avoid being drafted into the army, I reenlisted in the navy.

In September 1944, after the Normandy landings, I returned to the United States and received orders to report to the USS *Emmons* (DD-457/DMS-22). The *Emmons* had originally been a destroyer built in 1941 and was also involved in the Normandy landings. When it came back to the States, one of the after turrets had been removed and replaced with minesweeping gear. After the conversion was completed, we went through the Panama Canal and out to Pearl Harbor. From Pearl we were sent to Ulithi Atoll. On the way, we received a message that there was a downed aircraft and that we were to look for survivors. We found two survivors, and after they were brought aboard, I went down and poured each one of them a shot of whiskey. Afterwards, the captain of the ship, Commander Foss, asked me why I gave them the whiskey. I told him it was the best tranquilizer you could use in a situation like that. He said, "Okay, when we get to Ulithi, order some more, because we had some rough times at Normandy, and we could have used something like that." When we got to Ulithi I ordered ten more bottles of Old Granddad, and they sent me ten cases, but they later went down with the ship.

For the invasion of Okinawa we left earlier than the rest of the ships to go up and sweep for mines. We finished sweeping before the invasion, which started on 1 April 1945, and joined in with other ships and shelled the island. Then on 7 April we took ammunition from the USS *O'Brien*, a destroyer that had been hit by a kamikaze. The *O'Brien* was being sent back to the States for repairs. We were then sent up to join the radar picket line. If you could stay up there for five days without being sunk, you got relieved. We spent five days

Chief Petty Officer Claude Eaton Jr., who
lost a leg from a kamikaze attack, but
stayed on in the navy after the war until his
retirement.

up there, didn't see any enemy planes, didn't have any problems, and were
relieved. Then the *Emmons* and her sister ship, the USS *Rodman*, were assigned
to screen some wooden minesweepers that were sweeping for mines between
Okinawa and Ie Shima, where Ernie Pyle was later killed.

We were up there in what we thought was a nice peaceful area when
Japanese planes started coming over. I thought they were a long way away, so
I went below to inventory the ship's medical supplies. I put on a pot of coffee,
then heard our 5-inch guns going off, but not regular enough to be bothered
with. But when I heard the 40-mm guns start to chattering, I went topside to
see what was going on, and I saw a Japanese plane get shot down. It was quite
a ways away, so I figured the 5-inch guns got it. It got quiet again, so I went back
down to the chiefs' mess, and all the coffee was gone, and nobody had made
another pot. So I put on another pot of coffee and went back to work on the

books, and the same thing happened, except this time the 20-mms started chattering, too. I rushed back up topside and saw two more Japanese planes get shot down. Then it got quiet again, and I went back down, and the coffee was gone again. I put on another pot of coffee, then all hell broke loose. I went up topside again and was about midships. Just then a Japanese plane dived straight down at the ship and missed us by just a few feet. His wings stayed on the water, but the fuselage went right on down. I was never so afraid in my life. I was trembling, and I thought about a song that was popular at the time, "It Must Be Jelly, Because Jam Don't Shake Like That."

There I was about amidships, and the doctor on the ship was at the battle dressing station in the wardroom just below where I was, and if we had been hit right there our whole medical department would have been wiped out. I had a battle dressing station in the after part of the ship, so I went back there. We had a housing there where a gun turret had been, and there was a door on both sides of it. Inside this housing was a ladder that went down to a compartment where I had a large chest containing medical supplies that was hooked to the bulkhead so that it could be lifted down.

I started to go in there and was a few feet from the door when these men started running in my direction from the stern of the ship with fear on their faces. Some of them were white with fear. I stepped aside and let them go by. A little roly-poly officer had started out in the lead, but was now in the rear. Just as he passed me, a plane hit the ship. They had seen the plane, but I hadn't.

We had a gun on the very stern of the ship that could fire parallel to the water, but the one on the next level up, for safety reasons, could not depress its barrel enough to fire that low. That Japanese pilot was smart. We were firing proximity shells from our 5-inch guns that would explode near the plane, but if the plane was down close to the waves, those shells could be detonated by the proximity of the waves just as easily as proximity to a plane, and that pilot knew it. He came in at the stern just above the water. He got the screws and the rudder and put us dead in the water.

While we were sitting there dead in the water, another kamikaze hit on the other side of the housing that I had been about to go into. By that time, I was lying down on the deck. The engine from the plane went completely through the housing, and I would have been killed if I had been standing up. Some time after that three more kamikazes hit the bridge, pretty much wiping out the bridge personnel.

We were hit by five kamikazes within about forty minutes of each other. The captain was blown overboard and was temporarily blinded, but eventually recovered. The executive officer also survived.

The ship was on fire, and we had to abandon ship. And to abandon ship, life rafts were put into the water on the lee side of the ship and casualties who were thought to have a chance of surviving were loaded into the rafts. Those who weren't wounded got into the water next to the rafts and kicked their feet to propel the rafts away from the ship.

After the last of the kamikazes hit the bridge, it was quiet. I looked down at my lower body and could see that I was hit pretty bad and knew I was going into shock. I had distributed morphine throughout the ship and had given each chief petty officer one box to carry in his pocket. I started to reach for the morphine in my pocket and noticed one of my index fingers was missing. I looked around and found it lying beside me. I picked it up and held it in the palm of my hand and gave up trying to give myself a shot of morphine. Then a sailor came along and said, "Chief, you trying to give yourself a shot?" I said, "Yep, that's what I was trying to do." So he gave me a shot of morphine, but I forgot to tell him to mark an "M" on my forehead with my blood so that I wouldn't get another one. Then another sailor came along and said, "Boy, you look like you are going into shock," and he gave me another shot of morphine.

I actually didn't feel any pain from my injuries. I felt no discomfort other than the fact that I was lying on my back on the deck with no clothes on. They had all been blown off, except for my shirt. Most of my injuries were from the waist down, although I did have some shrapnel in my face and head, but not enough to cause much trouble.

Some of our mess attendants decided to abandon ship on the windward side of the ship and couldn't get away. They would push away from the side of the ship and the wind would push them right back against it. The kamikazes that got me also knocked a big hole in the hull. Pieces of metal were pointing away from the ship around the hole and the raft worked its way down to it. One of the mess attendants grabbed hold of a piece of metal sticking out from around the hole, and it lifted him out of the raft as the ship rolled. The raft then went inside the ship. They got lost inside the ship, and you could hear their voices. A chief radioman, who was badly burned, jumped into the water and went inside the ship and helped them out and brought the raft around the stern of the ship to the leeward side. The mess attendants were then made to get out of the raft to make way for more wounded who had a chance of surviving.

I was among the wounded left behind because it was felt I didn't have a chance of surviving. My injuries were described as "multiple-extreme." There were about six of us like that, and there were about ten men who weren't wounded who refused to leave as long as we were on the ship. One of them was a Lieutenant Griffin, and he was the senior officer left aboard at that time.

I can vividly remember a young crewman with two white hats, using them as semaphore flags in an effort to get some wooden minesweepers to come over and take us off. Finally, one of them did come alongside, and one of our crewmen yelled, "Throw me a line!" The skipper on the wooden minesweeper, who was a chief petty officer, said, "You're not tying me up to that burning hulk! Just jump aboard." Our man said, "We could have gone on the life rafts, but we have some casualties we need to bring aboard." So the skipper of the wooden minesweeper said, "Okay, I'll get some crewmen up here, and you hand them over the lifelines and bring them aboard."

I was put in a wire basket stretcher and passed to the other ship, and taken down to the mess deck and put on a table. I was asked, "What would you like, Chief?" I said, "Coffee." And one of the first things a pharmacist's mate first class gave me was a shot of morphine, because I still didn't have an "M" marked on my forehead. I went to sleep after that, and woke up a little bit when I felt myself being moved. When I woke up again, I was aboard the USS *Gosper*, and we were in Kerama Retto. We stayed there for about three weeks and then went to Guam.

I stayed at the hospital on Guam for several months. Then one day the officer in charge of sending patients back to the States came in, and he was an old classmate of mine from Hospital Corps School by the name of Blanchard. The next guy to visit me was a chief warrant officer who had been with me on the USS *Savannah* when he was an apprentice and I was a pharmacist's mate third class. The next time Blanchard came by to see me I said, "Why can't you get me out of here?" I wanted to get back to the States.

I was put aboard a plane and was sorry I didn't stay on Guam until my fever went down because I had gangrene in my leg and the plane wasn't pressurized. When we reached altitude, my infected leg started hurting. When we got to Hawaii, I was put in the hospital at Aiea Heights, and there I languished while the flesh on my leg rotted away. The tibia and fibula were sticking out, and every time I turned over they rubbed together, causing me a great deal of discomfort. I finally talked the doctor into removing the leg where the two bones were sticking out, the foot having been amputated earlier, while I was on Guam.

When I was wounded I was hit by a piece of shrapnel in the groin that nicked both the artery and the vein, which lie side by side. The artery was bleeding directly into the vein, and as a result I was getting no blood to the lower leg. They first amputated my leg at the ankle. I eventually had two more surgeries until my leg was removed to two inches below the knee.

My wife was worried about me. I had been on the serious list for months, and she was afraid that I was going to die. She contacted her local congressman, who happened to be my father's cousin, and asked him to get her permission to fly out to Hawaii. Civilian travel at that time was severely restricted. Then one day the commanding officer of the hospital came down to my bunk and said, "Do you feel capable of flying to the States?" I said, "Captain, I've been begging to do that for months." The captain turned to the doctor and said, "Get him ready to leave tomorrow. If you don't have a planeload of casualties going back, put him on one by himself."

It seems the captain received a letter from the congressman telling him to do one of two things. If he was able to, get me sent back to the States immediately. If not, then make preparations to receive my wife and provide her with housing, food, and transportation. He decided it would be easier to get me the hell out of there. I was then transferred to the Naval Hospital at Mare Island, California, where I stayed until I healed well enough to get a prosthesis.

Bill Keen, who owned the Bay Meadows Race Track, provided all the money for the brace shop at Mare Island, where they made artificial limbs. He paid the salaries of all the civilians who worked there, and once you were fitted with a prosthesis, you would go to school where you learned to use your prosthesis. Once you learned how to use your prosthesis, you could take it back to the ward with you until the navy decided to release you.

I remember one man who was brought in. He had both hands blown off, and he was blind. When he was discharged, he went to work as a police dispatcher for the city of Sacramento. He had a wife and kids, and was able to support them.

I was a pharmacist's mate. My only trade was in the nursing profession, and I was no longer physically able to do that. I wanted to stay in the navy because I had a wife and a child to support. I told Dr. Thomas Canty there at the Naval Hospital that I wanted to stay in the navy, and he said, "Okay, Chief, we'll see what we can do." The next time we had an inspection, he told the captain I wanted to stay in the navy. The captain said, "No! There's no way." Dr. Canty said, "We'll still try." Then we had a big inspection with the admiral from the Twelfth Naval District. When he inspected the brace shop, Dr. Canty told the admiral that I had planned to stay in the navy. The admiral said, "Too bad— can't do it."

When I was brought up before the Board of Medical Survey, I was declared fit for discharge. That's when Dr. Canty and I wrote a letter from me to the chief of the Bureau of Medicine and Surgery requesting that I be allowed to stay in the navy. Dr. Canty signed it and approved it. The captain signed it disapproved, but forwarded it. The admiral of the Twelfth Naval District signed it disapproved, but forwarded it. Then we received a telegram. It was short and sweet. It said, "The records in the bureau show that Eaton's enlistment expired during the war, but that he was kept on active duty by order of the President of the United States. If Eaton wishes to stay in the navy use this telegram as authority to waive all disabilities. If that is not what he wants, please wire the bureau his wishes." It was signed by Adm. Chalmers Carr, who had been the junior doctor aboard the USS *Republic* when I was aboard at the beginning of the war. That was what I wanted, and I reenlisted in the navy.

When I was asked where I wanted to go, I said I wanted to stay as close to the brace shop on Mare Island as I could. So I was transferred to the Naval Shipyard Dispensary on Mare Island. After a few months there I was asked if I wanted to transfer to the Naval Reserve Training Center in Vallejo, and that is where I spent the rest of my naval career. I retired from the navy on 30 October 1958.

CHAPTER 14

The Goldbrick

Don Hawley

Don Hawley was born in 1923 in St. Paul, Minnesota, and grew up in Sioux Falls, South Dakota. He served aboard an LCI in the Pacific during World War II and was discharged from the navy in January 1946. After World War II Hawley went to college and worked as a Christian evangelist in the United States and later as a missionary in Pakistan. He also served as a hospital chaplain and magazine editor. He has written eighteen books, mostly on religious subjects. He now lives in Gladstone, Oregon.

Over one thousand LCIs were built during World War II. They were meant for landing troops directly onto a hostile shore. Some were built or converted to other uses, such as close-in rocket ships and gun ships.

In January 1943 I signed up for the U.S. Navy. Ever since I was a small boy I knew there would be another world war and that I would be killed in it. I just

took that for granted, so when I left town to go into the navy, I gave away everything. I wasn't coming back. And since I wasn't coming back, I thought I might
as well join the regular navy, so I signed up for six years and went to boot camp
in Idaho. And I loved every minute of it.

I went on liberty with some friends from boot camp and went down to Coeur
d'Alene. We paid a guy with a huge motorboat to give us a ride, and as he roared
along parallel to the shoreline, I imagined myself with twin .50-caliber machine
guns raking the enemy on the edge of that shore. It was a good feeling. However,
when I actually went into battle for the first time it was at Empress Augusta Bay
in Bougainville, and my gun was not a twin .50, but a 20-mm automatic cannon.
I was raking the shore all right, but I wasn't feeling real good about it. There is
something different between the imagined and the real.

I had the highest grade in my company in boot camp in regard to aptitude,
which gave me the chance to choose the school I wanted to go to, and I chose
quartermaster school. I always wished it had another name because people
think quartermaster means I took care of a warehouse someplace. I think quartermaster is the best rating in the navy. It puts you on the bridge, and you have
to be able to do anything a signalman does. As a quartermaster, you are in
charge of the ship's log, the ship's chronometer, and all the charts. You help plot
the course of the ship, and are lead helmsman. So I went to quartermaster
school. I studied hard, and I loved it. I was at or near the top of my graduat-
ing class. Those few at the top of the class would graduate as third class petty
officers, and I was pretty sure I had that nailed down.

Unfortunately, I had an altercation with a fellow classmate who was put in
charge of our barracks. He came around one day and told me to swab the deck.
I told him what to do with the handle on the swab. He didn't like that but didn't
say anything, which surprised me.

Finally, graduation time came, and a list was posted. At the top were the
graduates who had made third class petty officer. I looked with great antici-
pation, but my name was not on it. I couldn't believe it; I was physically ill.
Then I looked at the list of graduates who made seaman first class. My name
wasn't there either, and it wasn't under seaman second class or seaman third

class. My name was at the bottom of the list all by itself: Don Hawley—Goldbrick!

That guy who told me to swab the deck really got even with me. I was disgraced. Most of the other guys got orders to ships right then. I was sent to Bremerton, Washington, and kind of floated around for a while. At Bremerton somebody came to me and said, "We see that you graduated from business college. While you are here would you help us with a desk job?" I said, "Sure, that would be great." "By the way," someone said, "the last person to work at this desk was Henry Fonda, the Hollywood actor."

I was kept at Bremerton for a while, then sent to Shoemaker, California, which was a jumping-off place for the Pacific. From Shoemaker I was sent to the Pacific aboard the Matson cruise ship *Matsonia*. They packed us in. I had a cabin meant for two people, and they probably had thirty men in there. The *Matsonia* was a fast ship, so they sent us off without an escort, and we zigzagged our way across the Pacific without incident.

Our first sighting of land was New Caledonia. However, we weren't allowed off the ship and continued on to Espiritu Santo, where we disembarked. I spent about three months on Espiritu Santo. I guess they were trying to figure out what to do with a "goldbrick." Around Christmas 1943 I was brought in along with some other men and told we had been assigned to some amphibious corps. That meant that not only could I fight at sea but also on land. Well, I already had this great big sea bag to lug around, and now they gave me a marine backpack. They gave me everything except dress blues. I had a pup tent, shovel, fatigues, a helmet, and worst of all, a rifle with a bayonet. That was the worst Christmas present I ever got, and I was decidedly unhappy.

Shortly after that I was put on a ship going somewhere, and I thought, "I can't lug both a sea bag and a backpack around." And I knew by that time that the military was so screwed up that I could probably get away with giving everything in my backpack away. So I gave away everything except the rifle. I figured if I got caught I might have to pay for that, but I never heard another word about any of the equipment.

Aboard the USS LCI(L)-66, somewhere in the Pacific, 1944.
Six members of the quarterdeck crew. *Back row, from left:*
Jack Owen Edwards, Joseph Alfred Ruskauff, Donald
Thomas Hawley. *Front row, from left:* Robert Joseph
Higgins, George Richard Skinner, William Hall Stamp.

Some time after that incident I was put on a destroyer—my first real warship—and ended up in the Russell Islands, which was part of the Solomon group. While in the Russells I was called into an office and told, "We see that you graduated from a business college. How would you like to be on the admiral's staff?" That looked like pretty good duty. First of all, there were only about twenty men that made up his staff, and they went with him wherever he went. They had cement walks right there in the jungle, their own mess hall, their own cook, and I'm sure they had their own food. They had their own movie theater. It was outdoors, but everybody on the admiral's staff had his own private chair with his name on it. I also figured that if you stayed close to the admiral you might never got shot at. It was a real temptation, but being a nineteen-year-old romantic, I said, "No thanks; I want to go aboard a ship."

Eventually I was sent to Tulagi on Florida Island, where there was an LCI base, and I went aboard *LCI(L)-66*. LCI stands for "landing craft infantry," and the "(L)" stands for "large." It was 150 feet long, and 23 feet wide at the beam. It was about the smallest ship in the navy that could go to sea on its own, if necessary. It had a crew of about twenty men and three officers. Because I came aboard as a seaman apprentice, I was put to work chipping and painting for awhile. There was a chief boatswain's mate aboard who was not too bright. He had been in the navy for hundreds of years and had hash marks from his shoulder to his wrist. He couldn't read or write, but as the chief boatswain's mate on the ship, he had power. He took a dislike to me and put me to work chipping paint. Then the captain took a look at my records and called me in one day and said, "You need to be in the quartermaster's department," and I agreed. Of course, this was a small ship, and the captain put me under the only other quartermaster on board. I already knew the job, and this guy left shortly after that, and I took over as the ship's quartermaster.

LCI(L)-66 was one of the early models. It had a flat bottom with a draft of only 4 feet when not fully loaded. When we made a landing, the stern anchor was dropped on the way in, and the ship would slide right up onto the beach. There was a ramp on either side of the bow; these were dropped down, and the troops would run down the ramp and onto the beach, hopefully into water that wasn't very deep. Then with the engines and the stern anchor winch, it would pull itself off the beach.

One day four of us were called ashore for special training. We were getting radar. We went to school for radar for one afternoon. That was our training for the new radar, which meant about all we could do was turn it on and off. The rest was on-the-job training. At about the same time I was made a gunner on the forward, port side, 20-mm cannon, and the only training I got on that was when we went out from Florida Island and a plane towed a target sleeve by for me to shoot at. That was it.

Eventually, I was in charge of the entire quarterdeck crew, which consisted of all the radiomen, signalmen, radarmen, and quartermasters, of whom there was only one—me. I spent a lot of time on the bridge with the officers and was responsible for getting the ship ready for sea. I also oftentimes plotted the course ahead of time for the captain.

When I first came aboard, I noticed that several of the men were wearing gold earrings, and I had to ask about that. I was told that it showed that you had served in the South Pacific. Well, it wasn't long before one of my shipmates took a needle with silk thread, and a piece of cork on the other side, and made a hole in my earlobe. I wrote home to my dad and asked him to send me a gold earring with a gold star on it.

Not long after I went aboard, we received orders for the landing on Green Island (15 February 1944), which is at the northern end of the Solomon Islands. This was before the *LCI(L)-66* was converted to a gun ship. At that time, we had five 20-mm guns, two aft, two amidships, and one on the bow. I was put on the bow, not to man the gun but to be the talker for the 20-mm. I felt a little exposed up there going into the beach, but the Japanese decided not to contest the landing, so nothing happened.

It was after this landing that we were converted to a gun ship, LCI(G). So now, instead of landing troops, we would go in close, ahead of the troops, and duke it out with the Japanese guns on shore. We ended up with twin 40-mm guns on the quarterdeck, four 20-mm guns, some .50-caliber machine guns, a mortar, and a 3-inch gun in a big gun tub forward of the conning tower. That was a huge gun for our small ship, and when we fired it, the ship rattled and we almost stopped dead in the water. I was first loader for awhile on the 3-inch gun, but that didn't last long because those were big heavy shells, and I was so skinny I couldn't handle too may of them, one right after another.

After our conversion to a gunboat we took on more crew. I think we eventually had sixty men and six officers on board to man all the guns. Unfortunately, the galley didn't change in size, and the poor cooks had to fix meals for all the men in a galley the size of a telephone booth. I'm sure there were some good cooks in the navy, but the ones we had on *LCI-66* were not the kind you would find in a four-star restaurant. And unlike the cruisers and other big ships, we didn't get the better food. We had mostly boned chicken in oil packed in a can, and after about the fiftieth serving of boned chicken it's hard to get it down anymore, so we ate mostly whole wheat bread, baked on board, and peanut butter. We also had dehydrated milk, eggs, and potatoes—mostly uneatable.

Sometime later we were sent to shell Torokina Point at the entrance to Empress Augusta Bay. The Japanese were dug in there, and we were supposed to go in there at night and shoot up the place. I strapped on my helmet and lifejacket, and got behind my 20-mm, not feeling quite like I did back in Idaho when I was on the lake at Coeur d'Alene. The thought struck me, "There are guys over there on the beach, and they want to kill me." Orders came down from the bridge to open fire. I started firing rounds into the beach. Immediately, my loader fell to the deck, and of course, I thought he had been shot, but it turned out his knees buckled out of fear. I managed to keep standing, and I kept firing away. Then I saw tracers coming back at us, and I thought they were going to come right down the barrel of my gun, when all of a sudden my 20-mm jammed. In fact, I think it jammed every time I fired it in action. Whenever that happened, there was a ramrod you were supposed to ram down the barrel to knock loose the defective round. Whenever I had to do that, I always held the ramrod between my forefinger and thumb out of fear of a hang-fire. I didn't want to lose my whole hand.

I don't know how long the firing lasted, but it seemed like a long time in my mind. After it was all over I was embarrassed to learn that not a single shot had been fired at us in return, and that all those tracers I thought I saw coming at me were actually our own tracers that I got mixed up in my mind as coming from shore.

One time we were awakened at about 0200 and told to get under way immediately, and go to Choiseul Island because a PT boat had got hung up on a reef up there. As the sun rose, we got ready to pull the boat off the reef. There were a couple of Corsairs flying overhead for our protection. One of our men swam over and tied a line to the PT boat. I was on the helm on *LCI-66,* and we were able to pull the PT boat off.

We often worked with the PT boats, and one day I was talking with the quartermaster on one of them in shorthand—what we called waving our hands but without the flags. We were close enough that I thought I knew the guy. As it turned out, we had been to school together. I invited him to come over and have lunch with me. His boat was getting ready to go on patrol, but he said he would come over the next day after they got back in. When I got up the next morning, I heard that we had lost a PT boat during the night. As it turned out, there were three PT boats on patrol together that night, and the lead boat had some high-ranking officer from shore who wanted to go along for the ride. They were ahead of the other two PT boats by quite a ways, and nearing the mouth of a river on the north shore of Bougainville, when they picked up a target on their radar. The skipper of the PT boat wanted to wait for the other two boats to catch up before making an attack, but the high-ranking officer from shore ordered him to attack at once before the enemy could get away. The target turned out to be a couple of smaller Japanese barges lashed together with a couple of larger ones, and mounted with guns. So, it was a crescent of pretty good firepower, and this lone PT boat went roaring right into the middle of it. The first shot fired from the Japanese barges hit the high-ranking officer, and he was never seen again. The second shot knocked down their radar mast and it fell on top of my buddy who was knocked out. When he came to, the boat was on fire, and everybody had abandoned ship but him. He jumped over-board and found the captain, who had severe abdominal wounds and was drowning. My friend held him up and helped save him, at least for that night.

The other two PT boats saw the fire and came at top speed to help. By the time they arrived on the scene, the Japanese had turned around and gone back up the river. Naturally, that next day I wondered if my buddy was still alive, whether it was his boat or one of the others that had been sunk. At noon he came up the gangplank very nonchalantly, and we had lunch. I thought, "Well, it wasn't his boat." As it turned out, it was his boat and I admired the way he took the situation with such equanimity. But the next time they went out on a night patrol and general quarters was called, he went to pieces, and they had to give him a desk job after that.

We had around sixty men on board, but only one of them was black. In general, we had a rather motley crew. The LCIs didn't always draw the cream of the navy. Quite often when we got new men aboard, they came from the brig. Many of them were not overly bright, overly clean, or overly educated. However, this one black guy we had on board was very good looking, clean, well educated, artistic, and altogether a rather outstanding individual. But the only thing he was allowed to do was to wait tables for the officers. In other words, he couldn't strike to be a gunner's mate or anything else—just wait tables. Not only that, but he had to live all by himself, away from the rest of the crew, and I cringe when I think back on that. I know it was common back then, but still I think there was something terribly wrong with that.

One thing I will say about the officers we had on board—they were fair. For instance, one time our ship got 106 cases of beer, and they split that treasure right down the middle—53 cases for the 60 enlisted men and 53 cases for the 6 officers.

We spent some time off Malaita, an island northeast of Guadalcanal where some of the men would swim to shore. The natives put their women in huts for safekeeping while our men traded their shorts for native souvenirs, and came back to the ship in grass skirts. I really liked the natives of the Solomon Islands, and when I wanted to go back overseas as a missionary after the war, I requested the Solomon Islands, but it didn't work out.

The best friend I ever had was a fellow by the name of Jack Stewart. We were in high school together, and he really had it all. He was 6 feet tall, very handsome, beautiful personality, a baritone singing voice, and a good sense of humor. He was a great guy, and we were really close friends. I joined the navy and went to the Pacific, and he joined the army and ended up in some special program in college. All of a sudden there were too many guys dying on the front in Germany, so they jerked him out of his special program and sent him over to the 78th Infantry Division.

One day I received a letter from home, and out fell a clipping from the *Argus Leader,* the newspaper from Sioux Falls, South Dakota. There was a picture of Jack, and above it said, "Killed in action." I could hardly breathe, and for about two or three days I could hardly think straight. After the war, I decided I had to find where he was buried, and found he was in a cemetery near an airport in Los Angeles. Still not satisfied, I wanted to know how he died, where he died, and what he was trying to accomplish when he died. I went on the Internet a few months ago and found out there was an organization of men who used to belong to the 78th Infantry Division. They have a newsletter, and I asked the editor to put in a little article in the next issue to help me find out about Jack Stewart and his death. I received the next newsletter in the mail at about four o'clock one day, and less than an hour later I received a phone call from a man who was with Jack when he died. According to him, it was Jack's first action, 30 January 1945. They started out to take a village in the Heurtgen Forest. During the attack he was hit in the leg by a shell that didn't explode, but it tore his leg off and he died. Fifty years later I finally found out what happened to one of my best friends.

LCI(G)-66 was made part of the force that invaded the Philippines. We were to take part in the last of six major landings, the landing on the island of Mindanao. We took our place in a long line of LCIs. The LCI(R)s—the rocket ships—went in first. They really tore the beach up, and I think the only resistance the Japanese offered after that was one lone machine gun, so it was an uneventful landing in that regard. But we relaxed a little too early, because we soon received an assignment for a special mission. We were assigned to a five-ship group, which consisted of our ship, another LCI gunboat, and three PGMs—sub chasers also turned into gunboats. Each of the ships, including the PGMs, had a 3-inch gun. Our assignment was to go up the Mindanao River and get close enough to Fort Pikit to bring our 3-inch guns to bear on it. The captain of our ship was in charge of the group of ships, and he was honest with us. He said the river wasn't all that wide, and it was covered with jungle along its banks, which meant we were going to be sitting ducks. There could be Japanese hidden in the jungle, and we wouldn't be able to spot them until they opened fire on us. This was not a choice assignment, and the captain ordered all of us to wear our life vests and helmets, and all guns were to be manned going up the river.

On the way up the river we would see Filipinos along the banks, and they would wave small American flags at us, and yell, "Welcome! Welcome!" After we had gone up the river a ways, we arrived at a little town called Cotobato, and tied up there. Only twelve hours before, Japanese troops had pulled out of there, and not too far away there was fighting going on. We spent a couple of nights there before going further up the river, and before nightfall we tied up to the bank, while the skipper of the other LCI put both a bow and stern anchor out and kept his ship in the middle of the river. That way it would be difficult for anybody to approach, which was no doubt smarter than what we did.

The main deck on our ship was the same height as the bank where there was some tall grass and beyond that some coconut trees. I thought that was a terrible arrangement, because if there were any Japanese in the area they could have fired on us, or even crawled through the grass and onto our ship. The captain had all the guns manned for the night, and all of us picked up small arms. My 20-mm was on the river side of the ship, which meant I couldn't fire it across the deck if we were attacked from the shore side. About four or five of our men armed themselves and went out to patrol the area. They met some Filipinos who said there had been some Japanese in the area only a short time before. The Filipinos were told to go home because anything that moved after dark would be fired at.

Shortly after dark I saw a light on the opposite bank and squeezed off one round in its general direction, and as soon as I did that, several other shots rang out after mine. The 20-mm on the opposite side of the ship from mine was manned by a fellow by the name of Teraz, and pretty soon he started imagining people crawling through the grass toward him. He started popping off with his carbine into the grass. Then he got a hold of a submachine gun and let off a couple of bursts with that. Then he started shooting his 20-mm. All of a sudden tracers started coming back at us, and this time it wasn't imagination. We were under attack! Then I realized what was happening. We had tied up in a loop in the river, and the three PGMs had tied up on the other side of the loop, and we were fighting it out with our own men. I started yelling into my phone, and by then the gunnery officer had figured out what was going on, and he started yelling into his phone for the entire crew to cease fire. In the heat of the moment it took some time before the last gun was silenced.

Finally, the PGMs got us on the radio, and they were exceedingly unhappy. After all, we were the ones who started this friendly war, and one of the skippers on one of the PGMs got on the radio and said, "If you fire one more shot, we are going to open up on you with our 3-inch guns." We capitulated right there. Our skipper was not only embarrassed, but also very angry because he knew this incident would have to be reported and he wasn't gong to look very good. He called us all up to the quarterdeck, and he stood on the conning tower looking down on us. He had a lot of salty language he had learned over the years, and he used it all on us that night.

Standing next to me was Shinners, a man I was training to be a quartermaster. The captain turned to him and said, "Shinners, is that carbine unloaded?" And Shinners said, "Yes sir!" And to prove it, he pulled the trigger. It was not unloaded, and the bullet whistled past the skipper's ear. Now the captain was ready to kill all of us. Instead, he ordered all of the small arms put away, and sent us to our bunks except for a skeleton crew to man some of the guns. Teraz was tucked into bed, and I was ordered to take over his gun on the shore side of the ship. Now, I was unhappy because I was staring into the grass just a few inches from my nose with orders not to fire without permission. I started seeing things crawling through the grass towards me, and I couldn't fire at them. I got a bayonet and sat on a bucket with just my helmet and eyes sticking above the gun shield, but nothing happened.

The next morning the PGMs took the lead and sailed past us. Their crews had a lot of nasty remarks for us as they went by. During the night they had hit our ship with several rounds and we had put a couple in theirs, but no one was hurt.

We kept going up the Mindanao River until the water got so shallow that we got stuck in the mud. There were no Japanese around, and the Filipinos were very friendly. My best friend on the ship was Jack Owen Edwards. We went ashore and

Quartermaster Don Hawley, strapped to a 20-mm gun
aboard *LCI(L)-66.*

met a Filipino who gave us some tuba, a coconut liqueur. Then he took us over
to his brother's house for some fresh hot roasted peanuts. While there I became
close to a Filipino preacher who had studied at Yale University. They didn't have
too much, but his wife made me a beautiful dish of avocado, covered with local
chocolate, sugar, and cream. It was delicious. I gave her an old mattress cover,
and she was thrilled because they had no material for clothing. She had a sewing
machine, but no thread, so she unraveled a sock and used that for thread.

The preacher's little boy had an interesting toy. It was the largest insect I had ever seen—a huge beetle. It wasn't much smaller than a sparrow, and he had it attached to a stick with a string. When it flew around the stick on the string, it sounded like a small fighter plane.

This preacher was especially proud of his small library, but the Japanese had taken some of his best volumes, so I promised him that after the war I would send him some religious books. I kept that promise and sent him a good-sized boxful, but was disappointed when he never wrote to say they had arrived or to thank me. Finally, after many months, he did write and explained his apparent rudeness. Something had shattered his life and left him unable to communicate. The countryside was littered with unexploded ammunition, and one of his little girls went out and played with a shell that exploded and shredded her into little pieces. In his letter, he described the horror of picking up the pieces of his little girl before the birds could carry them off.

While we were stuck in the mud, the preacher held some dances for us at his home. A nearby army unit provided a generator for lights, but some of the Filipinas couldn't come because they didn't have anything decent to wear. For a time, the war had passed us by, and we were living the good life. Word came down that if our ship remained stuck in the mud for three months it would be decommissioned, so we started praying for a drought, because we figured that maybe they would send us to Hawaii to pick up a new ship. Naturally, it rained, the river rose, and we came loose.

The invasion was over, and we were all feeling pretty good because we were all still alive, but it was no time at all before we received orders to form up with another convoy and get under way for the invasion of Balikpapan, Borneo. This was at the same time that all the action was going on up at Okinawa, with kamikazes attacking our ships. Balikpapan has a good harbor and rich oil fields, so this was a piece of real estate the Japanese had no intention of letting go of. Of course, our forces had other ideas. The soldiers going in to take it were Australian, and the man in charge of the invasion was Gen. Douglas MacArthur. He was on the USS *Wasatch,* and calling all the shots from there. This was July 1945. We had a long string of LCIs, both rocket boats and gunboats coming in abreast, and since our skipper was an old-timer, he was in charge of all the LCIs, and our ship was the closest to the mouth of the harbor going in. As quartermaster, I was the only enlisted man on the ship with access to the invasion plans. For this particular invasion I was almost sorry I had looked at the plans because there was a red circle for every known gun emplacement, and it looked like somebody had spilled red ink on it. There were lots and lots of Japanese guns waiting for us.

In order to make this landing possible, minesweepers were sent before the invasion, and that is horrible duty because those minesweepers couldn't do anything evasive. They had to go back and forth slowly clearing away mines to make it safe for the invasion force. I heard we lost six minesweepers before the invasion even started.

All the LCIs came in abreast, and after we had fired all of our ammunition, we pulled a 180-degree turn and headed back out to sea, reloaded, and made a second run. While we were making a final run, the landing vessels would filter through our lines and make the actual landings. And since we were the LCI command ship, we were on the left flank, which put us on the edge of the area cleared of mines. That edge was marked by some flagged buoys. I was usually on one of the 20-mm guns, but the skipper put me on the helm because it was important that the LCI not stray out of the cleared area and hit a mine. After we made our first run, firing everything we had, there was no response from the beach. After we pulled back and got ready for our second run, we thought, "Well, this is going to be just like Mindanao, where the Japanese had pulled inland." As it turned out, that was not the case. When we came in the second time, a Japanese gun emplacement of pretty good size fired a shell across our bow, and it landed in the water about 30 feet to our starboard. I think that must have been a signal to the other Japanese guns, because the rest really opened up on us after that. I was trying to maintain a steady helm while geysers of water erupted all around. One shell landed close enough to the LCI next to us to wound a couple of men aboard that vessel. As we headed back out to sea for the last time, the landing craft with the troops aboard filtered through our lines and started landing on the beach, and I felt very sorry for them. They were going in to do the really tough fighting as we pulled out of range.

One of my first jobs after we anchored out a ways was to send a message to another vessel by signal light. The signal light was at the top of the conning tower, which was higher than anything on the ship except the mast. As I was sending this message, shells from cruisers and battleships went lumbering over my head on the way to the beach. They sounded like a subway train going by. I knew they were well above my head, but regardless, every time one went over I instinctively pulled my head down between my shoulder blades.

Not too distant from the beach a low range of mountains rose up, and from the conning tower I was able to watch with my binoculars as the action progressed. It was like looking at a movie screen. It was unnerving to sit in perfect safety and see men die. I watched as an army patrol moved against some Japanese position, and I could see everything. I don't know what they were trying to accomplish, but they were sending men out one at a time, and one by one they were being brought down by Japanese gunfire. It was impossible to watch and feel detached.

Then I noticed a road that snaked its way up a mountainside, and there was a line of tanks going up that road. They were clanking along when all of a sudden the column stopped, and up ahead was a Japanese fortification. One of the tanks back in the column moved out of the column, passed the others in front of it, and got in the lead position. It moved up towards this pillbox, and I realized that it was a flame-throwing tank. A horrifying sheet of flame roared out of the tank and enveloped the concrete bunker and quickly fried anybody who might have been inside. Then the column moved on.

That first night, the Aussies were almost driven back into the sea. The Japanese had been there for a long time, and they had tunnels and caves all over the place. At night it was necessary to keep the area lit up so that anything that moved could be seen. A group of destroyers moved in and took turns shooting flares that hung from small parachutes. For thirteen nights that area was not dark for even one moment. As soon as one shell was about to go out, another one would take its place.

Again, we thought we were out of action and safe and sound while the army did its thing, when we received a message from the *Wasatch*, General Mac-Arthur's control ship, with orders to take aboard some special personnel and land them inside the harbor. A second LCI was to follow in our wake, hauling some additional personnel. The captain called me aside to explain the situation. Only one minesweeper had been used to sweep a lane for us, so the resulting channel was very narrow. I don't know why, but the minesweeper chose a zigzag course. It swept in one direction, dropped a buoy with a flag on it, then changed course. I think there were about five of these zigs and zags going in. The captain put me on the helm and told me to scrape the marker buoys, and to be very careful. That can be tricky because of tide and drift. We reached the shore without difficulty, landed the personnel we had on board, and began to retrace our course back out to sea with the other LCI following.

Now, we were sure our role in the invasion was over, until we received another, even more disturbing message from the *Wasatch*. I was standing duty on the signal bridge when it came by blinker light. It was orders to get under way immediately with instructions as to where we were to patrol. I took the message to the captain, and he told me to chart the course. I plotted it, and what I saw really stood my hair on end. Dashing up to the bridge, I reported to the captain, "They have us going back and forth all night in a known mine field." Well, the captain was a little upset too, and he got on the radio to the *Wasatch* and told them that they had apparently made a mistake. In a few minutes a message came back from the *Wasatch* that there was no mistake, and that we should proceed.

The captain called us all topside to explain the insanity of the situation, and since we were going to do this night after night, indefinitely, he didn't see how we could help hitting a mine eventually. So he ordered everybody to wear lifejackets at all times, and no one was to sleep below deck. If the ship blew, we wanted to get off quickly. Sacking out on a steel deck is not very comfortable, and everybody was tense with the situation we were in.

The first night nothing happened. The second night nothing happened. By the third night everybody was defying orders and sleeping below in their bunks. On that night, 10 July 1945, it wasn't even dark when we started patrolling, and I had just finished cleaning out my locker and was starting up the ladder when the ship rocked with a huge explosion. I looked back, and all the lockers had popped open and everything had spewed onto the deck. The railing on the ladder I was holding was blown out of its sockets and was lying on the deck. I rushed topside and opened the hatch to go out on deck. I saw two or three men in the water; they had been blown over the side. I then looked up, and a motorboat we kept on the fantail was in pieces in the air and was on its way back down, so I ducked back down so I wouldn't get hit.

Our engines had stopped, and we were dead in the water. Of course, we had hit a mine. It detonated at the stern of the ship, about 6 feet below the hull. The explosion split some seams. After steering was full of water, the number four hold was filling with water, and the water was over the deck plates in the engine room. We were listing to starboard, and the stern was settling, but no one was killed.

We got our pumps going, but the water was coming in faster than we could pump it out. It seemed obvious to me that we were going to sink, so I rushed below to get my picture album and a samurai sword I had picked up on Borneo. I headed topside, ready to depart the ship, when I ran into the executive officer who wanted to know what in the blankety-blank-blank-blank I was doing. He bellowed at me, "No one gave orders to abandon ship! Get rid of that junk, and take this pistol!" He gave me a .45 pistol, although I don't know why. Then he said, "If we do abandon ship, you are supposed to take the ship's records with you." He also reminded me that it was my job to destroy the ship's radar. Then, he told me to get topside and get busy.

The blast from the mine shut down not only our engines but just about everything else aboard ship, the radio and radar included. Since the radio didn't work, we sent up a red distress flare, and another LCI, a newer model, was sent out to help us. They tied up to us, and with their pumps and our pumps we were able to stay afloat and get towed into the harbor. Emergency repairs were made, and we were then towed to Hollandia, Papua New Guinea, where we were put into dry dock.

Hollandia was a welcome relief. There wasn't any fighting going on there, and while the ship was being repaired, the crew was sent to a camp in the mountains for rest and recuperation. The camp had a fresh-water lake for swimming, badminton, baseball, basketball, horseshoes, and ping-pong. We took boat trips, went to the movies; we had a crafts center, a rifle range with free ammunition, volleyball, a library, and everything else you can think of. This was like paradise, and there were no work details. All we had to do was bring a toothbrush. There was also a Red Cross installation that served sandwiches, doughnuts, and Coca Cola. Not only that, but they had Red Cross women serving these things—real, live women. Later, I had to break out my dress blues because we were invited to a dance with sixty-five WACs at the Club Tropicana, built by the Seabees. It had a bar and an orchestra; it was almost like being home.

On 6 August 1945 an atomic bomb was dropped on Hiroshima, and then another was dropped on Nagasaki, and suddenly and unbelievably the war was over. Today, some of the young people talk about how terrible it was of us to drop the atomic bomb on those poor Japanese people. I don't like being around people who talk like that because I'm liable to get ugly. As I remember rightly, we didn't start that war, and if we had invaded the Japanese home islands, the Japanese would have fought to the last man—the last woman. Yes, it was horrible! But the fact is, many lives were saved by the dropping of the atomic bomb on Japan.

The next dangerous situation came from celebrating the end of the war. I understand eighteen men died on Okinawa from the celebrations with all kinds of guns going off. I was on the ship when the celebrations started in Hollandia, and the tracers were flying overhead so low that I went below decks.

When the war was over, as far as I was concerned it was over. I didn't join the American Legion or Veterans of Foreign Wars. I didn't hang out in bars, telling war stories, and I didn't think the government owed me anything. I was appreciative of the help I received in the form of the G.I. Bill in helping me get a college degree, but the government didn't have to do that. The government didn't owe me anything. I served because I wanted to.

CHAPTER 15

◆ ◆ ◆ ◆ ◆

Steward on the Destroyer *Ramsey* (DD-124/DMS-16) and the Submarine *Pollack* (SS-180)

Hadwick A. Thompson and Lily Aubert Thompson

Hadwick A. Thompson was born in Willows, California, and is a fourth-generation Californian. His great-great-grandfather, Alvin Coffey, was brought out to California from Missouri as a slave to help his master work in the gold fields. He worked six days a week for his master, and one day a week for himself. In this manner he was able to buy his wife and children out of slavery and bring them out to California. Thompson's father was a rice farmer in northern California when Thompson joined the U.S. Navy in 1939. Lily Aubert Thompson was born in Oakland, California, and is also a fourth-generation Californian. She was in junior high school when she first met her future husband, Hadwick, who was eighteen years old at the time. They married while Thompson was serving in the U.S. Navy during World War II, and have been together ever since. Thompson was discharged from the navy in 1945, went to college on the G.I. Bill, and became one of the first two African Americans to join the Oakland, California, police force. He retired from the Oakland Police after twenty-five years. He is also retired from the Bay Area Rapid Transit Police Department, and the Bank of California. He is still active in a number of clubs and associations, including the Society of California Pioneers and the Navy League, and served on the Alameda County Grand Jury in 1998 and 1999.

The USS *Ramsey* (DD-124/DMS-16) was commissioned in 1919, was converted to a mine layer in 1937, served throughout the war, and was scrapped in 1946. The USS *Pollack* (SS-180) was one of the older fleet boats to see service in World War II. She was commissioned in 1937, won ten battle stars, and was decommissioned in 1946.

HADWICK

When I graduated from high school, I joined the navy. Because of the Depression there were no jobs. That was in 1939, and I was shipped to San Diego. Before that, I had never been out of Willows except for visits to the San Francisco Bay area. While I was in San Diego, I was told by one of the chief petty officers that if I signed a paper, in other words, changed my race, saying I was Caucasian, I could do anything I wanted. There was no explanation given, but I wouldn't do it, so I was sent to steward school in Norfolk, Virginia, on the USS *Henderson,* an old transport. I was with a bunch of Guamanians. They were going to steward school also, and since I spoke English better than they did, I was put in charge.

While I was going to steward school, I was put in charge of all the colored kids, teaching them how to swim. There isn't much to tell about steward school. It was just another navy school. The only problem I had was once when I went into Norfolk. Here I was, a kid from California, and I didn't fully understand

Hadwick Thompson, steward's mate. Photo taken in
Bremerton, Washington, before Pearl Harbor.

the segregation system back there. In Willows, I was the only colored kid,
although there were other colored families in the area, and I never had any
problems. In Norfolk one time, I got on a streetcar and the conductor had this
southern attitude, and I had my California attitude, and they didn't mix, so I
threw him off the streetcar and drove the streetcar back to the base. When I got
about a half-mile from the base I said to myself, "I better stop and go over the
fence." It's lucky I did, because there was a group of people waiting for me
where the streetcar normally stopped. I didn't go back to find out who they
were. I only found out about that later. After that happened, the commander
of the base said, "I better get Thompson out of here." So I was put on a ship
and sent back to California.

I was put on a transport, the USS *Cappela,* and went back through the
Panama Canal. When I got back, I got word that all of the people I was with were
going to be transferred to destroyers. I was up in Bremerton, Washington, and

about two hundred of us were put on the cruiser *Chicago* and sent down to San Diego. That is when I was assigned to the USS *Ramsey* (DM-16), an old four-stacker. I went to work chipping paint and got seasick about every other day.

After we got the ship ready for sea, we went up to Port Angeles. We stayed up there for about three or four months before we were sent over to the Hawaiian Islands. On our first attempt at leaving Bremerton, we got about 50 miles out and had to be towed back to Bremerton. On our next attempt, we made it out about 100 miles and had to get towed back again. The next time, we got out about 150 miles and were told we were on our own. Those old ships would just break down.

I was a steward, but I worked with the deck gang on the *Ramsey*. The captain kept me there and even wrote to Washington and asked if they could have my rate changed, because I was good working on the deck and I was good with men, but Washington said no. But the captain kept me with the deck gang anyway, and I was assigned to the 4-inch gun amidships. I was the number one loader and in charge of the gun. This was the later part of 1939.

In the early part of 1941 we got a new skipper, Lt. Cmdr. G. L. Sims, and he was prejudiced. I had quite a few confrontations with him. One time he said, "You know, Hadwick, on my plantation I never saw colored kids like you." I said, "Well, my dad has a big plantation in California and I never saw Okies like you, and you better get used to it because there's more of us coming along." This was where the dialogue went.

We used to have ship's parties on shore, and one time I brought this pretty girl along. There was a lieutenant who didn't like my bringing her. I guess it got to him, because when we got back to the ship, we went out to sea and did some gunnery practice. When we got done with that, he came down to the wardroom and started pushing me around, verbally, and I pushed him around, verbally. That's when I got thirty days on bread and water.

When the Japanese attacked Pearl Harbor, I had just come back from being on liberty and was standing on the quarterdeck at about 0755. This plane came over the bow of our ship; it looked like it was only a couple of hundred feet off the water. There was another sailor standing next to me and he said, "They sure are flying low. You know how those crazy navy fliers are." And I said, "Navy, hell! Look at the rising sun on that wing." A second later that plane dropped a bomb on Ford Island.

We were tied up at Lock-3, Aiea. That's near Pearl City, which was just across from Ford Island, where there were some battleships tied up, and I ran up to the flying bridge to one of the machine guns and manned that during the entire attack. The Japanese were dropping torpedoes in the water, trying to get the battleships. I would shoot my machine gun for a while, then look over at the battleships, see one get hit and start to roll, then I would shoot some more. You could see the Japanese pilots, they were so close. I didn't worry about them dropping bombs on us. They wanted the battle wagons. They weren't going to waste a torpedo on a tin can.

I think everybody who was at Pearl Harbor thinks they shot down a Japanese plane. I was shooting a .30-caliber and I was pretty good, but I don't know for sure if I shot any planes down. There were also some .50-caliber machine guns firing, and we were all aiming at the same planes as they came in, so I couldn't tell for sure if I hit any of them.

We were the senior destroyer of our four-destroyer squadron, and about ten minutes into the attack we cut loose from where we were tied up and headed out of the harbor. We were the second ship out of the channel, and while we were going out, some B-17s were coming in from the mainland. They flew in right over our ship, and they were all shot up. I guess they ran into some Japanese fighter planes on the way in.

While we were trying to get out of Pearl Harbor, a Japanese dive-bomber tried to sink us, but when he came down at us, we blew him apart. While we were going out of the harbor, there was a Japanese midget submarine coming in, and we put a shell through its conning tower and sank it. Later, while we were outside the harbor and on patrol, we depth-charged another midget submarine that we had picked up on our sonar, and I think we sank that one, too.

We were out for four days because there was supposed to be a lot of Japanese submarines out and about near the channel. After we came back into Pearl Harbor, we refueled and went right back out and laid mines all around

Hadwick Thompson and Lily Aubert
Thompson. Photo taken shortly after the wedding, while Thompson was a steward's mate
aboard the submarine *Pollack*.

the New Hebrides and Samoa. My job was to sink mines. See, a lot of times
when we laid mines, they would pop back up, and I had to lay up on deck with
a gun and shoot at them until they blew up.

At this time, the United States had more submarines than men, so when
the *Ramsey* came back to Pearl from laying mines, I found my bags had been
packed and were sitting on deck. When I saw that, I said, "Oh skipper, you're
giving me shore duty?" He said, "Yes son, you see that little bit of a ship over
there? You stop by there and talk to the skipper." That was the submarine, the
USS *Pollack*. I reported aboard the submarine, and two weeks later we were off
the coast of Japan.

The skipper's name was B. E. Lewellen. We called him "Loopy-Lew" because
he thought he could do loops with a submarine as if it were an airplane. During
the war, I think we sank eleven ships, including one cruiser. That is why I have
four Bronze Stars. See, I made four patrols, and if each patrol was successful,
the enlisted men got a star.

In May 1943, when we sank a Japanese cruiser, we failed to see the destroyers that were with her, and they boxed us in. That's when we were down for fifteen hours. You're only supposed to stay down for twelve hours because you
run out of oxygen. Well, about midnight the skipper said we were out of oxy-

gen and we had to surface. We surfaced, and luckily we were far enough away from the destroyers that we were able to get away. I think that was on my second or third war patrol with the *Pollack*.

On the next patrol we went after a Japanese task force, and one of our torpedoes went off prematurely. When we fired it, it went out about 20 yards, then went straight down and blew up underneath us. When that happened, we had one Japanese destroyer on our right, and one on our left, so the skipper ordered a hard dive. We went down at a 53-degree angle to about 450 feet, and the test depth for those older fleet subs was only 270 feet. I was on the gyroscope, and the sub was actually breathing from all the pressure. The hull was hitting me in the head as it went in and out.

I remember the engineering officer saying with his Texas drawl, "Captain, don't you think we ought to go back up about now?" We finally pumped enough air into the ballast tanks to slow our descent, and we started going back up. We pumped so much air into our ballast tanks that it was an uncontrolled ascent. Now, our problem was that the Japanese were still up above us, and we accidentally came up underneath one of the destroyers and hit the bottom of her with our conning tower. Then we went back down and got away.

One of our patrol areas was the Bungo Straits, between Kyushu and Shikoku. That is where we lost some of our subs to Japanese subs. There was a Lieutenant Hartley on the *Pollack,* the electrical officer, who wrote me a letter years later and said, "Hadwick, I can tell you this story now, but if I had told it earlier they would have put me in the nut house. Once when we were operating off the coast of Japan during the war I was asleep and dreaming that somebody was shaking me awake. The person in my dream was a female. She shook me once, then she shook me twice. After she shook me the third time I woke up from my dream. Once awake, I got up and went into the conning tower and found the guy on the radar sound asleep." The dream woke Hartley up, and he looked on the radar screen and saw a Japanese submarine waiting at the entrance of the Bungo Straits. So he took our submarine down, went underneath it, and came up safely on the other side. See, the Japanese knew our submarines were operating in that area, so they would plant some of their subs out there to get ours.

After that cruise, I came home and got married. Lily, my wife, isn't a small-town girl, and after we got married we went to a high school football game in Willows where I had been a star athlete, and when we walked onto the field, the game stopped and the band played the wedding march and "Here Comes the Bride." Lily had never seen somebody get so much attention. So you can understand why somebody like me—coming from a small town like Willows where there were only a few families of color and no racial tensions—would have run-ins with people like those I met in Norfolk and the captain of the *Ramsey.*

When my leave was up, I had to report to a submarine in San Francisco that was going to take me back to Hawaii. For me, that was the hardest part of the war—seeing Lily on the dock as we headed out. I said, "To hell with this war!" I was going to dive off that sub and swim back to shore. The skipper said, "No, you don't, son. Get down below." Lily said she cried all the way back to Oakland.

LILY

Every day I read the paper and looked for names of ships that had been sunk. It was hard.

HADWICK

When I got back to Pearl Harbor and reported back aboard the *Pollack,* I passed out. The pharmacist worked on me and got me back on my feet, and I passed out again. Then I was shipped off to the hospital where they found out I had ulcers. That ended my submarine duty, and I was in the hospital in Hawaii for about six months. Then I was sent to Oak-Knoll Hospital in Oakland, California, a U.S. Navy hospital. They patched me up at Oak-Knoll, then sent me to Tanforan Race Track in San Bruno, where they kept some Nisei. They had a concentration camp there, and the Nisei were kept in these horse stalls. This was in 1943.

While there, I was put in charge of about two thousand or three thousand colored sailors who were waiting for orders to various ships. I got that job because I had a little confrontation with the commanding officer, Captain Green, who was white. This is at a time when colored sailors were going into San Francisco and getting into trouble—getting into fights, and this and that. Captain Green said, "Goddamn it, Hadwick, these people can't be controlled!" I said, "Captain, don't tell me they can't be controlled! They are your people. You whites raised them in the South; you told them Negroes were no good. Now, you expect them to listen." So he said, "Oh, you think you're so smart," and he put me in charge of all of them. I was a second class steward then.

I gave them lectures every day about how to behave while on leave. I would say things like, "You wonder why you are treated this way or that. Well, look how you act; look how you look. Goddamn it, I can smell some of you from up here. Some of you don't even take baths." Consequently, they started shaping up. I ran into some of them later in life who told me that if it hadn't been for me, they probably would have been dead. Some of those guys hated whites so much.

There are some blacks that are far more prejudiced than whites. I had black sailors who hated me because my hair was straight. Some hated me because I wasn't as black as them. There were some who thought that I thought I was better than them.

Also, at this time the navy had given permission for stewards to have gold buttons on their uniforms. So one time this steward came running up to me and said, ""Hadwick, Hadwick, they cut all my gold buttons off!" I said, "Who is 'they'?" He said, "The guys at the main gate." So I put on a coat with gold buttons and walked out the gate, but nobody did anything. I came back in, and walked back out again. I wanted them to cut my buttons off. So I walked through the gate again, and this time I was called over, and the men on duty at the gate did cut my buttons off this time. I picked one of them up and threw him across the counter, and I ended up in the brig. I then called Captain Green, and he asked what happened. He came down, and I said, "Now, you were wondering why you have a problem with your colored sailors. Well, let me tell you what happened. See this coat? See these buttons? The chief at the gate cut these buttons off when I walked out, and he cut the gold buttons off of a couple of other stewards when they walked out. And here is the order that says they can wear gold buttons." Captain Green got me out of the brig, and that chief got busted down in rank.

Lily

I was working in civilian personnel at the naval hospital and was secretary to the nurse in charge of dependents. Hadwick didn't talk about his wartime experiences for the first seven years we were married. In fact, when he first came home, we were having dinner with this other couple, and they were interested in what Hadwick had done in the war. This girl kept asking him, and Hadwick just looked at her. Finally, I said, "Mary, don't ask any more questions. He doesn't like to talk about it." But Hadwick looked at her like she was crazy. He didn't say anything about the war for a good seven years. He would tell me about his friends, but nothing about the war itself. He wouldn't talk about Pearl Harbor, about the bodies floating in the water. I remember right after we were married, one night some planes flew over, and Hadwick jumped out of bed and ran to the door yelling, "They're coming! They're coming!" He still doesn't like to talk that much about the war.

CHAPTER 16

Me and "Corky" Carkin

Ralph S. Bailey, USN (Ret.)

Ralph S. Bailey was born in Lake Stevens, Washington, in 1922. He was living in Edmonds, Washington, when he dropped out of high school at the age of seventeen and joined the navy. Throughout most of World War II he served aboard two destroyers, the USS *Smith* (DD-378) and the USS *Radford* (DD-446). Late in the war, he served aboard the *Thetis Bay* (CVE 90), an escort carrier. He retired from the navy in 1966, having served in both the Korean and Vietnam Wars. He now lives in Bremerton, Washington.

The USS *Smith* was commissioned in 1936, earned six battle stars during World War II, and was decommissioned in 1946. The USS *Radford* was commissioned in 1942, and earned twelve battle stars during World War II. She went on to serve in the Korean and Vietnam Wars, before being decommissioned in 1969. The USS *Thetis Bay* was commissioned in 1944. In 1955 she was converted to the first assault helicopter aircraft carrier.

Navy buddies. *From left:* Chief Boatswain's Mate Ralph S. Bailey, a cousin of his, and Clayton "Corky" Carkin.

This narrative begins when Pearl Harbor was not nearly so well known—in 1940. At that time those of us in the Pacific Fleet were aware we would find ourselves in a war, but expected it to commence in the Atlantic, followed by a declaration of war by Japan in support of the Axis countries, a time referred to historically as the "National Emergency." I was a seaman first class assigned to the captain's gig aboard the USS *Smith* (DD-378). My older brother, Bill, was already aboard, and had been since 1939. Before the Japanese bombed Pearl Harbor, he commissioned another destroyer, the USS *Fanning*. Later in the war, he was transferred again to another destroyer, the USS *Sullivans*, and also served on a number of ammunition ships. He was a chief machinist's mate when he retired on a disability.

One day, several new men reported aboard the *Smith* fresh from boot camp, one of whom, Clayton Carkin, was assigned to the gig as replacement for my mess-cook-bound "bow hook." Carkin acquired the nickname "Corky" and carried it for at least the next nineteen years. Corky was a very sharp person, equipped with an inquiring mind. During the following two to three months he literally mined my mind. His questions became less frequent, finally coming to all-stop. From that time on, I asked the questions. Corky acquired a copy of the *Encyclopedia of Knots and Splices,* and during this same period absorbed the contents. In his spare time he busied himself with McNamara lace, which is better known as macramé—square knots, and other fancy knot work.

About the middle of November 1941, the USS *Smith* headed back to the States and Mare Island Navy Yard for overhaul. Corky and I were returning to the ship on Sunday morning, 7 December 1941. Our ship's engineering officer stopped his car alongside us and said, "The Japs have attacked Pearl Harbor." Momentarily, we thought it was some kind of joke. Then we noticed his pale, drained face.

Our ship had just started "rip out," meaning to disassemble machinery, piping, and so on, for overhaul. The crew quickly gained respect for the shipyard workers. They worked until they were ready to collapse. Then they would find some place to flake out and, after about an hour or two, be back at work. Often, we would find our bunks occupied by yard workers. No problem, we would leave them be and find another bunk elsewhere. This did cause some confusion when looking for the relieving watch, but the problem was not insurmountable. These same workers refused to leave the ship when we shifted to the ammunition depot, and worked alongside us as we loaded ammunition.

The USS *Smith* was assigned to escort the Matson liners, *Lurline, Matsonia,* and *Mariposa* on 25-knot convoys between San Francisco and Honolulu. I do not recall which trip, but on the second day out on one of them we were credited with sinking an enemy sub. That was the first blood drawn by the USS *Smith.*

Whenever smoke was spotted on the horizon, our captain, Francis X. McInerny, would jump up and down and scream, "I hope it's a goddamn Jap battleship!" I cannot honestly say I shared his enthusiasm. At such times I was inclined to consider the 2,500-pound shells that could be hurled about 25 miles by a Jap battleship as just a little much to counter with our 5-inch shells, weighing in the neighborhood of 50–60 pounds, with a range of about 3.5 miles.

I was briefly detached from the *Smith* in Hawaii when I came down with a case of mumps, and was sent to the hospital. After I got out of the hospital, and was waiting for the *Smith* to come back to Pearl, I ran a motor launch around in Pearl Harbor, picking up "floaters." Floaters are dead people and parts of people. It was nasty business.

During rough weather, while standing my watch on the bridge, it seemed every roll of the ship would cause me to step on Captain McInerny's toes. Needless to say, his remarks were considerably less that laudatory.

We finally were detached from convoy duty and ordered to Bremerton, Washington, to escort three repaired battleships to San Francisco. I'm not sure, but I believe they were the *Colorado, Pennsylvania,* and *Tennessee.* I had been home only once since joining the navy in 1939. While entering Puget Sound, I was the stern lookout. As we steamed past my parents' house in Edmonds, Washington, I spotted someone in our yard. Corky had brought me coffee and was enjoying the scenery. Knowing how much I wanted to visit home, he laughed and said, "I would say your chances of making it are less than one in ten." He knew very well that thoughts of jumping over the side of the ship and swimming for shore had entered my mind.

During the Battle of Midway, we received orders to head for the Gulf of Alaska to cut off any Japanese attempts at landings up there. We found nothing, and after the Battle of Midway was over, we headed back to Pearl Harbor. A draft of men was being sent from the *Smith* to new construction. I was asked three different times if I wanted to go. Each time I declined. Then one day, one of the men on the draft was taken to the hospital. Corky was on the draft, and he persuaded me to take the open spot. We were off to our new assignment aboard the USS *Radford* (DD-446). The date was 15 June 1942.

My battle station on the *Smith* was trainer on the number one 5-inch forward gun. This was also my station aboard the USS *Radford.* Later, after I left the *Smith,* at the Battle of Santa Cruz Island, the *Smith* shot down a Jap torpedo plane with the torpedo still intact. The plane crashed into the side of the *Smith* near the number two 5-inch gun, and fell onto the main deck near the number one 5-inch gun. The flames from the burning plane caused the torpedo to explode, blowing up the ammunition handling room for both guns. The resulting explosion killed many of the men forward of the bridge. Corky had saved my life by persuading me to take the transfer to new construction.

While at the receiving station in San Diego, Corky and I were on a detail, stowing lumber in the hold of a 3,000-ton coastal freighter being converted to a Q-ship, a harmless looking vessel being used for coastal antisubmarine work. Its appearance was deceiving, as it bristled with hidden antisubmarine weapons. While we were busy at work, some men who had been goofing off came over and relieved us. We were then approached by a man in dungarees, astride a bicycle. He asked us our names, and we thought we were in trouble for something. But he said, "Go on up to the Personnel Office and tell them I said to give you liberty, now." He was yelling at the goof-offs who took our place as we passed out of range of his voice. He was called Captain "Mac," and although he didn't have a sea command, Captain Mac did have a good reputation for the way he ran that receiving station.

We eventually boarded a train and headed east, where we would find our new ship, the *Radford*. The cars were ancient, but they were Pullmans. Although soot from the coal-fired steam engines filtered through the windows, we slept on sheets in real beds that folded into place from the seats. The ever-so-solicitous porters practically tucked us in at night. We ate in the dining car, set with starched linen tablecloths, and napkins in napkin rings. The food served was excellent. Even so, some of the sailors still bitched and griped. One afternoon, we slowed to two or three miles per hour as we passed a sidetracked troop train way out in nowhere, among sagebrush and tumbleweeds. The soldiers were lined up with their mess kits, getting their meals from a field kitchen. Corky sounded off with, "While all you assholes are bitching and moaning, take a good look. If you had been luckier you could have gone first class, along with those dogfaces." We heard no more bitching after that.

Once in New York, we checked in at Pier 92, adjacent to the burned and capsized SS *Normandy*. That was quite a sight, but didn't begin to equal the experience of Receiving Station, New York. It was not the commanding officer, but the commanding officer's wife who was in command. She held inspections, assigned work details, granted and withheld liberty, and stood on the quarterdeck at liberty call with the marines on watch, and canceled liberty at whim. The captain (I use the term out of respect for his uniform only), his wife, their daughter, and her ensign husband, lived aboard the old cruiser, USS *Seattle,* which was tied up alongside the pier.

The ensign, it was claimed, came up through the ranks after he had impregnated the daughter. His duties consisted of overseeing the marines holding close order drill performed by the sailors. Sometime later, the radio announcer, Walter Winchell, gave the situation publicity on one of his broadcasts. Subsequently, I heard the captain was transferred to Timbuktu, and supposedly never commanded a ship after that. However, it was reported that he later became commanding officer at the Treasure Island Receiving Station in California.

After we arrived at the Brooklyn Navy Yard barracks, an event occurred that changed my life. Corky and I went on liberty, and we had two things in mind, liquor and thoughts related to our hormones. We eventually ended up in Prospect Park. Soldiers were camped all over the park, and we wandered into a canteen where volunteers were handing out coffee, soft drinks, doughnuts, and so on. There were three girls working there, and we ended up walking them home. One of the three in particular caught my attention. Corky and I made no more liberties together in Brooklyn, and I was married to that girl for nearly fifty-five years.

One time, or should I say several times, Corky was AWOL. This one time he had given me an address where I could get in touch with him. I decided to go get him and found myself walking into Harlem for about one and a half blocks. I didn't like the daggerlike looks I was getting, so I turned back and hailed a taxi. The cab went straight through Harlem and out into the Italian area of town. How did I know it was an Italian area? I like pasta, but I like it even better when Italians make it, and there was no mistaking the aroma. I found the address that Corky had given me, but found no Corky. He and the daughter were not there, and the irate parents bluntly and unceremoniously failed to invite me for dinner.

Corky returned to the ship, but another crewman who had been AWOL with him did not and was eventually given a bad-conduct discharge. After the war, I ran into that ex-sailor in Charleston, South Carolina. He was living high on the hog, owned a fancy nightclub, and was the local bootlegger.

Corky was awarded ten days in the brig on bread and water after one of his escapades. He came out weighing more than when he went in, much to the consternation of the wardroom crowd. The guards were kept busy unlocking the door to his cell to admit visitors. Cooks, mess cooks, and mess attendants, with the best chow on board, all paid him visits. Others came bearing candy bars and cigarettes, even torpedo alcohol, properly distilled, of course. Corky claimed it was the best vacation he ever had.

Corky and I acquired a Coca Cola syrup barrel in which we dumped gallon cans of peaches, apricots, pineapples, applesauce, and other fruits, and yeast and a sack of sugar. We stashed this mess in the starboard peacoat locker, covering it with piles of peacoats behind the hanging ones. After too long a time watching this mixture boil and churn, we strained it through a sugar sack during the midnight watch. Shipmates lined up to help us sample it. When the barrel bottom finally appeared, the dregs were still boiling like a cauldron.

On one occasion, when we were loading depth charges aboard, and lowering them down through the Second Division compartment, a jug of raisin-jack in the starboard peacoat locker exploded. It made so damn much noise, I thought one of the depth charges had gone off. All we could find of the jug was the handle.

One night while we were in the Solomon Islands, we made a night raid on the island of Munda. Jap Betty bombers were circling overhead in the darkness, showing us the way. The stars were out, and it was a bright moonlit night, and we could actually see the red meatballs on the wings of the Jap planes. After we bombarded Munda, the whole destroyer division went hell-bent for the cover of a rainsquall. The *Radford,* or at least her crew, thought her to be the fastest destroyer in the fleet. However, we received a message from another destroyer, either the USS *Fletcher* or *Nicholas,* which said, "Move over or we will climb up your fantail!" They were serious, and they were coming on fast.

On another occasion we came under air attack off Rendova Island. The water was full of burning Jap planes, some with Jap pilots standing on the wings, shooting at our passing ships with pistols. We also did target practice on long strings of Jap barges loaded with soldiers retreating up the "Slot" to Bougainville. We were assigned to fire star shells to illuminate targets, and in return received machine gun fire from a line of Jap barges close by—too close to see on our radar. When our 20-mm guns opened up on them, it was mayhem.

One morning word was passed to fall in for inspection by our new destroyer squadron commander. At the time I didn't know who the new squadron commander was. All hands, with the exception of those on watch, assembled. Second Division assembled amidships, portside. My position was on the left, front rank, facing inboard. Out of the corner of my eye I observed the approach of the inspecting party, and my god, there was Capt. (now commodore) Francis Xavier McInerny! "What in God's name is he doing here?" I thought. Upon commencing inspection, the commodore leaned over and, speaking very softly, said, "Don't I know you?" "I don't know if you know me, sir," I replied, "but I know you." "Where was that?" he asked. "On the USS *Smith*, sir," I said. "Ah, yes. The name is Bailey, isn't it? What are you doing on deck? Weren't you an engineer?" "No, sir," I said. "That was my brother, Bill." "Oh, I see. You were that damn seaman who couldn't stay off my toes." He suppressed a chuckle as he moved on.

As the inspection party moved by, I caught the quizzical look thrown my way by Lieutenant Knox, who had been some kind of department head at Macy's before the war. After we fell out from quarters, I proceeded to my assigned cleaning station, the after deck house, which included the area around gun number three. Because of the operations we had been involved in, the ship was in bad shape. In desperation, the previous day I had mixed paint dryer with haze gray paint and applied a wash-coat over everything, rusty hot-shell case netting and all. During their approach to my cleaning station I could hear Lieutenant Knox using his salesmanship, attempting to interest the commodore in his pet project, a latrine at the end of bridge so the officers wouldn't have to leave the bridge during underway watches. I also noticed the commodore was not impressed.

"Good morning, Commodore. O-1 level ready for your inspection, sir," I reported, saluting smartly. "Well, Bailey, very impressive. Freshly painted, I see—even the hot-shell case netting," he replied. "Yes, sir!" I said, quite elated at his compliment. Leaning over, and again softly speaking in my ear, he replied, "But you didn't see me watching you yesterday from up forward while you slapped paint over all that rusty mess, did you?" He chuckled again as he walked away.

It has been well past fifty years since that inspection. Admiral McInerny [his rank at retirement] is long dead, and now I can answer your questions that followed that inspection, Lieutenant Knox. No, Commodore McInerny was not a relative. He was my grouchy, crusty, salty, and well-liked taskmaster on board the USS *Smith.* In a way, Admiral McInerny was a father figure to me—sort of a hand-on-the-tiller, guiding me, among others, during our formative navy years.

I was saddened after the war to read in a San Francisco newspaper that while serving as a senior officer of a general court-martial board at Goat Island, San Francisco, Admiral McInerny was requested to retire because his explosive verbal performance allowed a man to beat a general court-martial. I knew he had an explosive temper, but he also had a sense of humor, depending on the situation. Yes, Lieutenant Knox, I would have been very proud if I had been able to claim him as a relative.

Corky and I left the *Radford* in Pearl Harbor when we returned from the war zone in December 1943, and had thirty days' leave before reporting to Bremerton, Washington, for reassignment. Corky and I were assigned to the USS *Thetis Bay* (CVE-90). However, while still at the receiving station I was notified to report to the office of some lieutenant (jg). When I reported to his office, he was sitting slouched in a chair with his feet on the desk. He said, "What do you want?" I explained to him that I was told to report there, but I hadn't the slightest idea why. After asking what my name was, he reached into a drawer, withdrew an object, and tossed it onto the desk alongside his feet, saying, "This belongs to you." That was the manner in which I received my

Presidential Unit Citation for my service aboard the *Radford*. After the *Thetis Bay* had been put into commission, Corky received his. The whole crew of that little carrier lined up for a full-dress inspection. Corky was called to step forward, the PUC was pinned on him by the captain of the ship, and Corky led the inspection party. Somehow, and in some ways, I have always felt that I was cheated.

One time we were supervising the loading of cases of beer into one of the holds of the ship, and Corky talked the officer in charge of the working party into giving us a case. In our hiding place, in the line storage area, we proceeded to lighten the case. Having no church key, we used our sheath knives to open the cans. Things became somewhat hazy, and then Corky had to cook up an excuse when he went to sick bay with a stab wound, as he missed the can with his knife, but not his foot. Our flight surgeon, Cmdr. Joel Pressman, the husband of Claudette Colbert, covered for us on that one.

Corky was in Second Division on the CVE-90, and one of his duties was taking care of the life rafts surrounding the flight deck. One day when supplies came aboard, an enormous amount of raisins disappeared. After we departed for parts west, the odor of fermentation began to waft about the ship. Officers were detailed to search for the source, but never found it, while Corky went about his business of changing water on the life rafts. If we had had to abandon ship, we wouldn't have had water to drink while in those life rafts, but we would have been the happiest bunch of castaways in the Pacific.

I can't remember which one of us left the *Thetis Bay* first, but Corky went to a picket ship off the waters of Okinawa. Hearing nothing from him, I presumed he had been killed, but I was wrong. From 1950 to 1952 I served aboard the USS *Nicholas* (DD-449), our companion ship at the Battle of Kula Gulf. Having convinced myself that my old buddy was dead, I was overjoyed to collide with him while on the beach at Pearl Harbor. He had become a navy diver, and it was from his fellow divers aboard his ship that I heard about his exploits. They at least equaled what we of the *Radford* had witnessed after the Battle of Kula Gulf when Corky had helped in the rescue of survivors from the sunken cruiser, *Helena*. Corky had been awarded a medal, but which one I don't know. He never told me, but it was for voluntarily making a deep, hard-hat dive in

Pusan Harbor to retrieve secret material from a plane that had crashed there. He did it while his crash boat was under bombardment from shore batteries.

By the time I ran into Corky again, he had married, and he and his wife had two children, George and Katie. I was married by then, and had my family with me there in Hawaii. Our two families became close. We spent many days at the beach picnicking. Our wives shopped together and kept each other company while we were away at sea. It is a time I look back on with pleasure. I was later transferred to Guam, and Corky was sent to the diving school in Washington, D.C., for a helium-oxygen refresher course. I heard no more from or about him until November 1958. That is when I entered diving school myself. Corky was the skipper of the *Mary Anne*, a harbor craft somewhere between 120 and 150 feet in length that was used for training in helium-oxygen diving. I saw him off and on during this school, but the school was intense, and I didn't have much time for visiting. Unfortunately, I never heard from him after that. I heard he had retired from the navy after his last tour of duty at the diving school, and shipped out in the Merchant Marine. I also heard that Corky had failed the physical that would have allowed him to continue diving, and that is why he was used as the skipper of the *Mary Anne*. He should have had twenty years of service in 1960. After he retired from the Merchant Marine, he and his second wife retired to Florida. Years later, I was able to track her down and learned from her that Corky had died of cancer just six months earlier.

CHAPTER 17

◆ ◆ ◆ ◆ ◆

All the Ships and All the Battles of . . . Charles Link

Charles Link

Charles Link was born in 1921 in Goble, Oregon, at a time when few people lived in that part of the United States and when the largest city, Portland, had only a few thousand people. His father worked in the logging industry, and the family moved often. There was no electricity, no telephone, and few radios. Children either walked or rode horses to school. Every boy carried a pocketknife, and every girl knew how to use needle and thread. The Link family had a love for music and dancing. They made their own music and danced at the local Grange Hall. Link joined the U.S. Naval Reserve while still in high school and volunteered for active duty in 1941, just three weeks before he would have graduated from high school. Before Pearl Harbor, he served briefly aboard the battleship USS *Oklahoma*. While the Pacific Fleet was still on the West Coast, he was assigned to the battleship USS *California* and headed for the Hawaiian Islands soon thereafter. By war's end Link had served on five ships, two of them having been sunk beneath him. He left the navy soon after the surrender of Japan, but returned in the summer of 1946 to serve for a total of nineteen and a half years, leaving before retirement because he was tired of going to sea while his children grew up without him. He retired from his civilian job in 1983 and now lives in Fairfield, California.

My mother was a schoolteacher, and both of my parents believed that if you were going to school you should go all day, come home and do your chores, then do homework and go to bed. Depending on where we lived at the time, I would walk anywhere from three to eight miles to get to school. That meant I had to leave while it was still dark out and get to school just as the sun was coming up. School got out at four-thirty in the afternoon, and I might not get home until maybe seven o'clock at night. When I got to the sixth grade, I started to ride to school on horseback. We had eight grades in one room and one teacher teaching all eight grades.

There was no such thing as after-school social activity, except once a month on Saturday night we could go to the Grange Hall with the adults and visit with people our own age. That was it. That was also a time for young men and ladies to meet each other and get acquainted. So there was practically no social life. What social life we did have revolved around our families. When Christmas came, we didn't get presents. We made things for each other with a pocketknife or, in the case of the girls, with a needle and thread. We didn't have any toys unless we made them ourselves. Our parents might give us an apple or an orange. We were a very close family.

When I started high school, we moved to the big city, Portland. It had electricity and indoor toilets. I thought it was a big city—it had ten thousand people. And while I was still in high school, I joined the Naval Reserves in 1939. In late 1939 and 1940 there was a lot going on, and the navy started putting more ships into service and moving them from one place to another. But they didn't have enough people to do it with, so they started using the reserves to take ships from one port to another. We were doing that just about every other weekend.

I think it was in 1938 or 1939, there was a World Exhibition—something like a World's Fair—in San Francisco, on Treasure Island, and since I was in the reserves they took our group from Portland and put us on the USS *Oklahoma*. The *Oklahoma* left Bremerton, Washington, and went down to San Francisco. And because we were sailors, we had free entry to the fair. We also took visitors onboard and gave tours of the battleship. I went ashore every day for about four or five days, and I thought that exhibition was the most fabulous thing I had ever seen in my life—all these things from different countries and different places. Plus, I got to see all these modern things like radios and telephones—all kinds of things.

I was about to graduate from high school in 1940. In fact, I only had three weeks to go before graduation when President Roosevelt declared a national emergency, and the navy was asking for reservists to volunteer to go on active duty. So that is what I did. I volunteered to go on active duty. My mother was very disappointed. She thought I should get my diploma first. But I said no, because I thought there would never be another opportunity like that again. Besides, I wanted to travel. I wanted to see something other than Oregon and trees.

When I went on active duty, I was put on the USS *California*. While in the reserves I was in engineering, but now they put me in the electrical shop. I was just a seaman first, but in less than a year I was a third class petty officer. It usually took four years to do that. I was in the lighting gang, which took care of all the normal lighting on the ship, plus the battle lanterns, which gave off a blue light and were down low to the deck so people could see where they were going at night but which couldn't be seen at a distance by other ships.

It was somewhere during those early days on the ship that I met my best friend. I'm not very good at names, and I don't remember the names of most of the people I served with in the navy, but his last name was Streeter, and he was from Denver, Colorado. In Colorado his father ran the movie projector at a new movie house, and he helped his father run the projector. On the *California*, he volunteered to run the projector and I volunteered to help him.

I was a slightly different kind of a guy than the other enlisted men. Most of them came from poor families, and most of them were interested in liquor and women. I was not interested in either one. I was interested in women, but in a different way. I enjoyed talking to them, and if they could dance, I was interested in them for that reason. If they couldn't dance, I wasn't interested.

Charles Link. Photo taken shortly after the end of the war.

What I was interested in was movies, parks, zoos, and music—bluegrass music. When I was growing up in Oregon, my aunt played the piano. I had an uncle who played the banjo, another uncle who played the accordion, and one of my brothers played the violin. They all played bluegrass. When we went to dances, we did the waltz and the foxtrot to classical music. I also liked operas and operettas and things like that. It took about three months' pay to go to an opera.

I had nothing in common with the other men on the ship, but Streeter was different. He was interested in the same things I was. We went ashore together and went to movies, parks, and the zoo. We got along very well together.

When I went aboard the *California*, our home port was Long Beach, California. Then the fleet was moved to Hawaii—Pearl Harbor. That was in 1941. All of the officers got to take their families and household goods, and the navy had housing for them when they got there. The enlisted men were on their own. They didn't get any of that. The officers could also spend their weekends ashore. The enlisted men had to be back aboard ship by midnight.

I had a terrible impression of Hawaii when I first got there. I didn't like it. There wasn't anybody there, except lots of prostitutes. The civilians didn't want anything to do with enlisted men. We were the scum of the earth. It was that way everywhere, not just Hawaii. Fathers punished their daughters if they even looked at a sailor. You couldn't go to the opera in Hawaii. There wasn't one.

There was only one hotel, the Royal Hawaiian. It was pink, and you had to be rich to go there. If you were a sailor and tried to go in there, they threw you out. The well-to-do didn't want anything to do with poor folks—sailors. So as far as I was concerned there was nowhere to go and nothing to do in Hawaii. However, one thing I did do was go to a civilian airport and take flying lessons. Streeter wasn't interested in that, but I was. So every other weekend when we were in port, and if I had the money, I would go take another lesson. On 7 December I was going to go to church, then take my final lesson. The weekend after that, if I had enough money, I was going to solo.

On 7 December 1941 reveille was at six o'clock. I had breakfast, then went to muster, and just as we were about finished with muster, general quarters sounded. Everybody started complaining about having a drill on Sunday, but we all went to our general quarters stations. I no sooner got to mine when the ship made a terrific lurch. We had been hit by a torpedo that lifted the ship in the air, then dropped it. It was like hitting a speed bump in a car doing about 30 miles per hour. The ship started listing right away. The port side went down, and the starboard side went up. We were tipping at a steep angle, and everything started sliding down the deck. Since I was in Repair-4, damage control, I was right in the middle of the ship, right above the voids, fuel tanks, and the fire rooms. We got orders to flood the fire rooms to counter the port list. Right below where I stood were two fire rooms with, I think, seven men in each room, and we were told to flood them. We asked if we could get the men out first and were told, No! The hatches were dogged down, and preventers were put on to keep the men inside from opening them. We heard the men inside begging and hollering as the water began to rise. But once we started the counter-flooding, the ship stopped rolling, and little by little it leveled out. Then there was no more noise from the fire rooms. That bothered me for years.

It still bothers me. I participated in killing those people. But if we had rolled over like the *Oklahoma,* thousands might have died. Instead, we lost fourteen, and the ship stayed afloat.

After the torpedo bombers hit us, the dive-bombers hit us, then the horizontal bombers came over. One bomb hit us. It went through the upper deck, the main deck, and exploded on the armored deck, which is 6 inches of steel. The explosion went upwards and started a fire in some of the berthing spaces. The mattresses were what caught fire, mostly, but it was confined to that one deck, over a large area.

I learned later that some other bombs hit near our starboard bow and sprang some plates, and the ship started taking on more water. Streeter's battle station was in the lead acid battery locker, which was below where my battle station was. The lead acid batteries were for the number three turret. The turret normally ran off the ship's electricity, but for backup they had these batteries. One of the torpedoes hit just forward of the lead acid battery locker. That was the only way out for Streeter, and it was flooded. The captain ordered abandon ship, and I went topside. The lead acid battery locker had a good-sized vent, but it had bars across it so Streeter couldn't get out that way either. I stopped at the vent, and I could hear Streeter playing his "sweet potato," a round flutelike instrument. I stayed there and talked to him for about ten minutes. He told me to go on and abandon ship, but I said, "I can't just go off and leave you!" "There is nothing you can do," he said. "I'm stuck in here. It looks like this is it." I said, "What is your condition down there?" and he said, "Well, water is coming in and it lacks about one inch before it comes over the top of the batteries. And once it does that those batteries will start bleeding chlorine gas and that will be the end of me. So I've got maybe twenty minutes, then I'm gone." We stopped talking, and he went back to playing his sweet potato. I listened for a few minutes, then left.

I went to the stern of the ship and stood there for a while. There was open water between the ship and Ford Island. I went into the water and started swimming. I was a good swimmer and could swim quite a long distance. I was swimming along, and all of a sudden my arms started stinging, and I was gagging on black smoke. What had happened was, burning oil from the *Tennessee* and *West Virginia* came around and got between the ship and the beach, and I swam right into it. Both arms from the elbows down, and both legs from the knees down, were burned, and I lost all my hair. I finally made it to a beach on Ford Island and sat there. I looked back at the ship and saw all these guys going into the water and getting burned. Quite a few of them died. After about ten minutes the burning oil moved off and there was just water again. But just before the burning oil moved off, I saw an officer struggling in the water, trying to push the fire away from him. He was having an awful time, so I went back in the water, grabbed him by the wrist, and started pulling him towards the beach. By the time we got back to the beach, the fire was gone. We sat there on the beach for a while and talked. He said he was an ensign and new to the ship. He had only come aboard the week before. Shortly after that he thanked me and walked off.

I went over to a partially destroyed hangar on Ford Island where some wounded were being treated before being taken to the hospital. I asked if they could do something for me because my arms and legs were burned and I had no hair on my head. The skin was hanging off my arms and legs, and I was in a lot of pain. I was told, "You can walk, so get out of here! We are only taking care of people who can't sit up or walk." So I left and wandered around Ford Island taking in all the damage. I was standing with a bunch of other guys when a chief came roaring up in a jeep and said, "You, you, and you; go over to the other side of Ford Island, find some machine guns, and mount them some-place and shoot any planes that try to land that aren't American."

I walked across to the other side of the island, and when I got there, I saw the *Utah*. She was bottom-side up, just like the *Oklahoma*. There was a bomb crater, and near that was a PBY with two twin .50-caliber machine guns. A couple of us unclipped them and carried them to the bomb crater. None of us knew how to use them, but we thought if any planes tried to land, we would shoot them. When night came, everybody was feeling tired and sleepy, but my arms and legs burned and stung so much that I couldn't even think about sleeping, so I volunteered to take the watch while they slept. About dawn, the others woke up and told me to take my turn at getting some sleep. I finally did doze off. I was in a lot of pain, and I don't remember everything that happened over the next few days. But one morning when I woke up, right in front of me was this huge aircraft carrier, the *Lexington*. Well, I thought, they have a sick bay. Maybe they will take care of my burns. So I got up and walked up the gangway. The officer on duty looked at me and said, "Oh my God! Take this man to sick bay!" In sick bay a pharmacist's mate took scissors and cut the skin off my arms and legs, and some off my head. Then he took some kind of liquid that was black but turned brown when he poured it into the water and carefully wiped it where I was burned. He then told me to lie down and get some sleep, which I did.

When I woke up I was told to go topside and look around, then it would be time to eat dinner. When I went topside, I had the surprise of my life. We were out in the middle of the ocean. I ran back down to sick bay and said, "Hey! We are in the middle of the ocean!" I was told, "Yeah, you were asleep for twenty-four hours. We refueled and pulled back out." The *Lexington* had taken about fifty battleship sailors out with her. After the Japanese attack on Pearl Harbor, the carriers needed extra crew, and rather than going through channels requesting this and that, they just took up battleship sailors, since there were no more battleships. They gathered us in the hangar bay, and people brought clothing up, and we took whatever fit us. We were then told that they were in the process of permanently transferring us to the *Lexington* as part of the crew.

I was walking around the ship and ran into a chief electrician's mate. I said, "Hey, Chief, you need a hand? I'm a third class electrician's mate." He said, "Yeah, we need help in the motor room." The *Lexington* had sixteen boilers to make steam, and two engine rooms. And both engine rooms had generators to turn the propeller shafts that drove the ship. I was put in the number three motor room with two gigantic electric motors for turning a 3-foot-diameter propeller shaft. That was for the starboard inboard propeller. There were four all together. The whole time I was on board the *Lexington,* that is where I was assigned. My sleeping compartment was along one side of the ship, right behind where torpedoes were stored.

In March 1942 we were east of Australia and south of New Guinea. We sent our planes north over a range of mountains [the Owen Stanley mountains]. The Japanese didn't think we would do anything like that because there were headhunters in there. Our planes flew over those mountains and sank a few of their ships near Salamaua and Lae. It was around that time that Tokyo Rose said the Japanese had sunk the *Lexington* with the loss of all the crew. We all had a lot of fun with that.

During the Battle of the Coral Sea, I was in motor room number three. The captain zigzagged the ship to get away from the torpedoes that were launched against the *Lexington,* but she turned way too slow and got hit by two of them. That was in the morning. That afternoon I could hear the sound of aircraft hitting the flight deck, so I knew we were taking our planes back aboard. They were refueled and rearmed, and ready to go again. Then along about four o'clock in the afternoon there was a terrific explosion one deck below and forward of the bridge, and fires started burning out of control. This was not the result of a bomb. It wasn't found out until later, when the survivors were interviewed, that one of the torpedoes had ruptured an aviation fuel storage tank and the fumes drifted out and filled the whole forward part of the ship, going from compartment to compartment. Then a spark from a generator or something set it all off. We didn't find that out until later, after the ship sank.

So the ship was burning, and the fire was getting out of control. The fire made its way all the way to the bow of the ship, then started working back all the way to the forward elevator. There was then another explosion, this time under the forward elevator. The explosion blew the elevator up into the air, tilted it up on its side, and it fell back into the hole.

People in the engine rooms were passing out from the heat. It got up to 150 degrees where they were, so they were told to secure everything and go topside, and that's what they did. We shut down the boilers and everything else, including the salt water pumps. It was the salt water pumps that gave the firemen salt water to fight the fires. Then "Handy Billies," gas-powered pumps—hundreds of them—were put on the hangar deck with hoses hanging over the side, into the ocean. They were then used to pump seawater to fight the fires.

But still the fires gained on the firemen. In the meantime, a destroyer pulled up alongside of the *Lexington* and started taking all the wounded off. We got all of our stretcher cases off that way. Then the captain ordered abandon ship.

I went topside to the flight deck, and there were all of our planes sitting there fueled and armed with bombs and torpedoes, all ready to go. The fire-fighters stopped fighting the fires, and people started leaving the ship. Some jumped, but most climbed down ropes. My abandon ship station was just aft of the island. There was a rope hanging over the side with a knot tied in it about every two feet. I started down that, and the next thing I know there was a steel deck under my feet, but there was so much smoke I couldn't see anything. I got down onto my hands and knees and crawled along until I came to the barbette of a gun turret. Then I turned my back to it and sat there. Others were coming down. Some came down on the destroyer I was on, and others came down into the water.

After all the survivors were picked up, one of our destroyers fired six torpedoes at the *Lexington* to finish her off, but only two of the six torpedoes detonated. Our torpedoes weren't very good in those days. The destroyer circled around and fired six more torpedoes. Again, only two of them detonated, but the *Lexington* sank. The stern didn't go up; it just settled into the water. Immediately all the smoke disappeared. Then the *Yorktown* and all the other ships headed south to Tongatabu in the Friendly Islands [Fiji Islands]. Two American transports came to Tongatabu, and all the *Lexington* survivors went aboard. The next morning we headed for San Diego.

After we got to San Diego we heard about the Battle of Midway and the loss of the *Yorktown*. In San Diego we got a whole new seabag. The navy just gave it to us. Before, we had to pay for it. Normally, in order to go on liberty you had to be in the uniform of the day, but our captain arranged it so that we could go ashore in anything we had. That was unheard of, but our captain arranged it. He also arranged it so that we could be assigned to any ship we wanted. We couldn't say, "I want to be on the *Yorktown* or the *Helena,* or this ship or that ship." That wouldn't work, but what did work was, "I want to be on a cruiser or a destroyer." The captain said, "Whatever type of ship you choose, I guarantee you will get it." So one day I was looking out over San Diego Bay and saw this small ship, a YP—yard patrol. I had been on two ships that had been sunk, and I didn't like it, so I thought that if I got on a YP I could spend the rest of the war sailing around in some port, so I put in for a YP. As it turned out, I got on a yard patrol, just as the captain said. However, the yard patrol I got was a converted tuna fishing boat, built right there in San Diego. It was about 110 or 115 feet long, and almost the entire hull was made for ammonia refrigeration to refrigerate tuna.

Now, when the navy took over that ship, they called it the USS *YP-518*, but when it was a civilian tuna boat it was called the MV *Commodore.* This ship was under construction before the war started and was completed just after Pearl Harbor. But instead of sailing around in some port for the rest of the war, the next thing I knew we were heading off across the Pacific.

There were twenty-two crew members on that ship, and after we got out to sea, the captain called us all together. There was only one officer aboard, and that was the captain, and he was an ensign. In civilian life he had been a night desk clerk in some hotel in Chicago, but he had had two years of college, so when he joined the navy they made him an officer—a ninety-day wonder. The problem was, he had never been on a rowboat, let alone a ship, and here he was the captain of a ship. But he was very honest with us. He gathered us together and admitted that he didn't know up from down and that we would have to help him.

As it turned out, over half the crew had worked on ships just like this in civilian life. In fact the chief boatswain's mate had owned his own boat as a civilian. That is why he was a chief. The other half of the crew was like me— they came from the regular navy. This captain turned out to be a pretty smart cookie. He decided that since he knew nothing about the ship, but had a crew that knew everything about it, he would just let everybody do their job, and he would learn by watching. And that is what he did.

There were two other ships just like us, and the three of us set off across the Pacific to Pago Pago, American Samoa, then Suva, Fiji Islands. Then we went to New Caledonia and the New Hebrides. When we got to the New Hebrides, we discovered that the marines had landed at a place called Guadalcanal with only a three-day supply of food. We were supposed to go in and supply them with more food because two days had already gone by and they only had one day of food left. And that is what we did. We went up to Guadalcanal and got in real close to the beach, and the marines sent out work parties in amphibians and unloaded all the food we had on board.

For the next two months all we did was go to Espiritu Santo, load up with more food, and take it to Guadalcanal. And during that entire time none of our small ships were attacked. We had air raids almost every day, but they never attacked us small ships.

I don't remember when it was, but sometime during this campaign Eleanor Roosevelt paid a visit to the front lines. She came to Tulagi to give a talk to the troops. In order for everybody to see her, a large tower was built, and she had to climb up it. I was there, and the first thing she said was something like, "I hope you boys appreciate the fact that you are here to sacrifice your lives so that the American people back home can live the lives they have become used to." Now, a lot of these guys had lost friends, and they started booing her. They didn't want to hear that from her. The marines especially didn't like this at all, so they started shooting at the tower, right by her feet. Splinters were flying everywhere, and she screamed. She disappeared after that. I mean, she thought we should be proud to die.

The next place we went to was the island of Munda, and we resupplied the marines there. In July 1943 we were in on the resupply for the landings on Rendova Island. Again, the marines landed, and we went in two days later to resupply them. Also in July, we supplied the landings on Bougainville.

Now, our captain was a bit unusual in that he wouldn't let any of the men take tests for advancement in rating. His argument was that he wanted everybody to stay right where they were. He said everybody gets along fine and everything is running fine, so why change a good situation? But some of the guys wanted to make the navy their career, so there were some hard feelings. Finally, someone back in Washington got word of the goings-on on our ship, and they started transferring people off, and I was one of them. I was transferred to the USS *Whipstock* (YO-49), a very small oiler. I was assigned to her in 1944, just before the invasion of Saipan, and Saipan is where we went.

I went aboard the *Whipstock* at Espiritu Santo. Merchant marine ships brought food supplies from the States in big refrigerator ships. And while the merchant marine ships were in a combat zone, they got extra pay—hazardous duty pay—so they were all for staying there as long as they could before going back to the States, and they delayed our loading as long as they could. They were also eager to get souvenirs. From the marines we would get Japanese rifles, bayonets, helmets, flags—all kinds of things. We would take these things to the merchant marine ships and get all kinds of money for them. I found that I could get maybe $10 or $20 for a Jap helmet, but if I put a bullet through it first, I could get up to $100 for it. And these merchant marine guys would go home and tell their friends how they went up to the front lines and got all this stuff.

While I was on the *Whipstock,* we started off across the ocean carrying aviation gasoline. That ship was only about 40 feet long. It had a diesel electric engine and was originally intended to refuel ships in a harbor, but it had been refitted to refuel airplanes. For the landings on Saipan there were a lot of aircraft carriers with extra planes on them. Those planes were supposed to take off from the carriers and land on Saipan, and stay there and help the marines.

There was a small airstrip near the beach where the marines landed, and these planes were supposed to land there, and we were supposed to pull right up to the beach and refuel them from our ship. The only problem was there was a sandbar between the beach by the airstrip and us. So the captain had us load everything we could in the forward part of the ship: water, fuel, everything we could. Then he backed the ship up in the lagoon about a quarter of a mile and opened the throttle and hit that sandbar dead center. We then stopped the engines and moved everything aft. We took both anchors out into the lagoon, put the ship in reverse, and used the winches to pull on the anchors, while the crew went back and forth from starboard to port, which helped rock the ship from side to side. The combination pulled us off the sandbar. We did this about three times before we broke through the sandbar and drove the bow of the ship up on the beach, where we started refueling planes.

This was around two or three days after the marines landed, and there was still fighting going on nearby. There was no mortar or artillery fire, but we were being shot at with rifles. When a bullet hit the ship, you could hear it go *whing!* As soon as we emptied our fuel tanks, which was sometime the next day, we got out of there because if a bullet hit us in the wrong place, it would have been a catastrophe.

In July 1944 we did the same thing on Tinian, but instead of refueling planes directly, we emptied our fuel into 55-gallon barrels on a dock. We did the same thing on Guam later in July, and in October I received orders to go to Astoria, Oregon, and report to a new CVE—a baby carrier—and put it in commission. I also got twenty days' leave and went home to see my folks. By then I had two brothers in the navy. One was on the aircraft carrier *Franklin* when it was hit by a kamikaze. He survived. My other brother was in the Seabees.

The carrier I put in commission was the USS *Bougainville* (CVE-100). By then I was a second class electrician's mate, and I was put in charge of the battery locker—the aviation battery locker. All airplanes have batteries, and the batteries have to be taken care of—recharged and so forth. The only thing was, this carrier's flight deck and hangar deck were covered from end to end with new planes, and they all had cosmoline all over them. All the way across the Pacific the crew was busy cleaning the cosmoline off the planes so they could be delivered to other carriers. So basically, I didn't have anything to do. I just relaxed. I probably made eight or nine trips across the Pacific taking new planes out to Halsey's carriers. No combat, no work to do; I just enjoyed myself.

Then I was transferred to a new destroyer, the USS *Keyes*. It had just been commissioned and was going to join the fleet. The only thing was, this destroyer was a brand-new class and had all kinds of new electronics that the electricians had to take care of, and the school for that was in Norfolk, Virginia. So I was sent to Norfolk, to this six-week school. While I was there, the war ended, and people were being discharged according to a point system. I had enough points for two and a half people. I had been on all these ships, in all these battles, and been to all these places, and it all added up so that I could get out immediately. And that is exactly what I did. I was one of the very first to get out.

CHAPTER 18

◆ ◆ ◆ ◆ ◆

From Pearl Harbor to Manus Island, USS *ABSD#4*

Bob Addobati

B ob Addobati was born in 1922 in Canosburg, Pennsylvania, and enlisted in the U.S. Navy right out of high school. He was a seaman second class aboard the hospital ship USS *Solace,* anchored in Pearl Harbor when the Japanese attacked on the morning of 7 December 1941. He was later transferred to an auxiliary floating dry dock, the USS *ABSD#4,* that was towed in sections to Manus Island in the Admiralty Islands, where the sections were then assembled. Addobati received a medical discharge from the navy in 1946. He is now retired from the U.S. Postal Service and lives in Sacramento, California.

The USS *Solace* (AH-5) was originally built as a passenger ship called the SS *Iroquois* in 1927. She was acquired by the navy in 1940, converted to a hospital ship, and commissioned the USS *Solace* in 1941. She was decommissioned in 1946 and sold to the Turkish Maritime Lines in 1948.

I joined the navy the day after I graduated from high school in June 1941. I joined the navy so I would have something to eat. There were eleven of us in my family, and times were really tough. We lived in a little coal-mining town outside of Pittsburgh. My father was a white-collar worker who went to work every morning dressed in a suit, with a hanky in his breast pocket. He was an accountant.

After I graduated from boot camp, I went aboard the USS *Solace*, a hospital ship in the Brooklyn Navy Yard. We arrived at Pearl Harbor on 27 October 1941. We were there only five or six weeks before the Japanese attacked. I was a seaman second class, striking for signalman. The night before the Japanese attacked, I was ashore. The battleships each had a band, and they played the old music, the good music, the Big Band sound. That Saturday night, they had a Battle of the Bands. The band from the USS *Arizona* won the contest, and the next morning everyone in that band was dead.

The morning of the attack, Sunday morning, I was on the 0400 to 0800 watch and was on the gangway waiting to be relieved. In fact, I should have already been relieved. The watch was usually relieved fifteen minutes early. While I was waiting, I saw this plane coming down and drop something. I always thought it was the first Japanese plane in the attack that morning because the thing it dropped was the first explosion I heard. The bomb exploded on Ford Island, towards the end of Battleship Row, near the USS *California*. Then in just a matter of minutes, Japanese planes were all over the place. I think in all, there were over three hundred aircraft involved. They hit us in two different waves, the first one at 0800 and the second at around 0900.

After that first bomb fell, my relief came running up and said, "I'm relieving you. You have to get in one of the boats." We had about four boats in the water tied up alongside the *Solace*. I ended up being a deckhand in one of the boats, and we ran back and forth between the *Solace* and Battleship Row picking up the dead and wounded. We couldn't get near the *Arizona*, she was burning so bad. However, we were able to get to the *West Virginia*, which was also burning. We didn't try to go aboard her, but there were men in the water. A lot of them were dead or wounded. Then there were others who weren't wounded and were trying to get out of that oil-covered water. There were only about three or four of us in the boat, and we started picking them up, and I remember one of the guys in my boat reached over the side and grabbed a fellow by the arms and he literally pulled all the skin off his arms, he was burned so badly.

I was wearing my white uniform, and it was all covered in blood and oil. We continued to go back and forth all day long, all night long, and into the next day, mainly to the *West Virginia.* I remember a chief petty officer that we pulled out of the water. He was lying in the bottom of the boat with his hands covering his stomach. He kept asking me for water. When I handed him a canteen, he reached up for it and his stomach and everything else just fell out into the boat. He put the canteen to his mouth and died right there. You never forget things like that.

There were so many men we pulled out of the water, and many of them were burned to a crisp, like pieces of wood. We couldn't touch them. If we did, they screamed, "Don't touch me! Don't touch me!" One time we came back to the *Solace* with a boat full of wounded, and the medical officer was on the gangway. He yelled down at us, "Try to bring back as many living as you can. Half of the ones you are bringing back are dead." I thought that was a pretty hard decision for an eighteen-year-old kid to be making—which ones to pick up and which ones to leave in the water.

Everybody we picked up was taken aboard the *Solace,* whether dead or alive. We had a big incinerator aboard the *Solace,* and about six or eight operating rooms. Arms and legs that were amputated were taken down to the incinerator, and the incinerator was kept pretty busy, but I don't think we incinerated entire bodies in there. We took the dead ashore, over to Aiea.

We did this for two solid days, and we finally got aboard the *Arizona* but didn't find anybody alive. The ones off the *Arizona* who did survive swam over to Ford Island, just a short distance away. I was one of the few people who was right in Pearl Harbor while the bombing was going on, going back and forth in one of those motorboats. That was quite an experience for an eighteen-year-old kid. It was probably the biggest experience of my life.

We stayed in Hawaii until March 1942. Then we went to Pago Pago, then the Tonga Islands—Tongatabu. They were some of the prettiest places I have ever seen. From Tonga, we went to Nouméa, New Caledonia. Then U.S. Marines invaded Guadalcanal, and we were going back and forth out of Nouméa. When we had a shipload of patients, we would take them to Auckland, New Zealand. We made several trips to New Zealand, and that is about the prettiest place I have ever been to.

The captain of the *Solace* when I went aboard was Capt. Benjamin Pearlman. He was a good skipper—very conscientious and caring. When we were in Tonga in May 1942, he went aboard the USS *Portland*, a heavy cruiser. The skipper of the *Portland* got sick, and Captain Pearlman took command of the *Portland* for the Battle of the Coral Sea. Then he came back to the *Solace*.

Our executive officer was Lt. Cmdr. "Muddy" Waters, and he later took over the ship from Captain Pearlman. He was wild. Sometimes we called him "Tulagi Joe." If somebody screwed up he would say, "Send them to Tulagi. Put them on the beach." Tulagi is a small island just off Florida Island, not too far from Guadalcanal, and considered a less than desirable place to be.

I remember one time we were coming into Espiritu Santo just at dusk, when it is real hard to identify ships. A transport, the *Zeilen*, was coming out, and she opened fire on us with her 20-mm guns. I was up on the signal bridge, and Lieutenant Commander Waters, who was the skipper by then, was screaming at me to fire a flare. So I put a World War I vintage flare in the projector, and when I pulled the lanyard, it just fizzled. The *Zeilen* kept firing at us and damaged a bunch of our lifeboats. When the flare didn't go off, I got on the 24-inch signal lantern and identified us by Morse code. Then I flashed the message, "What ship?" They came back and said, "USS *Zeilen*." Waters was still screaming, "What are they saying? What are they saying?" I said, "Captain, that is the USS *Zeilen*, one of ours." Nobody was hurt, and it ended almost as soon as it started, but I'm sure a long report was written up.

The head of my division on the *Solace* was a big burly chief by the name of Schultz. He was a real nice guy, and he had about eight signalmen under him. The senior petty officer was a first class signalman by the name of Sanderson, and he was responsible for our training. Most of the men in my division were reservists from New England. We had a lot of guys from New Jersey, almost all of them of Polish descent, and everybody got along.

Of course, being a hospital ship, we had a large medical staff. The senior medical officer was Captain Jensen, and we had nurses on board. We didn't have any problems—none of them got pregnant—but there were a couple of nurses who got pretty wild when they were on the beach. I was very good friends with one of the nurses. Her name was Kitty Shaw, and I remained in contact with her and her husband until her death in Hawaii a few years ago. Her husband was a doctor—a lieutenant commander—on a destroyer. I think it was the USS *Lansdowne*. During the war they dated, and then got married after the war was over. Whenever the *Solace* was in port and the *Lansdowne* came in, the lieutenant commander would call over to the *Solace*. The message was always, "Tell Kitty Shaw, 'I'll see you on the beach.'"

On the *Solace* you could walk on deck and actually look in the windows— not portholes, but windows—of the operating rooms. Like I said before, there must have been six or eight operating rooms, and they were so busy after a landing, doing surgeries. At Guadalcanal we took most of the wounded to New Zealand, where there was a large hospital. We spent a lot of time in New Zealand, and a lot of the ship's company married girls from New Zealand. Most of the New Zealand men were in North Africa fighting the Germans.

Once, early in the war, we were in the Tasman Sea on our way to New Zealand, when we received an SOS from an Australian hospital ship, which had been torpedoed by a Japanese submarine. Before that happened, we ran with our lights on because we were a hospital ship and had a big red cross on both sides of the ship, but after that Australian hospital ship got torpedoed, we ran with our lights out.

We were in Wellington, New Zealand, painting the ship, when we got word that we were going back to the States. I believe that was in October 1943. When we pulled into San Francisco, I was the first guy ashore. If I remember correctly, we weren't in San Francisco very long, maybe three or four days. We dropped off some patients, refueled, and replenished our supplies. I thought I was going to leave the ship at that point, but for some reason they kept me and another signalman on board, and we sailed for Tarawa in the Gilbert Islands. We weren't in the Gilberts for long, just long enough to fill the ship with wounded marines from the battle.

Tarawa was a tragedy for the marines. When they landed, the tide was out, and they had to walk a long way to get to the beach. The *Solace* stayed out about where the battleships were, and the casualties were brought out to us in boats. There were hundreds of them, and getting them aboard was awkward. They were carried up the gangway on stretchers, and I don't think that procedure was ever changed. We didn't have cranes on board to hoist them aboard with. The medical staff was terribly busy, and I watched them in the operating rooms. The doctors and nurses were working in their bare feet. I don't know if it was for comfort or what.

We went to Pearl Harbor after that, but didn't stay very long. I thought we were then going to go back to San Francisco, but we ended up going to San Diego instead, and that's where I got off the *Solace.* I was given twenty-one days' leave with no extra travel time to go to Pennsylvania. I was home just a few days and had to come back to California. Then I received orders to report to Hunter's Point Naval Ship Yard. The navy was building floating dry docks in sections in Stockton, California, and some up in Eureka. This was something new, and these dry docks were huge. They could be used to dry-dock ships as big as carriers and battleships. They could hold two LSTs at the same time.

These dry dock sections were gathered together at Hunter's Point, and then towed across the Pacific to Manus Island in the Admiralty Islands. I think we left in August 1944. Our floating dry dock was the USS *ABSD#4* (Advance Base Sectional Dock Number 4). It was manned like a regular ship. We had a captain, an executive officer, and a crew. There were living quarters on the dry dock, which were awful. Each section was towed by a tug. We were like a little convoy. It took us forty-eight days to get from Hunter's Point to Manus Island—forty-eight days at sea. I think we made about 5 knots all the way over there. We were lucky we had good weather. I don't know what would have happened if we had hit some dirty weather.

The skipper of *ABSD#4* was a Captain Carnes. He was a four-striper—an ex-submarine skipper. I think he must have screwed up, and that's the way the navy penalized him—put him in command of this dry dock. I mean, a four-striper on a dry dock—it must have been the low point in his career. Captain Carnes was okay; he did his job, but at night he would go ashore to the officers' club and get smashed. We had an elevator on the dry dock, and one day it broke down with him in it, and he was stuck there for several hours, screaming his head off.

The crew wasn't the greatest, either. I think they too were screw-ups from other commands. I don't know how I got on there, because I was a pretty good sailor. I used to think to myself, "How did I get stuck on this thing?" Being on that dry dock always reminded me of the movie *Mr. Roberts*.

When we arrived at Manus, we spent weeks assembling the sections of the dry dock, which was a huge operation. After it was assembled, we started docking ships. The concept was good, because it saved time by not having to send ships all the way back to Pearl Harbor or the West Coast for repairs, and we docked a lot of ships while we were there.

There was another floating dry dock, the USS *ABSD#2,* not too far from us. One night in April 1945, some Japanese planes came in and torpedoed us and the *ABSD#2.* From the air they probably thought we were carriers. We were working at night with lights all over the place, because by that time in the war we thought we were far removed from the action. All the fighting had moved north up towards Okinawa, and west towards the Philippines, so we felt pretty safe. But the two Japanese planes that hit us might have come from the island of Rabaul, which wasn't too far from Manus.

One of the torpedoes hit *ABSD#4* and literally broke us in half. It was around midnight, and I was asleep when it happened. I jumped out of my bunk, and my first thought was to run over to the signal bridge on the other side of the dry dock. I started across this wooden catwalk to the other side of the dry dock, but had to turn around and come back because part of it had been destroyed when the torpedo exploded. I had to go clear to the other end of the dry dock and cross at that end. Captain Carnes's quarters were near the signal bridge, and when I got there, he was standing there in his skivvies, waving a .45 pistol. The *ABSD#4* was damaged so bad that we couldn't dock any more ships, and it was torn apart section by section and towed back to the States. Why they did that, I don't know.

About three days after the bombing, we got hit by a typhoon, and we had several barges tied up to buoys all around us, loaded with all kinds of gear. One of them had a huge crane on it, and this lieutenant was worried that the line holding the barge to its buoy might part. He asked for a crew to go out at night and secure an extra line to it. I was a second class signalman, and he asked me to take charge of the crew. We went out to the barge in a boat as the typhoon was starting to die down, but there were still whitecaps in the harbor. We got aboard the barge, but there was no way we could secure a second line in that rough water, so I told the coxswain to come in and pick us up. I made sure everybody made it into the boat. I was the last one, and just as I jumped, a wave hit the boat and the bow went up. I got my hands on the gunwale but the boat smashed into the side of the barge and crushed my left leg. I ended up in the water between the boat and the barge. The boat was smashing into the barge above my head, but because the hull of the boat was curved I was saved from being crushed. Then, the boat drifted away from the barge a little bit, and a guy by the name of Bob Londo from Minnesota reached over and pulled me into the boat. They took me over to *ABSD#2* and hoisted me aboard in a stretcher, using a crane. They loaded me up with morphine, but decided they couldn't do much for me there, so they took me ashore to an army dispensary.

I was later flown to a hospital on Guam, and while I was there I heard the doctors talking about gangrene. I was on Guam only a short while before I was flown to Tripler Army Hospital in Hawaii, and that is where they took my leg off. I was later transferred to the Vallejo Naval Hospital, and I have to say that that was the happiest year of my life. I went to San Francisco almost every night with a bunch of other amputees, and ate in some of the finest restaurants. We might not have had more than ten cents in our pockets, but we never worried about it because somebody always picked up the tab.

There would always be four, five, or six of us that would go together. We would go to town with three or four decks of ribbons on our uniforms—on crutches, arms missing, legs gone—and the women just threw themselves at us. It was crazy! They would fall in love with us. We would go into nightclubs, and our table would be covered with drinks, and we wouldn't even know where they came from. That's the way it was back then. It was so much different than the Vietnam War.

There was a Dr. Charles Canty at the Vallejo Naval Hospital, and he had the misfortune of having to amputate his own son's leg. His son was a navy carrier pilot. Dr. Canty was a great guy—he passed away about ten years ago.

There were brothels on Georgia Street in those days—a bar downstairs and rooms upstairs. The girls who worked there would come up to the hospital. We knew them all, and they would bring us cakes they had made and things they had knitted. They were super—really nice girls.

I was discharged from the navy in January 1946 and drove cross-country back to Pennsylvania, and took three buddies with me—three amputees. One lived in Dallas, Texas, and his name was Cecil Downey. He was a tough little marine, covered with tattoos. He lost both legs on Iwo Jima. His legs were removed so high up that there wasn't enough stump left for him to wear prosthetic legs. The other two guys went all the way with me to Pennsylvania. Gene Virgil was a sailor who had lost an arm, and he lived in Philadelphia. The other one was Rudy Hollingsworth, and he lived in Florida. He was a marine and also got hit on Iwo. I still see him.

Before we left California, Cecil Downey called his brother in Texas and asked him to meet him in Oklahoma City. When we got to Oklahoma City, we wanted to get a hotel room for Downey before continuing on. Three of us walked into this small hotel while Downey waited in the car. I talked to the guy behind the desk, and he said, "No problem." I went out to the car to get Downey and brought him in in his wheelchair. We had a wheelchair and all these spare legs in the trunk. The guy behind the desk was reading a newspaper, and when we brought Downey in, he said, "We can't take him. We don't have an elevator, and the only room I have is on the second floor. What if we had a fire?" I grabbed the newspaper out of his hands and swatted him across the face with it. I said, "When is the last time you had a fire in this flea trap?" Then Downey said, "Aw, come on, let's go. Take me to the bus station. I'll call my brother and tell him to meet me at the bus station in Dallas." Downey's wife had filed for divorce while he was in the hospital, but Downey remarried and he still lives in Dallas and is doing great. He is a Baptist preacher. He is a great guy—a terrific guy.

I spent about a year in Pennsylvania and said, "I'm going back to the West Coast." There is nothing like a Pennsylvania winter. They are brutal. I came back out here and went to work for the navy in San Francisco at the Military Sea Transport Service (MSTS). I went aboard ship and went to sea again for almost seven years. We were civilian crews under the Department of the Navy. I was a chief yeoman, and went aboard ship with a typewriting course in one hand and my spare leg in the other. I got married after my last trip, and my wife said she wanted me off the ship. I loved going to sea, but my wife didn't like it, so I went to work for the Post Office. I spent the next twenty-five years doing that, sticking letters in holes. They could have trained a monkey to do that.

◆ ◆ ◆ ◆ ◆

CHAPTER 19

Aboard the USS *Aldebaran* (AF-10) and the USS *Columbia* (CL-56)

Clyde Jeter, USN (Ret.)

Clyde Jeter was born on 1 January 1923 in Santuc, South Carolina, and was the youngest of twelve children. When Jeter was still quite young, his family moved to Brevard, North Carolina, where he remained until he joined the U.S. Navy in 1941, at the age of seventeen. He was at the submarine base at Pearl Harbor on 7 December 1941, when the Japanese made their attack. He served as a steward's mate on two different ships in the Pacific during World War II and remained in the navy until his retirement in 1963. Jeter now lives in Menlo Park, California, where he remains active as president of the Northern California Chapter of Unit K West and B East, a black navy veterans' association of former steward's mates and mess attendants.

The USS *Aldebaran* (AF-10) was commissioned in 1939 and was purchased and renamed by the U.S. Navy in 1940. She served throughout World War II and beyond, being sold as scrap in 1974. The USS

Columbia (CL-56) was commissioned in 1942, won ten battle stars during World War II, and was decommissioned in 1946.

I was the youngest of twelve children. My father worked on a farm in Santuc, South Carolina, that was owned by a Dr. Stokes. From what I have learned from one of my older brothers, Dr. Stokes pretty much owned us. I guess you could say he was our master. One day, according to my brother, Dr. Stokes just packed up our family and moved us to Brevard, North Carolina, where he had more land. He wanted my father to farm it for him.

Between the time of my seventh and ninth birthdays, both my mother and father died. Some of my older brothers and sisters went north to Ohio to find work, and some stayed in North Carolina. From then on I was just about on my own. I lived with my older brothers and sisters, but I was pretty much on my own and had to make it the best way I could. Pastoria was one of my older sisters by about fifteen years. She was not only my sister, but was like a mother to me. Like my other brothers and sisters, she made a living by working for other people. The girls cleaned house and did cooking for white families. One of my brothers was a chauffeur.

There were about seven of us in the house at Brevard after my parents died. My older brothers and sisters helped keep me on my good foot. If I got out of line, they put me back in line.

When I was eleven, I started working in a drugstore, doing cleaning. I got fifty cents a week for doing that. This drugstore was also the bus station. There was a white bus driver in town by the name of Joe Neely. He worked for Atlantic Greyhound, and he liked me. I worked as a porter, unloading his bus. Then after a while he started taking me on trips with him. He would leave Brevard for the city of Hendersonville, which was about an hour away. Brevard and Hendersonville were big tourist towns in those days, and you had a lot of people who would come to that area in the summertime for their vacations. So I worked there as a porter just for tips. If I could make $2 a day, that was big money.

When I got older, I started mingling with some guys who were in a gang—some other black boys. The chief of police for that area, Mr. Freeman, liked me. He had known my parents and was fond of them. So one day he came up to me and said, "Clyde, I want you to stay away from the Irving boys. They are nothing but trouble. You've seen how many from their family have been on the chain gang, and if you don't watch it you are going to end up there, too." About a week later I joined the navy, and I never looked back.

I was sent to Norfolk, Virginia, and our boot camp was called Unit K West and B East. We had Filipino and black steward's mates training us. Our training was not all that military. They taught us how to salute and march, but most of the training was how to make up an officer's bed, how to clean clothes, and how to set a table. We did that for about six weeks, every day. This is what we had to learn before we got sent to a ship.

After our training we went by train to California. When we got into the state of Mississippi, it was in the afternoon, and they pulled down the shades on the windows where all the black guys were so the white girls couldn't see us.

From California we went to Hawaii on the *Lurline.* I was sent to the submarine base, where I went through some training to qualify for submarines. I was only making $21 a month at that time, and if I got on a submarine I could make 50 percent more. This white guy told me, "Hey, man, if you don't want to get on that submarine, don't do what they tell you. Don't follow the instructions." One of the things they did to see if you qualified was to put you in a chamber about the size of a refrigerator and start filling it with water. After that experience I decided I didn't want to be in a submarine even if it did mean a 50 percent increase in pay. Anyway, I was told I wasn't qualified for submarines, and they had me working around the submarine base at the officers' mess, which was fine with me because the submarine I was going to be assigned to was later sunk off the Solomon Islands.

While I was working at the officers' mess at the submarine base, I met John Kennedy. He was a wonderful man. He liked scrambled eggs for breakfast, but he wouldn't let me cook them. He cooked them himself, and he wouldn't let me shine his shoes—he did that himself, too. He was just that kind of guy.

Later, when I was stationed at Moffett Field, President Kennedy spoke at the Officers' Club. He had a very good memory; I didn't even have to introduce myself. He saw me and said, "You're here?" Yes, he was quite a man. It's too bad he had to die. That's what happens to all the good people.

The first ship I was assigned to from the sub base was the USS *Aldebaran,* a supply ship. We sailed between San Francisco and Hawaii in convoy. It had about ten officers on board. I didn't like it too much. One time we were serving fresh strawberries to the officers for dessert. There was one bowl of strawberries left over, and I ate it. The chief steward told me I shouldn't have eaten them, and one of the officers overheard our conversation. That officer told the chief to put me on report. I went before the captain, and he said, "Clyde, I hate to do this, but we are at war, and you have to show respect to your seniors and follow orders." So he gave me three days in the brig for eating a bowl of strawberries.

Things were in short supply during the war, and whenever the captain went ashore when we were in California, he had me get things like hams, cheese, and butter so he could take them home. I did what I was told, but I always had him sign a chit for whatever he took. Then one weekend I was going to have a party, and I took some food from the ship. I was stopped as I was leaving the ship and put on report. I had to go before the captain on account of that and was reduced in rank. I argued that the captain had done the same thing, but he was the captain and I was a steward. The ship's chaplain felt sorry for me and arranged for me to be transferred to another ship while we were in the New Hebrides. It was the USS *Columbia,* a light cruiser.

It must have been about six months after the Japanese bombed Pearl Harbor that I was transferred to the USS *Columbia.* The captain of the *Columbia,* Captain Curtis, told me that if I could straighten things out in the officers' mess he would restore my rank. Well, there was this mess attendant, lower in rank than me. The captain said he carried a big knife around with him, and all the stewards and mess attendants were afraid of him. He was sort of a bully. I made friends with this guy and started giving him responsibilities—put him in charge of a few things—and he turned out to be a pretty good guy.

On the *Columbia* we fought in the Solomon Islands and in the Philippines. As mess attendants we didn't know where we were or what we were doing most of the time. We were in so many battles I can't recall all of them. The only way I know now is from what I have been able to read in books. However, I do

Clyde Jeter, steward's mate first class. Photo taken at Alameda Naval Air Station after the war, where he played football for the navy.

remember Leyte Gulf—the Second Battle of the Philippine Sea. I was the gun captain on a 40-mm gun, amidships. We were an all-black gun crew—all mess attendants and stewards. We were fighting for our lives. There were other mess attendants below decks, passing up ammunition for the 8-inch guns.

We got hit three times at Leyte. One hit blew away the gun control officer—blew him right away. He was up by the stack. The second time we got hit, number five turret got it, and we lost sixty-seven men.

After the fighting I was helping with the wounded down in the wardroom. I was holding this one white kid—I think he was a boatswain's mate from Brooklyn. He got hit with shrapnel in his stomach—tore his penis off, too. He was bleeding like mad and crying. I was holding him in my arms when he died. That battle was my most unpleasant memory of the war. It was something that will always stick in my mind.

When the *Columbia* came back to California for repairs, I was transferred to Alameda Naval Air Station. I was there when the war ended.

You know, it's funny: during the war the white enlisted men were very cooperative. We got along fine when we were at sea, but once that ship came back to the United States, the white sailors would separate from us just as soon as we passed under the Golden Gate Bridge. It was like they didn't know us anymore. But when we were fighting, they were right there beside us, hoping we would all survive.

What I liked so much about the navy, segregated as it was, was that I worked in the officers' area, and many of those officers were graduates of the Naval Academy, and I think some of their intelligence rubbed off on me. I found myself trying to act like them and speak like them. But when I first went into the navy, what I really wanted to do was become an aviator, but I never had the education to qualify as an aviator. Even though the navy was segregated, that was my dream; that is what I wanted.

The reason why I really wanted to be a pilot goes back to when I was a kid working in the drugstore. The man I worked for was a Mr. McAfee. He had a son who was in the navy, and he had a small airplane. On the weekends when he came home, he would fly it. I had to crank the plane's engine to get it started, and then I would climb in and fly with him. We landed in cornfields and everywhere else.

Yes, I had run-ins with officers and enlisted men, but I have always been the type of man who could overcome those things. I also played football for the navy for twelve years, and that made me popular so that I could pretty much do what I wanted to. I could even go into the Officers' Club and sit down at the bar. In 1947 we won the All-Navy Football Championship. We were known as the Alameda Hellcats. I was put in the officers' coffee mess. All I had to do was be there at eight o'clock in the morning to make coffee for the officers and clean the place up. After that I was free until one o'clock in the afternoon when I went to football practice. At Alameda Naval Air Station I played with Joe Perry, who was later drafted by the San Francisco Forty-Niners.

I have no regrets about having joined the navy. When I joined the navy, I had no job, no clothes—a little bit of nothing. Yes, I had a job with the Greyhound Bus Company, but they weren't paying me nothing; I was working for tips. So you see, it really wasn't a job. When I was stationed at Alameda Naval Air Station in California, I took correspondence courses and finished high school. I was at Alameda from 1945 to 1950. December 1948 is when President Truman signed the desegregation bill. I've never been very political. Even if the navy was segregated, it didn't mean much to me. I went where I wanted and did what I wanted. I had a good time in the navy.

CHAPTER 20

◆ ◆ ◆ ◆ ◆

The Fourteen-Year-Old Sailor

Richard H. Johnson

Richard H. Johnson was born in 1928 in Claremont, New
Hampshire. He was a freshman in high school when the United
States entered World War II. He enlisted in the U.S. Navy at the age of
fourteen and served throughout the war on the USS *Taluga* (AO-62).
He left the navy after eleven years and took a job as a police officer in
the state of Maine. For the next thirty-five years he served in law enforcement and retired as a chief of police.

The USS *Taluga* was commissioned on 25 August 1944. She spent
most of World War II operating out of Ulithi Atoll in the Western
Pacific, supplying the Pacific Fleet with fuel and other supplies. She continued in her role as a U.S. Navy tanker until May 1973, having served
in both the Korean and Vietnam Wars.

While still in grammar school I took an interest in navy ships and studied
everything I could about them. In October 1943 I went to the U.S. Navy recruit-

ing station in Claremont, New Hampshire, and asked to enlist. I was told I would have to have a birth certificate and the consent of at least one of my parents. Three times I went to the town clerk's office, and each time they typed a copy of my birth certificate. Then one day I went at noon and had the person make a copy in longhand in ink. I had a small bottle of ink eradicator with me, and the minute I got outside the office I put a drop of the ink eradicator on the "eight" of the year 1928. I then went home and got a pen with the same color ink and put a five where the eight had been. A friend of mine and I went back to the recruiting office. He stayed outside while I went in and showed the recruiter my birth certificate and filled out a bunch of papers. After that the recruiter gave me a consent form and told me to have one of my parents sign it. I left, and my friend signed my father's name on it. Later that day I went back to the recruiter and gave him the signed form, and he gave me a train ticket to Concord, New Hampshire, where I was to go the next day for a physical. The recruiter also told me to destroy the handwritten birth certificate, as it could get me in trouble later if it was discovered that I was underage. I asked him if I would need it again and was given a negative by the recruiter. He then showed me a check on a piece of paper showing he had seen it. The recruiter knew my mother because she was a nurse and had once taken care of him in the local hospital, so he knew my birth certificate was a forgery. He later told my mother that he had gotten in trouble with the navy for allowing me to enlist.

The next day I took the physical and was told to get in a line. A marine stamped my papers, ACCEPTED INTO THE UNITED STATES MARINE CORPS. I told him I didn't want to be a marine, and he told me I was a draftee and "you go where we put you." I told him I had enlisted in the navy, so they sent me to talk to some navy officer, who then stamped my papers, ACCEPTED INTO THE UNITED STATES NAVY. He told me that almost everybody taking the physical that day had been drafted.

I was then given a train ticket home and another one for Boston. I went home for twenty-four hours, then took the train for Boston, where I was put on a bus for the United States Naval Training Center, Newport, Rhode Island. My parents didn't know where I was until they received a box with my civilian clothes in it,

Richard Johnson, one of the
youngest sailors in the war.

and a letter from the navy saying I was at the Newport Naval Training Station. When I later came home on leave, they told me they didn't do anything about it because they were afraid of getting me in trouble with the navy. A few weeks later somebody from the navy contacted them, and they signed something allowing me to serve as long as the navy promised not to send me overseas.

We arrived at the training center at dusk, and the first thing they did was cut all our hair off, then feed us. We were then taken to a large drill hall, where we slept on bunks that first night. The next morning we had another physical, many shots, were issued new uniforms, and assigned to barracks. We were issued company flags, and for the next twelve weeks these flags went wherever we went, and we marched everywhere we went. Life was not easy in boot camp. Our instructors hit us occasionally, and we were sworn at and threatened, and we were punished whenever we did anything wrong. We were also threatened with being kicked out of the navy and our names given to the draft if we didn't keep up. The threat was that if we were kicked out, we would be drafted into the army. A few men did fall out, and we never saw them again. I don't know what happened to them, and I didn't dare ask.

We were also told there were three ways to do things in the navy: the right way, the wrong way, and the navy way. From that day on we did everything the navy way. We got so we didn't think; we just acted when given an order. We were told when to get up, when to go to bed, when to eat, what to wear, when to take a shower, and when to wash our clothes.

About nine weeks into boot camp I was told to report to the OOD, the Officer of the Day. When I did, he told me I was going to be court-martialed for a fraudulent enlistment. He then gave me the name of a person from my hometown who had turned me in. I was given a navy lawyer and a hearing. I told the hearing board that I loved the navy and wanted to stay in. I was then told I would be sent home and brought back to active duty one day before my eighteenth birthday and be discharged one day before my twenty-first birthday—a so-called "minority enlistment." I was also told that when I completed boot camp, I should turn in all of my navy gear. At that time I would be issued civilian clothes to go home in.

Upon completion of my boot camp training I did just that, but was told there was no record of my being sent home, so I was sent to an outgoing unit just like the other recruits who had completed their boot camp training. The outgoing unit said they had no orders with my name on them, but said I should stick around until they could find out what was going on. A couple of days later I was told that the Office of the Secretary of the Navy had contacted my parents and that I would be allowed to remain in the navy, but would not be allowed to go into combat.

I was given a train ticket home to Claremont for leave before reporting to Portsmouth, Virginia, Naval Hospital where I would go to hospital corpsman school. I went to the school and hated it. We had an instructor there that everybody called Rigor Mortis. One day he told me to do something, and I didn't hear him. I said, "Mr. Rigor Mortis, what did you say?" His reply was, "You are out of here!"

The next day I was at the Naval Receiving Station in Norfolk, Virginia. Later, I was sent to the Naval Landing Force depot in Norfolk, where I was taught to be a coxswain. During my training I was given a weekend pass but was gone for seven days. When I returned to the base, I was given a Captain's Mast and sentenced to ten days in solitary confinement on bread and water. On the ninth day I was taken to the captain's office and told, "You are a juvenile and headed for serious trouble." I asked the captain what he could do to help me, because I wanted to be on a fighting ship and see some combat, and if I didn't I would go AWOL. He then told me it was my lucky day, because he was getting ready to assign men to three different ships, an old cruiser, a mine layer, and a brand new fleet oiler. I picked the fleet oiler.

The next day I reported aboard the USS *Taluga* (AO-62), and I was the happiest juvenile in this world. In fact, it was the greatest day in my life. I was assigned to First Division, which was the deck force on the forward part of the ship. The captain of the *Taluga* was Cmdr. Hans M. Mikkelsen, who had been a ship's captain in the merchant marine before the war. The executive officer was Lt. George P. Koch, who had been a chief gunner's mate in the navy before receiving a commission. My division officer was Ensign Marvin Pregulman, a former All-American football player for Michigan State, who went on to play professional football for Detroit after the war.

My watch station was the 40-mm antiaircraft gun on the starboard wing of the bridge, and my battle station was a 20-mm antiaircraft gun amidships. Later, in the Pacific, I was made gun captain of a twin 40-mm gun on the port wing of the bridge.

The U.S. Navy was segregated at that time. If you were a nonwhite, you had your own compartment with other nonwhites, and separate from the rest of the crew. And the only job you could have was that of waiting on officers. About the only time we saw nonwhites was when we were on liberty. I was shocked to meet African American sailors on the beach and find out we were from the same ship.

We left Norfolk and went on a shakedown cruise. On 6 October 1944 we went to Aruba, Netherlands West Indies, escorted by two destroyer escorts. One was the USS *Albert Moore* (DE-442). I don't remember the name of the other one. In Aruba we filled our fuel tanks for the first time. There was another tanker with us, the USS *Assilla* (AO-56), and after loading up with fuel, we went through the Panama Canal. Along with our two destroyer escorts, we went to

San Diego, then on to Pearl Harbor, and from there to Eniwetok Atoll in the Marshall Islands. We stayed there for a few days and refueled ships, then went to Ulithi Atoll in the Western Caroline Islands and became part of the Third Fleet, refueling carriers, battleships, cruisers, and destroyers.

The fourth week of November 1944 we were assigned to the anchorage originally assigned to the USS *Mississinewa* (AO-59), because she was late in arriving. Once she arrived, she was to be given our anchorage. I think it was 0530 on 27 November 1944—I was sleeping on the forward well deck and felt what I thought was rain, but when I checked further, I discovered it was black oil. I stood up and looked around. The AO-59 was all on fire, and black smoke was going thousands of feet into the air. She had been hit by a kaiten, a manned suicide torpedo. I saw some of the crew from the AO-59 swimming away from the burning ship and the flames on the water sweeping over them, and that was the last I saw of them. At the same time, destroyer escorts were dropping depth charges in the area. Then, a float plane from a cruiser landed in the water near the burning ship and turned so that its propeller would blow the flaming water away from some men in the water so they could swim away from it and be rescued. One of the crew from the floatplane also threw out a line so that some of the men in the water could grab hold of it and be towed away from the flames.

We slept on the well deck because there were aviation fuel tanks just below our berthing compartment. If we were hit while sleeping above decks, there was a chance we would be blown over the side and survive. But if caught below decks when hit, the chances of surviving were almost nil.

It was at about this time that I was made coxswain of the First Division motor launch. So here I was a boat coxswain and a gun captain and still a juvenile. We continued refueling the Third Fleet, a job to be proud of. We would have aircraft carriers, or battleships, or cruisers on the port side refueling, and two destroyers on the starboard side doing the same. We would be 50 feet apart, making 8–10 knots, and all the refueling hoses and other paraphernalia would be going from us to the other ships. Besides fuel, we gave them food, ammo, mail, movies, and occasionally we transferred personnel.

Sometimes, even during refueling operations, we would see our escorts shooting down enemy planes trying to attack us. At other times aircraft would be taking off and landing on the carriers we were refueling. We were told that if we were washed over the side, no ship was going to stop and pick us up. An escort might slow down and throw us a line, but they could not jeopardize a ship and crew for one man. Knowing that made you realize how small you were in that war. You were nothing but a sand pebble on a big beach. Life was that cheap. And if you died out there, you were buried at sea.

During the third week in December 1944 we ran into a typhoon—the biggest one in many years, we were told. On my ship it meant that enemy submarines and planes couldn't get at us, but three of the destroyers that were with us capsized with the loss of 80 percent of their crews. Other ships lost men overboard or were badly damaged. We saw a cruiser afterwards with its forward turret and bow gone, and several destroyers with their masts gone and guns gone. We saw aircraft carriers with their flight decks damaged and planes lost or damaged. We found out the Japs were not our only enemy.

After the typhoon we went back to Ulithi, took on fuel, and continued our job of refueling other ships. While refueling ships of the Fifth Fleet, a sister ship of ours suffered an explosion. The front part of the AO had a hole in it big enough to drive a train through. We tried to find out what had happened but never did.

At a later date, we were refueling ships of the Seventh Fleet. When we were done and it had turned dark, we heard a crash and saw flames. Two battleships had run into each other, but I don't know how much damage had been done or if there had been any loss of life. We were told nothing out there. We never knew where we were until we read it in the ship's paper, and that would only be after we had left the area. Tokyo Rose gave us more information about where we had been and what we had done than our own navy.

Our letters home were censored. After the war was over and I was home, my mother showed me some of the letters I wrote home. The navy censors even took out of my letters where I wrote about the weather where we were.

On 11 March 1945, when we were anchored in the lagoon at Ulithi, we were not too far from the USS *Randolph* (CV-15). There was an explosion on the

Randolph, then another one on the island of Mogmog. Two kamikazes had sneaked in. One hit the *Randolph* and the other dove into the island—probably thinking it was an aircraft carrier. We discovered that going to Ulithi wasn't much safer than being near the front lines.

On 1 April 1945 we were sent to Okinawa to be Station Fleet Oiler, and anchored in the nearby islands called Kerama Retto. We refueled everything from landing craft to large ships. We were hit with air raids of hundreds of planes almost every night. We weren't allowed to fire on them, because we were told they would follow our tracer bullets and come right down into us. Instead, landing craft would put out a smoke screen so the Jap planes couldn't see us.

While we were there, we refueled the USS *Indianapolis,* which would later transport one of the atomic bombs to Tinian, and was sunk shortly afterwards by a Jap submarine with the loss of most of her crew. Also while we were there, President Roosevelt died. One of his sons was on a ship tied up beside us.

On the morning of 16 April 1945 we were leaving Okinawa. It was around 0900, and as we passed by Ie Shima we were attacked by ten kamikazes. I saw a couple of them get hit and explode, then saw another one come in from our starboard side and go over our stern. His machine guns were firing and I could see his bullets hitting our deck. He hit our main mast, just 20 feet above my head, then crashed forward on our well deck, close to where we had 300,000 gallons of aviation fuel. The Jap plane had a 500-pound bomb that exploded, and I heard our executive officer, Lieutenant Koch, yell, "Abandon ship from the stern!" There was a fire burning in the area of First Division, and I know no one from First Division made it over the side. From my battle station on the port wing of the bridge, I could see the flames and our men fighting the fire where the plane had hit.

The captain would not take any of the men back aboard who had gone over the side of the ship, even though the exec had ordered abandon ship. I thought that was a shame, as I had heard the second in command telling them to abandon ship. To this day I don't know if those men died in the water or were picked up by other ships. I know that twelve men from my division were wounded, one with burns over 90 percent of his body. One had shrapnel wounds, and another lost a hand, but none were killed.

I was a juvenile before that plane hit our ship. Seconds later I was an adult. I saw just what a hell war could be. Seeing other ships get hit, other ships sinking, and men dying didn't bother me too much, but when it happened to my ship, it was a whole different thing.

We often got up at 0300 to rig the *Taluga* for the refueling operations, and refueling might go on for as long as fourteen hours. Then we had to take gear down, and some of us had to go on watch. Sometimes I was so tired I fell asleep standing up.

After being hit, we went to Ulithi and pulled alongside of the USS *Jason* (ARH-1), a repair ship. She patched us up enough so that we could be involved in raids against the Japanese home islands. We were told the worst was ahead; we were going to invade the home islands and that there would be over a million American casualties. We weren't too far from the coast of Japan when the United States dropped the two atomic bombs. Needless to say, we were a happy bunch of sailors when that happened.

A couple of years ago I asked an officer I served under on the *Taluga* why they had put a juvenile like me in charge of a boat and a gun crew in wartime, where hundreds of lives might be at risk. He said, "At your age, we felt you were too young to be scared and would act without giving too much thought to it." He may have been right, since I remember older men being taken off the ship in straitjackets.

At one of our reunions, one man who worked down in one of the engine rooms told me that they could hear the machine gun bullets hitting the ship, then the explosion. He and at least one other sailor down there shit in their pants when that happened. It's one thing being up on deck when that happens, but being below decks with all the hatches locked is much more frightening, especially when you consider that on a tanker you have millions of gallons of aviation gasoline, diesel oil, and ammo.

After the Japanese surrendered, we went into Tokyo Bay with some of the first ships to do so. In fact, we operated with the Japanese Navy after the fighting was over, as they were bringing their men home from some of the islands. Their ships didn't have the proper gauges that would tell when their fuel tanks were full, so they would send a man down into the tanks on a ladder and he would climb back up as the fuel level rose inside. When we saw his head come up, we knew we had about ten minutes to shut our pumps off before the tank overflowed. One time, instead of turning off the pumps, we turned them up higher and watched as the pressure blew the Jap right out of the tank, and their decks became covered in fuel oil. At first they got mad, then they started laughing, and so did we.

One morning I came out of my sleeping compartment and looked up at Mt. Fuji and thought to myself, "You still aren't old enough to be in the navy, and you have been involved in some of the biggest naval battles the world has ever seen, and you have ribbons and battle stars to prove it." When I first went aboard the *Taluga* in 1944, it was like being back in high school. We were a bunch of young kids under a few teachers. When we first went to general quarters during our shakedown cruise, it took us thirty minutes. Three weeks later we could do it in a little over a minute—all stations manned and ready. It was the same with all of our drills—fire drills, collision drills, abandon ship drills. When we came back from that shakedown cruise, we were a fighting machine, and we continued to drill, whether in a combat zone or peaceful waters.

I think if we hadn't fought World War II, most of the world would be speaking German and Japanese. Most of us who grew up during the Depression knew hunger and poverty, and when we went into the service, we found we had more than we ever had before in our lives. In the service, we had it all—good food, nice clothes, and most of us got to see the world.

I stayed in the navy after the war was over because I had no trade. But later I got married and had four children, and couldn't make ends meet on navy pay. When I was in Newport, Rhode Island, I was an instructor, and I had a brother who was on a fleet oiler. We would go home to Fairfield, Maine, where our parents then lived, and this policeman in our town kept bugging us for no reason and giving us warrants. I finally went to the police station to lodge a complaint. The police chief said to me, "My motto is, if you can't beat them, join them." Then he asked me how much longer I had to do in the navy. I told him I had five days. Seven days later, I started as a police officer, on the night shift, six days a week. Twenty months later, I was twenty-seven years old and was named police chief in Hampden, Maine. At the time, I was the youngest chief of police in the state of Maine. Thirty-five years later I retired. I feel the navy had a lot to do with my success in civilian life. The navy taught me how to take orders without question. The navy also taught me how to supervise other men, which I did during my law enforcement career.

I started the first USS *Taluga* reunions with the one we held at Unity College in Unity, Maine, in 1989. It was a big success, but since then many of the crew from World War II have died, so now we include former crew members who served aboard the *Taluga* during the Korean and Vietnam Wars.

CHAPTER 21

◆ ◆ ◆ ◆ ◆

Wake Island Survivor

John Unger, USN (Ret.)

John Unger was born in 1920, in Austria, and moved to the United States when he was eleven years old. In 1939, with work hard to find, he joined the U.S. Navy. He was married, and his wife gave birth to a son shortly before the Japanese bombed Pearl Harbor, a son whom he would not see until the war was over. When the Japanese attacked Wake Island in December 1941, the island was defended by approximately five hundred U.S. military personnel, mostly marines, and twelve hundred civilian workers, some of whom were Chamorros from the island of Guam. The highest ranking officer in charge was Cmdr. W. Scott Cunningham of the U.S. Navy. Maj. James P. S. Deveraux was commanding officer of the First Defense Battalion, U.S. Marine Corps. Forty-four military personnel and eighty-two civilian contract workers died while defending Wake Island. After the fall of Wake Island to the Japanese, ninety-eight

civilians who were left behind to work for the Japanese were executed before the war ended. A total of 1,462 individuals, including
Unger, were taken from Wake and sent to POW camps in China and
Japan. Before the war was over, 231 of them would die. Unger stayed
in the navy after the war and retired after twenty years. He now lives
in Vallejo, California.

I volunteered to go to Wake Island. I figured I could save some money by being
stationed out there. We were only on the island for about four months when
the Japanese bombed Pearl Harbor. The Japanese bombed us on the same day
and at the same time they hit Pearl Harbor. I had just finished breakfast when
the air raid alarm sounded, and was at my gun position on Peale Island, one of
the islets that make up Wake, when the first Japanese planes arrived over the
island. As a matter of fact, we were waving at the Japanese planes until they
started shooting at us. We thought they were ours. However, most of the bombs
were directed at the main island, where the airstrip was. Most of our planes
were destroyed on the ground. I think only about four survived.

After that, the Japanese came over just about every day and bombed us.
They stayed up high because our gunners were pretty good. Some of their
bombs hit the island and some hit in the lagoon, but Wake isn't very big, so
every bomb that hit felt like an earthquake.

I was kept running because I was a pharmacist's mate and people were getting hurt—shrapnel wounds and things like that. One day, I was called from
my position on a 3-inch gun to go to where a 5-inch gun was. Just before I got
there, we got hit by Japanese dive-bombers and fighter planes. I dove for the
nearest bomb shelter head first with bullets hitting the dirt all around me. I
came in through the opening of the bomb shelter so hard and so fast that the
people inside thought I was a bomb, and they stepped all over me trying to
get out. I mean I didn't just walk in—I dove.

I was lucky, though, because my position on the 3-inch gun took a direct hit from a bomb and destroyed all of my gear that I kept there, including a bottle of whiskey I was saving for Christmas. It also killed the marine first sergeant who was there.

Our commanding officer was Cmdr. W. Scott Cunningham of the navy. Maj. James P. S. Deveraux was in command of the marine battalion. He got all the credit for keeping the Japanese from taking the island sooner than they did. We prevented the Japanese from taking the island on their first attempt with the help of our 5-inch guns and the few fighter planes we had left. But on their second attempt the Japanese had that little island surrounded by ships. Deveraux told everybody to stay down and not to shoot. So when the Japanese sent their planes over and nobody fired on them, they must have thought that they had wiped everybody out. But when the Japanese moved in with troops to take the island, our guns opened up and sank some of their ships, and they had to back off. I heard at one point that Deveraux was asked by somebody if they could send him anything, and said, "Yes, send us more Japs." But I don't know if it is true he said that.

Then, in order to get on the island, the Japanese took some of their ships full of troops and ran the ships up on the reef. The marines killed a lot of them, but we were outnumbered. Finally, everybody was ordered to concentrate on the main island where Deveraux was. I left my position on a 5 inch gun, crossed the bridge to the main island, and hung around the command post until we received orders to surrender. Deveraux told one marine to get a white flag. Then he noticed me and said, "You come with us," probably because I was wearing a red cross on my arm, and he thought they wouldn't kill us if they saw that.

We marched down the road, the three of us. A bunch of Japanese started coming toward us. When we were about 50 feet apart, a marine in the bushes opened fire on the Japanese and hit one of them. There was some more shooting, and the Japanese killed the marine in the bushes. The wounded Japanese was down and bleeding. They noticed my red cross and indicated that I should look at him. I went over. It was the first time I had ever seen a Japanese. He was shot through the throat, and blood was going everywhere. I passed my finger across my throat to indicate there was nothing I could do. They then took my first aid kit away and made me take all of my clothes off down to my shorts. Then they tied my hands behind me with communication wire. Everybody who surrendered ended up like that and we spent that first night, Christmas Eve, on the airstrip, which Deveraux had mined earlier.

The next morning they gave us some water but nothing to eat. That night they put us all in some underground bunkers. It was that evening that a Japanese doctor and one of the Japanese officers came in. They announced their coming by shooting into the air inside the bunker. The bullets ricocheted around inside and killed three of our guys. What they were looking for was somebody who could speak German. Our doctor, Capt. G. Mason Kahn, a reserve medical officer, said, "We have a pharmacist's mate here. He can speak German." I guess some of their officers had been trained in Germany. So they took me to another part of the island where all of their wounded were. They had captured all of our medical supplies, and they wanted me to take care of their wounded.

They had a wounded officer, a pilot who had been wounded on one of the bombing runs against Midway Island. He was wounded pretty bad, and I was given a bunk right next to him. That is where I would stay and do whatever was needed. There were also three or four of our wounded that they had moved over there. One of them was a marine who had been shot in the head, and you could look right through the hole where the bullet went through his head. It was along the side of his head; not too deep, but still it was a hole. That marine is still alive. I saw him at our last reunion in Fresno just a couple of months ago.

Some of the other Japanese pilots and crew members would come in to see their friend, and they saw me there. For all I know, I might have been the first American they had ever seen. They were pretty small compared to Americans, and for some reason they wanted to wrestle me. I could pin them down pretty fast, but I found out they would treat me a lot better if I let them win. They would do things like bring me candy bars. One time they even brought me some sake.

I guess they held us there on the island for about ten days. I treated their sick and wounded; I even treated a Japanese admiral by the name of Masatake Okumiya. He came in one day along with the Japanese doctor. He spoke in

German, and said he couldn't sleep. We had some phenobarbital. The recommended dose was one and a half grains. I think I gave him four grains. He came back the next day and thanked me. He said it was the best night's sleep he ever had.

Anyway, these Japanese pilots kept coming in, and they were being pretty friendly. I had picked up a few Japanese words, so I said, "The next time you go to Midway Island, take me along and drop me off in a parachute." So one morning at 0500 they came over in their flight gear and woke me up. They said, "Let's go. We go Midway." It then flashed through my mind, "You think they will give me a parachute?" We ended up having a wrestling match going on there. These three or four guys were trying to drag me out to their plane, and I was hollering and trying to fight them off. We finally woke up the wounded pilot I had been taking care of, and he called them off. Otherwise, I might have been off to Midway. Even if they had given me a parachute, the Americans on Midway would have shot me coming down.

Pretty soon, orders came that all of us prisoners were to be taken off the island. They took all of the military and civilian personnel, but left ninety-eight of us behind to help do work on Wake. They picked people with certain skills. This included a doctor and two male nurses. I asked the Japanese doctor if I could stay, too. I got along pretty good with him, and he said I could. But after they had everybody loaded on the ship, he came in and said, "The admiral says, 'All U.S. military personnel must go.'"

The ninety-eight who were kept behind to work for the Japanese were later killed. According to the Japanese, they ran out of food, and that is why they executed them. So it was a good thing I didn't stay behind. I would have been executed, too. [The executions took place on 7 October 1943, by order of the island commander, Admiral Shigimatsu Sakaibara. For this crime Admiral Sakaibara was hanged on the island of Guam on 18 June 1947.]

That trip on the *Nitta-Maru* was quite a trip. As we all walked aboard, the ship's crew was lined up, and they beat us up as we passed between them. They put us in the holds of the ship, and the holds weren't big enough for all of us to lie down and sleep, and there was only one bucket to go to the bathroom in. I started to volunteer to take the bucket topside for emptying just so I could get a little fresh air.

Every day, about a dozen Japanese would come down into the hold with baseball bats and beat us up. Once a day, sometimes twice a day, they gave us a cup of water and a cup of rice. At some point during the voyage five prisoners were taken topside and their heads were chopped off.

The ship stopped in Japan, and about thirty or forty prisoners were taken off. Then the ship continued on to China. We landed at a port in the area of Shanghai. From there, we were marched to Woosung, not far from Shanghai. The camp commander was a Colonel Otera, and he had an interpreter by the name of Izamu Ishihara who spoke perfect English. At this camp there were seven long barracks. They put thirty-six of us in a section, and there were about six sections to a barracks, so they were pretty long. They put over a thousand of us in there, but the officers were in a section by themselves, and the entire camp was surrounded by an electric fence.

We also had the North China Marines in our camp. These were U.S. marines who had been doing embassy duty in China. When they were brought in, they came with their own doctors, Dr. Foley and Dr. Tyson.

On 6 December 1942 we were transferred to another camp, also not far from Shanghai, called Kiangwan. It was located between two airdromes. Colonel Otera, Mr. Ishihara, and most of the guards went with us to the new camp. There was a different Japanese doctor there, but again I was able to talk to him in German, and there was a dispensary on the other side of the fences with a path from the barracks area to the dispensary. It was guarded, but they allowed me to go back and forth, and the guards never stopped me. In fact, one time one of them saluted me. They wouldn't let anybody else through, not even our doctor. For about six months I had free passage. Our doctor would tell me what kind of medicines he needed, and I went over to the dispensary and told the Japanese what I wanted, and took it back.

The mosquitoes were eating us up, and I think everybody came down with malaria except me. And the reason I didn't come down with it was because every time I went over to the Japanese side I would steal some of their quinine.

Here again, because I spent a lot of time with the Japanese and got to know them, I received better treatment. I would get a candy bar or something to drink—little extras like that. After about six months, the Japanese allowed us to take one of the barracks and make a hospital out of it. That allowed our doctor to work directly with our sick.

We did have one appendicitis while we were in that camp. I acted as an anesthesiologist. We had a little bit of ether, and the surgery was performed on a table. We didn't have any surgical equipment, so the doctor operated on the patient with whatever was available, including kitchen knives. It was crude, but the patient survived. However, we lost one man who touched the electric fence that went around the barracks, and was electrocuted.

The prisoners were all forced to work. The Japanese had them making a mountain with shovels of dirt, just to keep them busy, I think. They were worked pretty hard, considering they didn't get much to eat. But I never had to do that. I always stayed in the hospital. I felt guilty about that, and at one point asked to be relieved of my duties and put to work with the others. But Deveraux told me I was doing a good job and to stay with what I was doing.

The future did look pretty bleak. The Japanese were always telling us that if we didn't obey the rules they would kill us. They also told us that we would never go home, that this was going to be our life forever.

Our food over there was basically rice, and we had a lot of problems with dysentery. What we found out was that the burnt rice at the bottom of the pot was good for dysentery. Sometimes we might find a mouse in the cooked rice, and that might have caused some of the dysentery, but people ate it. If a dog or cat wandered into the camp we would cook it up and eat it. We got seaweed, and during the three years we were there, we received several Red Cross packages. The Japanese would let us have them after they helped themselves.

The Japanese also gave everybody three cigarettes a day. At the time, I didn't smoke, although after a while I did take it up for the different taste it put in my mouth. Cigarettes were like money over there. For three cigarettes I could get a bar of soap. There was a bathhouse, but no hot water, and in the winter China gets pretty cold, but I stank so bad that I broke the ice one day and scrubbed myself down.

The Japanese gave us Japanese uniforms to wear when it got cold. Plus, the North China Marines arrived with all their gear, and since they had garments, they shared some of them with us, such as sweatshirts and jackets.

For sleeping we had raised platforms with a little straw matting, and we were all given three, not very good blankets. We slept close to each other—side by side. We also found that if we used old newspapers we could keep fairly warm. And as long as you could stay healthy it was okay.

A. T. Brewer was a friend of mine. He was also a pharmacist's mate, and he came up to me one day and said he couldn't take it any more. He was real finicky, and over there you couldn't even brush your teeth or keep clean. It was driving him nuts. He said he and a marine were going to try to escape. And sure enough, they escaped one day. But they didn't have a chance. First of all, the Chinese would turn them in, and the Japanese would give them something for doing it. They were gone only a couple of days before they were brought back, but they weren't allowed back with us. They were isolated, and we never did see them again until after the war. And since they were a part of our thirty-six-man section, we were blamed for not reporting them, and put on half-rations for about two weeks.

Our commanding office, Commander Cunningham, also tried to escape, along with several other officers. He managed to get out with two or three others, and I think they were gone for about a week, but they were caught and brought back, too. The Chinese turned them in. The only one who succeeded in escaping was a Marine Corps pilot by the name of John Kinney. He escaped from a train that was transporting all of us to Korea, but that was late in the war.

After keeping us about three years as POWs in China, the Japanese decided they needed us in Japan to do some work. We were put on cattle cars, and we were pretty weak by then. After about two days we arrived in Beijing and stayed there long enough to take care of our sick. Then we were put back on the train, and went to Manchuria, and then down to Korea, where we were put on a boat to Japan.

When we got off the boat in Japan, we had to march for three or four hours to get to the railroad cars that were going to take us to northern Japan. When the Japanese civilians—mostly old people and children—found out there were some American prisoners coming through their town, they came out, and the stones were flying. The Japanese soldiers were beating the civilians to keep them from getting too close to us. By then American planes were bombing the Japanese home island. We could hear the bombing.

Then they separated some of us. One of the doctors who was with the North China Marines, Dr. Tyson, myself, two other pharmacist's mates, and about a dozen of our officers were sent up to Hakodate, Japan. John Howard and Ernest Vaale were the two pharmacist's mates. The Japanese took us to this place that was one big barracks, and when we got there, we found some other officers. They were British and Australian.

There were coal mines up there, and the Japanese were using POWs to mine the coal. However, as officers, they didn't have to work in the coal mines. It was the enlisted POW that had to do all the work. The officers did gardening and stuff like that.

We weren't there too long, maybe four or five months, then the atomic bomb was dropped. All of a sudden, we started getting more food. When Japan finally surrendered, some Japanese officers called us together. One of them made a statement: "Due to the dastardly Americans' dropping of the atomic bomb, Japan surrenders." The officer said it in English. Then the Japanese turned their guns over to us and said the camp was now ours. It was such a surprise after forty-four months of captivity. Nobody was jumping up and own. There was no real celebration to speak of.

I think we were up there for another week. They gave us food, and we were free to go out and roam around. We went to the nearest village, but not alone. The civilians looked at us kind of funny, but they knew the war was over, and there were no incidents, and the POWs didn't try to take advantage. I mean there were no rapes, for instance, because when you haven't had enough to eat, you don't have a sex drive. So there was no problem with that. For instance, when we were in camp, we didn't talk about sex, we talked about food and freedom.

Also, while we were still in the camp, our planes flew over and dropped food, medicine, and clothes. They also dropped a radio. Then some of our

P-51 fighter planes came over and circled the camp. Over the radio that had been dropped, they told us to march to the nearest railroad station, where we would be taken to the nearest airport. We had to walk for about two or three hours to get there, and these P-51s followed us the whole way. There were only about fifty of us in this group, mostly officers. On the way, the only person who couldn't make it was me. I mean I made it, but I wasn't feeling good.

We got on a plane that was to take us to Tokyo, and I started throwing up. One of the doctors looked me over and said, "You have an appendicitis." The plane radioed ahead, and as soon as we landed in Tokyo, there was an ambulance waiting. I was taken to a hospital, and they took out my appendix. Most of the other POWs were flown home, but I had to go by hospital ship.

The hospital ship was pretty nice, but it was several days before we left for the States. In those days the routine was seven days of bed rest after an appendectomy, so this female nurse came in and said, "You need a bath," and went out to get some stuff to give me a bed bath. While she was gone, I got out of bed and took a shower. After all those years of not being around women, I didn't want to embarrass myself.

The ship finally arrived in Oakland, and we were all transferred to Oakland Naval Hospital. I was there for about four months as a patient, but much of that time was spent on convalescent leave. My wife and son lived in nearby Benicia, and they didn't know I was back, so within a few days after my arrival at the hospital I was issued a new uniform, and they gave me some money. I made my way to Benicia by hitchhiking. I walked up to our house. My wife was working, but my wife's sister was there. After four years I wasn't sure if she was my wife or sister-in-law. But when I realized she was my sister-in-law, I had her call my wife at work. She came home and never went back. This youngster came up to me and said, "Are you my daddy?" That was the first time I had ever seen my son. He lives nearby and calls me almost every day, and we still spend quite a bit of time together.

For the first three years of the war my wife thought I was dead. The War Department reported that the defenders of Wake Island had fought to the last man, but she never said if she believed it or not. Other women who had husbands on Wake remarried while their husbands were POWs because they thought they were dead. The way my wife found out that I was still alive was through a ham radio operator. American propaganda had it that the Japanese were killing all of their prisoners, and to counter this the Japanese had all of us go on a shortwave radio and say our names, where we were from, and so on. This was while we were still in China, and some ham radio operator here in the United States picked up my message and called my wife to tell her that I was still alive. We were also allowed to write postcards from time to time while we were POWs, and I received some letters from my wife in return.

I was given three months' convalescent leave while still a patient at the Oakland Naval Hospital. My wife had some money, and I had some money, so we went to Reno and had a blowout. I drank a lot and ate a lot. I couldn't get enough to eat. Even later, when we went out to eat, I would hope that my son wouldn't eat all of his food so I could eat it. Boy, I put on a lot of weight and after a while I couldn't fit into my uniform.

Also, when I came back, everything seemed so strange. I was not a normal guy, and I was probably hard to put up with. I would wake up in the middle of the night with nightmares, groaning, and thrashing around. I remember my wife wanting to go to parties, and before we got there, I would say I didn't want to go, and we would turn around and come home. Even now I don't like to be around people too much. I'm perfectly happy to be by myself. Still today, if I go to a restaurant, I always look for the exits so I can get out of there in a hurry. My wife, years later, said I left for the war as one person and came home as another person, but she never asked me about what happened during those years that I was a POW, and I think that is why I came out of it all right. There are others who never got over it.

I didn't start going to Wake Island reunions until 1973. People kept asking me to come. Some of them even wrote me letters, so my wife and I decided to go. They treated me awfully good. Having been a pharmacist's mate in the camps, I treated a lot of them, so more of them remembered me than I remembered them. In the beginning there were about five hundred guys who would come to those reunions, and with their families there were about one thousand people. I think only about eighty came to the last one. Of the one doctor and six pharmacist mates in the medical department who were with me on Wake, I'm the only one left, and I still think about the guys who didn't make it back from the war.

◆ ◆ ◆ ◆ ◆

CHAPTER 22

Survival at Corregidor

Richard Harralson, USN (Ret.)

Richard Harralson enlisted in the U.S. Navy in 1937 upon gradua-tion from high school. After boot camp in San Diego, California, he went on to become a radioman and served on the USS *Saratoga* (CV3) and the USS *Lexington* (CV2). Before Pearl Harbor he trans-ferred to the Asiatic Fleet, where he served on the USS *Augusta* (CA 31) under Adm. Thomas C. Hart, commander in chief of the Asiatic Fleet. After the fall of Corregidor in the Philippines, he served out the war as a POW. He stayed in the navy after World War II and retired as a lieu-tenant commander. He lives in Shingle Springs, California.

In early 1941 Admiral Hart moved his headquarters to Manila. Some of the "flag radiomen" went with him to Manila, and the others went to Radio Control, Cavite, a big center for all communications going back to the States. I was one of those who went to Cavite. I was very happy there through the rest of 1941 until Pearl Harbor was bombed. In the Philippines, that was 8 December, a Monday. By Monday noon the Japs had bombed Clark Field, and the war was full upon us.

On the third day, Wednesday, 10 December, fifty-four Japanese bombers flattened Cavite. What wasn't flattened was burned. After that, the radio gang was transferred to Corregidor. Corregidor is an island at the mouth of Manila Bay. Manila Bay is a very large bay that opens to the South China Sea to the west. The Bataan Peninsula makes up the western edge of the bay, and its tip is two miles north of Corregidor.

Most of the guns on Corregidor were installed to train to the west to protect from invasion by sea. The Japanese landed to the north and to the south on the main island of Luzon and formed a pincer movement. General MacArthur's troops then fled to the Bataan Peninsula.

I would like to point out here that our total forces in and around Manila were 20,000 trained American infantrymen, and 10,000 Filipino Scouts, who were excellent soldiers, for a total of 30,000 trained fighting men. When MacArthur was sent out to the Philippines as high commissioner and adviser to the Philippine government on military matters, he convinced the American government to defend the whole of the Philippine Islands, which was contrary to war plans [War Plan Orange]. He said he could do it with 150,000 Filipino soldiers. He had 150,000, but they had absolutely no training and very few weapons. As one wag put it, "The only thing they knew was to salute and ask when the next meal was." Most of these Filipino soldiers faded into the boondocks as soon as the war started. I don't mean to say anything derogatory against the Philippine people; their Philippine Scouts were excellent soldiers. It's just that the Philippine Army had no guidance, no equipment, and no leadership. So for the most part, it just disappeared. It was the Philippine Scouts that protected the rear of U.S. troops when they moved into the Bataan Peninsula, and they lost heavily.

When we got out to Corregidor, we radiomen from Cavite were moved out to a tunnel on Monkey Point. Corregidor looks something like a polliwog. It's about 3 miles long. The head of it is towards the west, and there's a large mountain there. Around the sides of the mountain, facing the sea, were these big gun emplacements—14-inchers, but everything was facing the sea. Now, if you look at Corregidor as a polliwog, the tail is to the east and curves south, and about

Richard Harralson in 1938, when he was a seaman
2/c, radioman striker.

where the anus of the polliwog would be is where Monkey Point and its tunnel are. The famous Malinta Tunnel was at about the waist of the polliwog. In
our tunnel was the Foreign Radio Unit. We called them "gumshoes." They were
the code breakers. They occupied the deep part of the tunnel. We occupied the
front half. This was for equipment and men on watch only. Dividing us from
the code breakers was a heavy curtain, with an armed marine guard. They were
very, very secretive about these foreign radiomen, so we had no contact or dis-
course with them. Our equipment filled our part of the tunnel. We had to live
and eat outside. We, as radiomen, did the same thing we did at Cavite. We handled high-speed radio communications, what little there was of it.

Our last decent meal was supposed to be Christmas dinner, 1941. There were some apartment buildings out there for navy dependents, but they had sent all of the navy dependents home long before, and the apartments were empty. The cooks put together a Christmas meal, and we were just about to sit down to eat it when an air strike hit us, and they hit us good. We ran from there and sought low places in the ground. All of the apartments were destroyed, and it was after that that everything started to go downhill with regards to food. We went to two meals a day. For awhile, we got rice and beans for our evening meal, but that soon petered out. What we got a lot of after that was spaghetti. Now, we're not talking spaghetti with tomato sauce and meatballs; we're talking spaghetti. For breakfast, we had ersatz coffee and bread. For the evening meal we had more ersatz coffee and spaghetti. We did get a share of government mules that were killed, some of them by bombs. They were good, but very tough.

The bombing intensified, and the Japs brought some big guns up to the south shore of Bataan and started shelling us from there. Water became hard to come by. There were several wells on the island, but what we got out of them was more towards the bottom side, and it had to be purified with chemicals. For a while we could take bucket baths, then it became canteen cup baths, then wet-rag baths, and then nothing.

At one point I talked to a soldier who had been at the Bataan front. He told me how terrible it had been on Bataan. He said they had been starving to death. Marivales was a small town at the southern tip of the Bataan Peninsula, and from there they would send out trucks with supplies to the front. When the trucks got to the front, there would hardly be any food in them. Who was responsible for the loss of the supplies, I never found out. Another thing was the sickness on Bataan. There was almost no quinine to fight malaria with.

MacArthur left tons and tons of food supplies in and around Manila. There seemed to be very little logistics in the whole effort. MacArthur didn't tell Admiral Hart when he was going to declare Manila an open city, so we lost a lot of supplies that way. Plus, the airplanes we had were virtually all destroyed on the ground the first day of the war. MacArthur had eight hours of warning.

Admiral Kimmel and General Short on Hawaii didn't have eight hours of warning, and their careers were ruined.

There were four of us radiomen who came out to the Asiatic Fleet together. There was Bill Lauer, Herald Hooper, and Mudge—I can't remember his first name. Mudge was the only one of us who was married and had a child. He was transferred off the *Arizona,* and you know what happened to the *Arizona.* We all went to the *Augusta* together. We all went to China together, and we all went to prison camp together. Mudge was killed somewhere along there. It might have been at Cavite.

Things got worse and worse on Corregidor. We were in pretty bad shape. We were losing weight, and there was constant bombing. After Bataan fell, the Japs didn't waste any time. Bataan was mountainous, and they established observation posts on top of those mountains. They moved up their big guns, and when I say big guns, I mean 250-mm, and proceeded to rake Corregidor from one end to the other. The island became just a bunch of craters. I spent most of my time hiding in holes.

Out on the point, not far from the mouth of our tunnel, the marines had an ancient-looking gun, a one-pounder that overlooked the beach to the east. And it was out towards there that I dug a hole in the ground for my sleeping quarters. I got acquainted with a marine corporal there; his name was York. He was a cool and courageous person—somebody to be with during a shelling or bombing. I have often wondered whatever happened to him. We used to sit out there and chew tobacco and spit out over the cliff. By that time MacArthur had left the island. I think it was March 1942. This was at the direction of the president—probably the only time MacArthur ever did what he was told to do. I guess you can tell by now I didn't like MacArthur. Anyhow, he left, and we all felt as though we were racing down a highway towards a brick wall. We knew early on that the "Rock" was written off. We were doomed, and nobody there thought otherwise.

I think it was around 5 May 1942 that we suffered an intensive shelling, and it went on into the night. For some kind of protection we all jammed ourselves up in the mouth of the tunnel. There was a sunken walkway just above our tunnel. It was concrete-lined, and if we weren't on watch, we were supposed to go up there when the Japanese landed. That was our defensive position. At about 11:30 that night the shelling stopped, and we were told to man our positions. I grabbed my rifle, two bandoliers of ammo, two hand grenades, and ran out the mouth of the tunnel. It looked as though the ground was on fire, so I turned around and ran back into the tunnel. I knew I couldn't stay in there, so I ran back out and managed to get up to the sunken walkway. It was dark, and you could hear guns going off—rifle fire and machine gun fire. You could see tracers in the air, and hear the sound of bullets ricocheting, but you couldn't see anything else.

We spent the night staring into the dark until our eyeballs ached. Come the first light of day, I looked up to the ridge to my left, and I could see people firing down towards the beach. I ran up there and jumped in a hole. We were on top of the ridge, and to my left—maybe 20 feet away—was a water-cooled, .30-caliber Browning machine gun. The men manning it were remnants of the Fourth Marine Division, originally stationed in Shanghai. They had been brought down to the Philippines just before the war. This regiment was supposed to be 3,000 strong. It was actually 1,600, and divided up into three battalions. The battalions had been filled out to 1,000 men each with army office personnel, navy personnel, and Philippine Scouts. The marines didn't like doing it that way, but the army had its way.

One of these battalions was put around the base of the western end of the island, another battalion about midpoint, and the third battalion just on the other side of Monkey Point, where we were. I was up there with this battalion of marines, filled out with army, navy, and other personnel. The Japanese had landed, and we were looking down at them. Everybody was shooting down at them, and I started shooting down there too. Sometimes I saw something to shoot at; sometimes I didn't. Then the Japs started to drop mortar shells down on us. They put one right in the middle of that Browning machine gun position. I have a vivid picture of one of the marines staggering down the hill backwards, trying to stay on his feet. He had a mangled leg. I guess the rest of them were killed.

To my right there was nobody. There was a small airstrip, but there were no airplanes on it. There came a lull in the fighting, and I looked over towards the end of the airstrip and saw the top of a white flag. I jumped out of my hole, and I started jumping up and down, and yelling, "They're surrendering! They're surrendering! The Japs are surrendering!" Then the flag moved forward, and there was a red meatball in the middle of it, so I got back down in my hole. The flag was on a tank. There was a road there, and the tank came down the road and stopped at an angle off to my right. It wasn't more than 25 feet away. In effect, it was enfilading—shooting right down our line at our troops. I tried to shoot through the slit just above the gun barrel on the tank. I thought if I could put a bullet in there, it would ricochet around and cause lots of damage. Of course, that didn't get anywhere. I threw my hand grenades; one of them went off, and the other didn't. That's another thing—all of our equipment was World War I or before.

After that, the firing faded off, and word came up the line for everybody to return to base. General Wainwright had ordered us to surrender. It was a good thing, because I hardly had any ammunition left. I got up and walked back down to the mouth of the tunnel. Everything was just a mess in there. I went over and took a box I had made for my personal possessions and took out a pack of "dobbie" cigarettes. That was a term used throughout the navy for anything local or native. Anyhow, I took those and threw everything else on a pile of junk because I didn't think I was going to be around much longer.

The navy had moved out the FRU—the Foreign Radio Unit—about a week before Corregidor fell. They were moved out by submarine. When they moved out, the curtain came down, and in their part of the tunnel were some concrete stairs that went up to a back door. It was a big iron door, and it had a big iron bar across it on the inside. We were milling around, wondering what was next. The Japanese were pounding on this iron door, so I went up and opened it. Standing back about ten or fifteen feet was this Japanese soldier, a little bitty guy. He was wearing a helmet with leaves and twigs on it. He was just standing there with his gun butt on the ground. We stood there looking at each other, then he waved me out. He pointed me to where he wanted me to go. As

I went by him, he handed me a cookie. It was like hardtack. When everybody was out of the cave, we started down the trail and passed a bunch of bodies. They were all Philippine Scouts. There hands had been tied behind their backs, and they had been bayoneted through the throat.

I can't keep the first few days after the surrender in order. I know in the evening the Japs pointed us to an area where there had been an old World War I searchlight that they used to aid the antiaircraft guns. It was paved with crushed rocks, and that's where we had to sleep the first night. It's funny, I don't remember if we got any food or water.

I remember another night when we were assigned a stretch of railroad tracks for our sleeping quarters. This was by Malinta Tunnel, which was about a mile from Monkey Point Tunnel. Malinta Tunnel was a huge affair. It went completely through the mountain, and had deep laterals. They had all kinds of things in there—hospital wards, stores, and offices. It was quite elaborate. Anyhow, it was outside of Malinta Tunnel where we stayed for awhile. Then I had the great fortune of being picked with three others to go with a squad, supposedly a work detail. By that time the Japanese soldiers there on Corregidor were occupation soldiers, not the soldiers that took the place. I have to say that the soldiers that took the place were veterans. They had been at war in China and all, and they were somewhat reasonable, but these occupation soldiers were kids and mean as snakes. Anyway, I got in this work squad, and they took the four of us out past Monkey Point and sat us down. They were jabbering among themselves, then took two of our men down the side of this hill, and out of sight of us. Then we heard gunfire. When the soldiers came back without the other POWs, the other kid and I were looking at each other and thinking this was it—we're next. Then here came a Japanese officer. He was aristocratic-looking, and he started shouting at these soldiers, and they seemed scared to death of him. Then he told us to follow him.

He took the two of us and allowed us to get a drink out of a 5-gallon can. Then he took us down to the beach. There were some other Americans there, along with some Japanese soldiers. The bay was just full of dead bodies— Japanese bodies. This Japanese officer put us to work pulling in those bodies.

We had to take off one legging and the belts from each body. I remember when I first saw all those bodies, I thought, "Gosh, all these Japs are fat guys." Then I realized that all those bodies had been floating in the water in the hot sun for several days and they were all bloated. That made it hard to get the belts off.

The reason we were taking off one legging was because they had identification sewn in them. I don't know why we were taking off the belts. After we did that, the Japanese officer took a sword and chopped off the left hand of each dead soldier.

After awhile this Jap officer called me over and handed me his sword and told me to cut off hands. I think a lot of the Jap officers spoke English. They were probably graduates of USC or Harvard. Anyhow, I discovered how hard it is to cut off a hand. I discovered you had to have something solid underneath when you did it.

We were in sorry shape by this time. I think I was down to about 130 pounds. I was put on another work party unloading a landing barge that had gotten to the beach and was partly sunk. We were getting matériel off that, and had to climb it up this bank. We were carrying the barrel to a field piece, and I remember there were six of us trying to move that thing up the bank and having a hard time of it. This Jap officer took out his sword and whopped us over the butt with the flat of it, and we went right up that bank.

When we got to the top, there was a dead American, but they wouldn't let us bury him. They left all of our dead unburied. Then once the bodies got good and ripe, after about four or five days, they went around and poured kerosene or gasoline on them and burned them. I was horrified that they wouldn't let us bury our dead.

On another work party there was this older Jap soldier. He told us he was an English teacher. I spent about four or five days on this work party, and this old Jap soldier was pretty fair-minded. He gave us our own C-rations, and he was always concerned that we had water to drink. He let us sit down to rest, and sometimes he gave us smokes. He was a pretty decent sort.

When that job was through, we were put in a compound near where they used to bring up seaplanes. I found some navy people, and they had rigged up a tent out of blankets. I took off my clothes and put my C-rations underneath the clothes. Then I went down to swim in the ocean to try and get clean. I probably got dirtier because the water was so foul from all the dead bodies. When I got back to where I had left my clothes, my C-rations were gone.

There were no provisions to feed us. We were strictly on our own, and there were only a few navy people on the island. The bulk of the people were army, and they formed cliques. It was like anarchy. Nobody was in charge; it was just these groups, each trying to survive.

The only source of water that I was aware of was a small hydrant, and the water didn't come out very fast. There must have been about ten thousand of us on Corregidor, and this long line of people waiting to get water. What people would do is have one man get in line, and he would have scores of canteens hung all over him, so it would take a hell of a long time for him to fill all these canteens. It was almost impossible to get any of that water.

I managed to get on another work party that was hauling C-rations and loading them onto Japanese ships. I accumulated a few more cans of C-rations before I went on this work party, and I had them tucked inside my shirt. However, when I went back to the compound, the Japs shook me down and found these C-rations in my shirt. I didn't take them from the boxes we were loading. I would have if I could have, but there was no opportunity to open the boxes and get at them. They accused me of stealing those C-rations, and I got worked over with rifle butts, and they took my C-rations. I was in even worse shape after that.

When I got back to the compound, one of my buddies had somehow gotten a small sack of lima beans. We thought if we could get water and build a fire, we could cook them. We were trying to do that in the middle of the night when the first rain of the rainy season hit. It put out our fire, and we couldn't cook the beans. It was the most miserable, god-awful place the next morning. All of our clothes were sopping wet. Then about ten o'clock that morning the word came that the Japs were going to move us out.

The Japanese had moved three merchant ships up close to Corregidor. They hauled us out to them in boats. It took an awful long time to move us all out, and we were jammed into those ships for the trip to Manila. When we got to Manila, the Japs marched us all over the city. Filipinos all along the way put their lives at risk trying to give us food and water. They had Japanese soldiers riding horses up and down both sides of our formation. When they went by, the Filipinos would come out with cans of water and give us some, then run. Others would come out and give us rice balls and things like that. I have to say I really like the Philippine people. They risked their lives to help us.

We stayed at different camps in the Philippines for awhile. While we were in one camp Bill Lauer saved my life. Before we surrendered on Corregidor, he took a bottle of sulfathiazole from the dispensary on the tug *Genesee,* where he had been stationed. We had lots of dysentery. When you had it bad, the Japs sent you across the road to what amounted to a death camp. Lauer gave me one of those pills for dysentery, and if it hadn't been for that, I would have gone across the road.

Another thing was ulcers—they started like blisters, then became big festering holes. I got one on my neck and couldn't stop it from getting bigger. Lauer took one of his sulfathiazole pills, smashed it up, cleaned out the hole, and put this sulfathiazole in the hole. That did the trick.

Lauer, Hooper, and I were together all this time. Then in September of 1942, about three hundred of us were singled out. They said we were going to Japan as guests of the emperor. They put us on the *Lima Maru,* and we headed out. They put us in quarantine on Taiwan for about two months, then put us on the *Dai Nitchi Maru* for Japan. We were down in the lower hold. There were three hundred of us, and about two hundred British from Hong Kong. It was terribly crowded, and the only way we could get a little air was to use the toilets that were built out over the water. They had about three or four of them on deck, so we would go up and stand in line to use them.

A lot of people had diarrhea. We were only at sea for about three or four days when we got caught in a typhoon, and they had to batten down the hatches. When you get that many people together the way we were, and many with diarrhea, you've got a problem. My memory is not very clear on the rest of it, but I think we were on that ship for three weeks before we got to Japan.

I spent the rest of the war in Japan. In Yokohama I worked in the Mitsubishi Ship Yard. I am now suing Mitsubishi.

Hooper stayed in the navy after the war, as I did. He was a chief petty officer. He married and had a couple of kids. Then in 1950 he put the barrel of a .45 pistol in his mouth and pulled the trigger.

Lauer also stayed in the navy after the war and retired as a chief warrant officer. He used to live in Cupertino, California, and we got together several times after the war and had real good times. He died about two years ago.

After the war a lot of guys held things inside—they never let it go. They're all dead now. I had two things going for me. I stayed in the navy, and that didn't give me much time for brooding. The second thing is, I found a good wife. She is a stable person. I would get depressed sometimes, but she was always there and helped me through it.

CHAPTER 23

◆ ◆ ◆ ◆ ◆

Mare Island Naval Hospital

Syble P. Kendrick Robinson and Lee Robinson

Syble Kendrick Robinson was born in 1920 in Atlanta, Texas. She enlisted in the U.S. Navy in June 1944 and did her early training at Hunter College in New York City and the U.S. Naval Training Center in Bainbridge, Maryland. Taking the advice of her sister, who was in the Naval Medical Corps, she requested transfer to the Naval Medical Corps and was sent to the National Naval Medical Hospital in Bethesda, Maryland, for her advanced training. After completing her training, she was sent to the U.S. Naval Hospital at Mare Island, California, where she met her future husband, Lee Robinson. Robinson was wounded while serving aboard the USS *Birmingham* and was discharged from the navy as a result of the injuries he sustained aboard the *Birmingham.* Syble Robinson was discharged from the navy in April 1946 but continued her work at the hospital as a civil servant, later transferring to the Industrial

Mrs. Syble Kendrick Robinson, Mare
Island Naval Air Station.

Dispensary, Mare Island Naval Shipyard. The Robinsons are both now
retired and live in Vallejo, California.

SYBLE

I arrived at the Mare Island Naval Hospital in February or March 1945 and
stayed there until it was closed in 1950. We had mostly amputees and mental
patients. Our "brace" (prosthetics) shop was world famous. That is where they
built new arms and legs for amputees. At first, prosthetic legs were held in place
with belts around the waist. Then they invented the kind with suction cups to
hold them on. The technicians who worked there did a lot of on-the-job
inventing and improving of artificial arms and legs. They received recognition
in the form of citations from the navy for their work.

There was a woman who came to the hospital. She was the wife of a ser-
viceman and had lost a leg in an accident, and was fitted with an artificial leg
that was like a bucket at the top with a suction device to hold it on. When she
got fitted with her artificial leg, she went right into the captain's office and danced
around to show him what she could do with that new leg. She even pulled up

her dress to show him that leg. It was the funniest thing I ever saw. She stayed on at the hospital after that and helped other amputees learn how to walk again.

LEE

They would have dances for the amputees, and this woman with the prosthetic leg would go and ask some of these men to dance, and they would say they couldn't because they were amputees. Then she would pull up her dress and say, "I have an artificial leg, too. Watch me." That gave them the will to help themselves. She was a big help.

SYBLE

When I first arrived at Mare Island, I worked at the Medical Survey Desk, surveying men either back to service or out of the service. At the Medical Survey Desk we met on Mondays, Wednesdays, and Fridays. On Mondays we did medical boards, Wednesdays was neuropsychiatric boards, and on Fridays we did the orthopedic patients. Two naval officers would come from the Twelfth Naval District in San Francisco. They were both lawyers; one would represent the navy, and the other would represent the patient. These boards were handled like court cases to make sure the patient received all of his rights, especially if he was going to be discharged because of his injuries.

I remember we had one army air force amputee at the hospital who had lost four fingers off one hand, but he still had his thumb. The brace shop made him a rubber hand that even had hair on it, and it looked identical to the other hand. He wore it like a glove. It looked so real that when he came before the Survey Board we couldn't tell which was his real hand and which was the artificial hand.

Of course, when I was in the navy we didn't make much money, so I worked part-time at the local theater selling tickets. There was a young sailor who had lost both arms up to the elbows, and when he came to the theater, I would have to reach out and take the dime from his pocket. Then one night he came through the door smiling from ear to ear. He had two prosthetic arms. He took one hook and held his pocket open. Then he took the other hook and reached

USS *Princeton* (CVL-23). Photo taken off Seattle, Washington, in 1944, before her fateful day off the Philippines.

in, took his dime out, and handed it to me. For the first time since he lost his arms, he was independent, and that was the greatest thing in his life at that time. He had been practicing that one act so that he could come to the movie theater and show me. It was things like that that made me feel we were really doing wonderful things at the hospital.

We had hundreds of amputees at the hospital at any one time. A lot of them lived around here after they got out of the service, but they are just about all dead and gone, now. There was one fellow, Roy Risk, who was a marine and lost a leg somewhere in the Pacific. He received a full medical discharge, but never let that leg stop him. He went to work at the Mare Island shipyard after his discharge.

Now, after we did all we could for these amputees, all they needed was convalescent care. I had maps showing where all the VA hospitals were across the United States, and I would make arrangements to get these patients to a VA hospital nearest their homes after they had been discharged from the service at Mare Island. From there, they would get medical care as veterans until they were able to go home on their own.

Taken from the cruiser USS *Birmingham* off Leyte in October 1944, while she was tied up alongside the carrier *Princeton,* before the explosion that killed so many men on both ships, and doomed the *Princeton.*

There was a Captain Smith who was the head of the psychiatric department, and I was really interested in all aspects of the work at the hospital. I figured the more I learned, the better I would be at my job, so I asked him one day if I could sit in while he was with one of his psychiatric patients and take notes. I hadn't had much training in the psychiatric department, so he called me in while he was interviewing one of the patients. Before Dr. Smith started, he told the patient that I was one of the clerks and would be taking some notes. Dr. Smith asked the patient, "When was the last time you went out?" and the patient said, "Oh, last night." Then Dr. Smith said, "Did you have a good time?" The patient said, "Oh, yeah! There was a whole bunch of us, and we really had a good time." I was listening to all this and writing it all down. Then I found out the guy had been locked up the whole time and hadn't been out at all the whole time he had been at the hospital. This man had been sent to us from a ship in the Pacific because he had become psychotic from some sort of mental trauma.

We had a "lock up" unit at the hospital where people were kept in padded cells, and some of them were given electric shock therapy. I remember

Crew members of the cruiser *Birmingham* helping to fight fires aboard the stricken carrier *Princeton*. Before the day ended, many of the men in this photo would be dead.

one patient was given shock therapy and died three days later. But others were helped by it. We didn't have drugs in those days the way they do now. We also had a unit at Napa State Hospital for military personnel, and if we had a psychiatric patient we couldn't handle at Mare Island, he was sent up there.

After the war was over, we had some men come through who had been in Japanese POW camps. There was one who couldn't talk because he had been hit in the throat with a gun butt. After his discharge, he worked as a guard at the shipyard.

LEE

I think most of the psychiatric patients were marines and soldiers, because they were the ones who saw the most action; I mean real blood and guts. But when I was on the USS *Birmingham* when the *Princeton* blew up alongside us, it almost drove me crazy. I can get on a crying jag real easy talking about that. The bombs, the gasoline on board—everything blew up. We almost had the fire under control, when we received a submarine alert and had to pull away for about thirty minutes. By the time we got back to the *Princeton,* the fire got the best of us.

During the submarine alert I went down below to get a sandwich. I was supposed to go aboard the carrier and help fight the fire from there when we tied up for the second time. I was with one of the ship's barbers, a little red-headed guy, and we were getting ready to come up on deck near the quarter-deck, when we saw the executive officer coming down the ladder. We didn't particularly like him, so we went through the quarterdeck to come up on deck from the starboard side to avoid him. It was then that the *Princeton* blew up. The explosion knocked me down and dislocated my elbow on my left arm and did something to my neck and shoulder. When I looked up, all this metal and debris was falling through the air, so I rolled under a 40-mm gun mount before everything hit the deck. That was the only thing that saved me.

The number four 6-inch turret on the aft of the *Birmingham* was hit pretty bad. The chief who had the watch on the turret was cut in half from the explosion, and everybody else who was inside that turret was killed by the shock from the explosion. Their bodies were removed with shovels. So many people died so fast, and the blood was just running off the sides of the ship. We had to spread sand around on the decks to keep from slipping in it.

In spite of my injuries I was still able to work and was part of the burial party, collecting the dead and dumping them over the side. One of our surviving surgeons weighed at least 300 pounds, and he worked on men for thirty hours straight without a rest. I went to work in the laundry room with another guy, doing one load every thirty minutes and taking the dressings to the sick bay. But none of us would go in there alone. We went in in pairs because of what we had to look at when we went in.

About a week later I went to the sick bay because my arm, neck, and shoulder were still bothering me. There were a lot of us who were wounded but still able to work, and there were so many others who were wounded worse than me and needed help more than I did, so that is why I waited as long as I did before trying to get help for my injuries.

Syble

When the explosion hit the *Birmingham,* it killed most of the people in their medical department. And there were a lot of men up on deck who were there to fight the fire, and when the *Princeton* blew, it killed most of them too. Lee said he went over to some chief petty officer who had lost both legs and tried to help him, but the chief knew he was going to die and told Lee to go help the others.

When the *Birmingham* came in for repairs, Lee was put in the hospital, and that is where I met him. While he was waiting to be surveyed out of the navy, he was put to work in the hospital laundry. He was doing the dry cleaning and pressing uniforms for the staff.

After I was discharged from the navy in 1946, I was asked to stay at the job as a civilian. I was planning to move back home to Shreveport, Louisiana, but decided to stay for a while. So I moved into town, and I would still visit Lee in the laundry. Lee was wearing a wedding band, so I thought he was married. I told his supervisor that I thought Lee sure was a good-looking guy and that I would be interested in him if he wasn't married. See, there were 350 WAVEs on that compound and no more than half-a-dozen men. She said to me, "He isn't married. He's wearing that wedding band to keep those WAVEs from bothering him." Six weeks later we were married.

When we first got married, Lee had nightmares like you wouldn't believe. It was hard, but we made it. We are still married fifty-five years later.

GLOSSARY

◆ ◆ ◆ ◆ ◆

Technical Terms

ABSD	auxiliary floating dry dock
AH	hospital ship
AKA	attack cargo ship
AO	fleet oiler
APA	attack transport
APD	high-speed destroyer transport
AS	submarine tender
ATR	auxiliary tug, rescue
BB	battleship
CA	heavy cruiser
CAP	combat air patrol (defensive)
CL	light cruiser
CV	attack aircraft carrier
CVE	escort carrier (smaller than a CV)
DD	destroyer
DE	destroyer escort
DesRon	destroyer squadron
DMS	fast minesweeper, mostly converted old four-stack destroyers
fleet boat	U.S. submarine type. Replaced smaller, older models from World War I and after
hedgehogs	a throw-ahead explosive device used against submarines
JICPOA	Joint Intelligence Center Pacific Ocean Area

kaiten	manned suicide torpedo (Japanese)
knot	one nautical mile (equal to 1.15 land miles) per hour
LCI	landing craft infantry
LCI(G)	landing craft, infantry, converted to a gun ship
LCI(L)	landing craft, infantry (large)
LCI(R)	landing craft, infantry, converted to launch rockets
LCM	landing craft, medium
LCP	landing craft, personnel
LCT	landing craft, tank
LCVP	landing craft, vehicle and personnel
LSD	landing ship, dock
LSO	landing signal officer
LST	landing ship, tank
LVT	amphibious tractors
MTB or PT	motor torpedo boats
NAS	naval air station
PC	patrol craft
PGM	submarine chaser (patrol craft) converted to a gunboat.
radar picket	usually a destroyer or destroyer escort, used primarily as an early warning system against kamikazes
S-boat	Pre–World War II submarine, later replaced by newer, bigger fleet boats
the "Slot"	the channel of water running northwest and southeast in the Solomon Islands where most of the naval activity took place during the struggle for control of these islands
TF	task force
TG	task group
tin can	destroyer
UDT	underwater demolition (frogmen)
vector	a magnetic heading, used to direct planes to a potential target
VF	navy fighter squadron
VMF	Marine Corps fighter squadron
VPB	navy patrol bombing squadron
YO	small oiler
YP	yard patrol craft

NAVAL RANKINGS AND OTHER TERMS RELATED TO PERSONNEL

Adm.	admiral
AWOL	absent without leave
Capt.	captain

CINCPAC	commander in chief, Pacific Fleet
Cmdr.	commander
CO	commanding officer
Ens.	ensign
Lt.	lieutenant
Lt. Cmdr.	lieutenant commander
Lt. (jg)	lieutenant junior grade
ninety-day wonder	USNR officer rushed through three months of training; sometimes, but not always, a college graduate
petty officers	enlisted ratings
POW	prisoner of war
R. Adm.	rear admiral
Ret.	retired
USN	United States Navy
USNR	United States Naval Reserve
V. Adm.	vice admiral
WAC	Women's Army Corps
WAVE	female members of the U.S. Navy
W.O.	warrant officer

U.S. Naval Aircraft

F4F	Wildcat, fighter
F4U	Corsair, fighter flown mostly by the Marine Corps
F6F	Hellcat, fighter
PBM Mariner	seaplane built by Martin Aircraft Company
PBY	Catalina seaplane used mostly for reconnaissance; also carried bombs
SOC	floatplane, flown for the most part off cruisers and battleships
TBM and TBF	torpedo planes (Grumman/General Motors)

A Few Japanese Aircraft Types Mentioned in This Book

Bombers: Bettys, Jills, Vals

Fighters: Zeros/Zeke

SELECT BIBLIOGRAPHY

Blair, Clay, Jr. *Silent Victory: The U.S. Submarine War against Japan.* Annapolis: Naval
Institute Press, 1975.

Brokaw, Tom. *The Greatest Generation Speaks.* New York: Random House, 1999.

Costello, John. *The Pacific War, 1941–1945.* New York: William Morrow and Company,
1981.

Dunnigan, James F., and Albert A. Nofi. *The Pacific War Encyclopedia.* New York:
Checkmate Books, 1998.

Dunnigan, James F., and Albert A. Nofi. *Victory at Sea: World War II in the Pacific.* New
York: William Morrow and Company, 1995.

Madsen, Daniel. *Forgotten Fleet: The Mothball Navy.* Annapolis: Naval Institute Press,
1999.

Morison, Samuel Eliot. *The Two Ocean War: A Short History of the United States Navy in
the Second World War.* New York: Little, Brown and Company, 1963.

Prangle, Gordon W. *Miracle at Midway.* New York: Penguin Books, 1983.

Veigele, William J. *Patrol Craft of World War II.* Santa Barbara: Astral Publishing
Company, 1998.

Y'Blood, William T. *The Little Giants: U.S. Escort Carriers against Japan.* Annapolis: Naval
Institute Press, 1987.

USEFUL INTERNET WEB SITES

DANFS Online. Dictionary of American Fighting Ships. Maintained by Andrew Toppan.
URL: www.hazegray.org/dnfs/

Pacific Wrecks Database. Maintained by Justin Taylan. URL: www.pacificwrecks.com/

WWII U.S. Veterans Web site. Maintained by Dick and Dave Berry. URL:
www.ww2.Vets.org/default.asp/

INDEX

◆ ◆ ◆ ◆ ◆

Bruce Petty was an aviation ordnanceman during the Vietnam War and served for two years on the USS *Yorktown*, (CVS-10). He graduated from the University of California at Santa Barbara with a bachelor's degree in history and eventually entered the medical profession, working for fifteen years as a nuclear medicine technologist.

In 1995, Petty and his wife moved to Saipan, where he researched and wrote his first book, *Saipan: Oral Histories of the Pacific War.* Upon their return to California in 2000, he began researching the role of navy enlisted men who served in the Pacific during World War II.

Petty and his family currently reside in Riyadh, Saudi Arabia.